Introduction

Qualifications covered

This book has been written specifically to cover the Unit 'Business Awareness' which is mandatory for the following qualifications:

AAT Level 3 Diploma in Accounting

AAT Diploma in Accounting – SCQF Level 7

The book contains a clear text with worked examples and case studies, chapter summaries and key terms to help with revision. Each chapter concludes with a wide range of activities, many in the style of AAT computer based assessments.

Osborne Study and Revision Materials

Additional materials, tailored to the needs of students studying this unit and revising for the assessment, include:

- **Workbooks:** paperback books with practice activities and exams
- **Wise Guides:** pocket-sized spiral bound revision cards
- **Student Zone:** access to Osborne Books online resources
- **Osborne Books App:** Osborne Books ebooks for mobiles and tablets

Visit www.osbornebooks.co.uk for details of study and revision resources and access to online material.

1 Understanding businesses

this chapter covers...

In this chapter we will cover different types of business, their structure, governance, and the legal framework in which they operate.

We will start by looking at the standard organisation types and their key characteristics, including how they are governed, the way in which they are funded.

We will then move on to the legal framework for companies and partnerships. This will include the key elements of company legislation and of unlimited liability partnerships.

The next section will identify common features of businesses before considering the difference between manufacturing and service businesses.

Businesses will have a range of internal and external stakeholders. In the next section of the chapter, we will look at the needs of the different stakeholders of a business.

Finally, we will consider the stakeholders' attitude to risk.

Business Awareness

Tutorial

Jo Osborne

Published by Osborne Books Limited
Tel 01905 748071
Email books@osbornebooks.co.uk
Website www.osbornebooks.co.uk

Design by Laura Ingham

British Library Cataloguing in Publication Data
A catalogue record for this book is available from the British Library

ISBN 978-1-911198-59-8

Contents

TYPES OF BUSINESSES

There are a number of types of business organisations which operate within the UK. Although the common perception is that the majority of businesses are keen to make a profit, some of these organisations will actually be run as 'not-for-profit' organisations.

The standard types of organisation are:

- **sole trader** – as the name suggests, this is an individual who owns and runs the business and is completely responsible for it
- **partnership**, a number of individuals working together in business and sharing the profit (or losses)
- **limited liability partnership and limited partnership**, a number of individuals working together in partnership which has been incorporated as a separate legal entity; this means that the partner can limit their personal liability for the debts of the business
- **private limited company**, an incorporated business with its own separate legal identity that is owned by shareholders and run by directors. The shares of a private limited company **are not** traded on a stock exchange
- **public limited company** – like a private limited company this is an incorporated business with its own separate legal identity that is owned by shareholders and run by directors. The shares of a public limited company **are** traded on a stock exchange
- **not-for-profit organisation** – this includes charities and public sector organisations. The money that is received by a not-for-profit organisation is used to achieve the organisation's objectives. For charities this will be for charitable purposes, and for public sector organisations this will be to provide public services to the community

SOLE TRADERS

Sole traders are individuals who run their own businesses. This may include anything from a plumber or a bookkeeper to a car repairer or a farm. Sole traders are also referred to as 'self-employed'. The businesses are generally smaller because the owner usually has a limited amount of capital and works alone. However, sole traders can, and do, employ other people to work for them. Profits are often ploughed back into the business after the owner has taken out drawings.

key characteristics of sole traders

- the owner is independent and can run the business as he or she wishes without consulting others

- once business expenses are covered, all profits belong to the owner
- the business is, legally, easy to set up – either using the owner's name, or a trading name such as 'Coleridge Garage' or 'Samira Tyler Bookkeeping Services'
- the owner has unlimited liability for the losses and debts of the business – this means that if the sole trader should become insolvent, the owner's personal assets may be used to pay their business debts
- the owner can grow the business by introducing more of their own capital, retaining and reinvesting profits, or by borrowing using bank loans or similar
- the owner must often work long hours and it may be difficult to find time to take holidays; if the owner is ill the work of the business will either slow down or stop completely until they are better

financial statements of a sole trader

The financial statements (final accounts) of a sole trader comprise:

- statement of profit or loss
- statement of financial position

Such financial statements are produced annually at the end of the financial year (which can end at any date – it doesn't have to be the calendar year). The financial statements can be produced more often in order to give information to the sole trader on how the business is progressing.

There is no defined format for sole trader financial statements, and they are not governed by specific legislation. Sole traders do not need to make annual returns to Companies House.

The sole trader is responsible to HM Revenue & Customs:

- for annual income tax returns, stating the profit of the business
- if the sole trader is registered for VAT, they must make quarterly or annual VAT returns with the accompanying payment if VAT is owed (the sole trader will receive a repayment if one is due)

PARTNERSHIPS (UNLIMITED LIABILITY)

Partnerships normally consist of between two and twenty partners (exceptions being large, professional businesses, such as solicitors and accountants). Partnerships are often larger businesses than sole traders because, as there is more than one owner, there is likely to be more capital. A partnership may be formed to set up a new business or it may be the logical growth of a sole trader introducing partners to the business to increase the capital.

The rules of the partnership are either set out in the Partnership Act 1890 or in a partnership agreement made between the partners (which may be written or oral).

key characteristics of partnerships

- all partners will contribute capital to the partnership thereby increasing access to capital. Further capital can be raised by the introduction of new partners
- the profits of the business are shared in accordance with the terms of the partnership agreement
- each partner is liable in law for the dealings and business debts of the **whole** business, not simply the share that they have in the partnership
- as there is more than one owner, decisions may take longer because other partners may need to be consulted
- individual partners may specialise in particular areas of the business
- with more people running the business, there is cover for illness and holidays
- the retirement or death of one partner may adversely affect the running of the business

financial statements of a partnership

Like a sole trader, a partnership prepares:

- statement of profit or loss
- statement of financial position

The financial statements show how the profit from the statement of profit or loss is shared out amongst the partners and incorporate the accounting rules either of the Partnership Act 1890 or of the partnership agreement between the partners.

There is no defined format for partnership financial statements and they are not governed by specific legislation (although the Partnership Act 1890 may apply regarding sharing of profits or losses). Partnerships do not need to make annual returns to Companies House.

The partnership is responsible to HM Revenue & Customs for VAT, if it is registered for VAT, and must make quarterly or annual VAT returns with the accompanying payment if VAT is owed (the partnership will receive a repayment if one is due).

Each partner is responsible to HM Revenue & Customs for his or her annual income tax return, stating their share of the profit of the partnership.

partnership agreement

Although some partnerships will not have a partnership agreement and will be governed by the Partnership Act, most partnerships have their own partnership agreement. The partnership agreement – which may not always be a formal document – will usually cover the following main points:

- division of profits and losses between partners (which may be expressed as a ratio, fraction or percentage)
- partners' salaries/commission
- whether interest is to be allowed on partners' capital, and at what rate
- whether interest is to be charged on partners' drawings, and at what rate

goodwill

Partnerships will have often built up an element of goodwill. This intangible asset may be as a result of various factors including a strong and loyal customer base, a positive reputation, a highly skilled workforce, or a successful and unique product.

Goodwill can be defined in accounting terms as:

'The difference between the value of a business as a whole, and the net value of its separate assets and liabilities.'

For example, if the assets and liabilities of an existing business are worth £650,000 and the business is sold for £800,000, the goodwill in the business is £150,000.

It is not always easy to value goodwill and will often require some negotiation between the people concerned. This will need to be done when one of the partners retires and/or a new partner joins the partnership.

When a **partner retires** it is necessary to calculate how much is due to them in respect of capital and profits. The partnership agreement normally details the procedures to be followed when a partner retires. The most common procedure requires goodwill to be valued and the retiring partner to be paid their share. There is an accounting process to do this which you don't need to know about for this unit. However, you should appreciate that if there is insufficient money in the partnership to pay the retiring partner in full, they may leave some of their capital in the business as a loan which is paid back over a number of years by the partnership.

A **new partner** can only join the partnership if all the partners agree. The new partner will be expected to 'buy in' to the partnership and will normally be charged a premium for their share of the goodwill at the time they are admitted. This is because the new partner will start to share in the profits of the business immediately and will benefit from the goodwill established by the existing partners. Again, there is an accounting process to account for this.

When there is a change of partner in a partnership, whether it is due to retirement or admission of a partner, this will result in the partnership agreement being changed. The revised agreement must be updated to reflect the new profit-sharing ratio following the change in partners.

LIMITED LIABILITY, AND LIMITED, PARTNERSHIPS

A limited liability partnership (LLP) is often the preferred business format for professional partnerships, including accountants and solicitors. Like unlimited liability partnerships the partners will normally take an active role in the running of the business.

An LLP is set up through a process of legal incorporation, which requires certain documents to be submitted to the Registrar of Companies at Companies House. It is also advisable – but not a legal requirement – for an LLP to have a Members' Agreement setting out the rights, duties and obligations of members – this may be written or oral. Although an LLP is a partnership, those owning the business are called members and not partners. All LLPs must have two or more 'designated members' who are responsible for ensuring that the legal and accounting requirements are carried out, eg keeping accounting records, arranging for the accounts to be audited if required, preparing, and submitting the LLP's Confirmation Statement and Annual Accounts to Companies House. The annual Confirmation Statement is submitted by LLPs and limited companies to Companies House in order to confirm that all the information required by the Companies Act 2006 has been submitted to Companies House.

The financial statements of an LLP are very similar to those of limited companies and comprise:

- statement of profit or loss
- statement of financial position
- supporting notes to the financial statements (the depth of information required varies with the size of the LLP)
- Auditor's Report (smaller LLPs may be exempt from audit)

The financial statements show how the profit from the statement of profit or loss is shared between the members and incorporates the accounting rules of the Limited Liability Partnership Agreement.

The accounting requirements, including the level of detail to be disclosed together with the order of items in the statements of profit or loss and financial position, are set out in FRS 102: The Financial Reporting Standard applicable in the UK and Republic of Ireland. Sample layouts of financial statements are given in FRS 102.

The LLP's Confirmation Statement and Annual Accounts must be filed at Companies House, by the designated members of the LLP, where they are available for public inspection.

limited partnership

A limited partnership is similar to an LLP except that it must appoint at least one general partner and one limited partner (an individual cannot be a general and a limited partner at the same time). Like an LLP, all limited partners will have limited liability. However, the general partner(s) will have unlimited liability. The general partner is normally responsible for the day-to-day running of the business, with the limited partner, or partners, not taking an active role in the managerial decisions. Limited partnerships are often formed for projects that will last for a relatively short period of time, such as a building project. Here the limited partners are predominately providing investment for the project in return for a share of the returns.

LIMITED COMPANIES

A limited company is incorporated as a separate legal entity from its owners (shareholders). There are two main types of limited companies:

- private limited companies
- public limited companies

Limited companies are owned by shareholders and managed by directors. A company may become a public limited company (**plc**) if it has:

- more than £50,000 of issued share capital
- at least two members (shareholders)
- at least two directors

The shares of a plc can be traded on a stock exchange, and bought and sold by individuals, limited companies and trusts.

A private limited company (**ltd**) is privately owned with:

- no minimum requirement for issued share capital
- at least one member (shareholders)
- at least one director who can be the same person as the sole shareholder

The shares of a ltd company cannot be traded publicly, but can be bought and sold privately.

Limited companies incorporate by registering under the Companies Act 2006 and by submitting certain documents to the Registrar of Companies at Companies House. The Articles of Association set out the written rules about running the company that have been agreed by the shareholders, directors, and the company secretary (model Articles of Association are available from Companies House at www.gov.uk).

Once registered, a company is run by the directors on behalf of the shareholders. It is a responsibility of the directors to submit the company's annual Confirmation Statement and Annual Accounts to Companies House. The company must ensure that access to this information is provided to all shareholders so that they can approve them. The company's Annual Accounts comprise:

- statement of profit or loss
- statement of financial position
- supporting notes to the financial statements (the depth of information required varies with the size of the company)
- directors' report to shareholders
- Auditor's Report (smaller limited companies may be exempt from audit)

Companies follow the accounting rules set out in the Companies Act 2006 and in Financial Reporting Standards (or International Financial Reporting Standards). Sample layouts of the statement of profit or loss and financial position are provided within these documents, including the level of detail to be disclosed, together with the order in which items are to be stated.

The company's Confirmation Statement and Annual Accounts must be filed at Companies House, by the directors, where they are available for public inspection.

advantages of incorporation

- the main advantage for a business of incorporation is the fact that the liability for members (LLP) and shareholders (limited company) is limited to the amount they have invested
- the continuing existence of the business as a separate legal entity
- an enhancement of the credibility of the business, eg a limited company sounds a more substantial business than a sole trader
- access to finance may be easier
- transfer of ownership of the business may be easier, eg the sale of shares in a limited company

disadvantages of incorporation

- the main disadvantage is the more complex requirements of setting up the business and then the additional costs associated with record keeping, maintaining documentation and filing an annual return

- information filed with Companies House is in the public domain so anyone can access financial and other details
- business finances must be kept entirely separate from those of the owners, which contrasts with a sole trader who can take drawings from the business as and when required

NOT-FOR-PROFIT ORGANISATIONS

Not-for-profit organisations include public sector organisations and charities. As the name suggests, unlike the businesses that we have looked at so far, the motive of these organisations is not to make profit.

public sector

Organisations in the public sector provide all public services in the UK. This will include education, health, emergency services, roads, rubbish collection and recycling, social care and many other things. It is 'owned' by central and local government and funded by taxes. Some public sector organisations form partnerships with private sector companies to provide a service, eg hospitals in the National Health Service. The amount of money that public sector organisations have to spend on these services depends on the amount that is allocated to them in the budget.

charities

Charities are set up to provide charitable activities within the scope of the charity. Most of their income is from donations, grants and funding; most of their expenditure is finance for their charitable activities.

The main rules governing charities are set out in:

- the Charities Act 2011
- the Charity Commission, which is the regulator for most charities
- the Statement of Recommended Practice (SORP) Accounting and Reporting by charities, or FRS 102, The Financial Reporting Standard applicable in the UK and Ireland

Charities are restricted in what they can do and how they work:

- they must follow charity law
- their purpose must be for public benefit
- they are governed by a trust deed, which sets out the name of the charity, its objects and powers, and deals with the appointment of trustees, how meetings are to be run, and the required financial statements (a model Trust Deed is available from the Charity Commission at www.gov.uk)

- they are run by trustees, who do not usually benefit personally from the charity but, under certain circumstances, could become liable for the debts of the charity
- they are independent of other organisations
- most charities must register with the Charity Commission

All but the smallest charities prepare financial statements which comprise:

- statement of financial activities
- statement of financial position (sometimes known as a balance sheet)
- cashflow statement (required for certain charities)
- supporting notes to the financial statements
- trustees' Annual Report (which must be available on request by interested parties)
- Auditor's Report (large charities) or Independent Examiner's Report (medium-sized charities), but no audit is normally required for small charities

These comprise the charity's Annual Return which must be filed by the trustees with the Charity Commission where it is available for public inspection.

COMMON FEATURES OF BUSINESS ORGANISATIONS

Whatever the type and structure of a business organisation, there are a number of common features that all organisations will share. These are:

structure – organisations are made up of a group of interrelated individuals. This group of people will be organised in such a way that they can work together efficiently and effectively.

common objectives and team working – the organisation will have defined objectives. These will be met by individuals working together as a team and ensuring **goal congruence** ie that the goals of the individuals coincide with those of the organisation as a whole, and its shareholders.

co-operation – to achieve the goals of the organisation, however it is structured, individuals must develop good working relationships and work co-operatively.

responsibility, authority, and division of work – within any organisation, whatever the size and structure, individuals will have defined responsibilities which identify what is expected of them and divides the work between them. Depending on structure of the organisation and their seniority, individuals will have varying levels of authority.

MANUFACTURING AND SERVICE BUSINESSES

Manufacturing businesses are those organisations that actually make and sell products. This could be a car maker, such as Volkswagen, or a business that makes and supplies parts to Volkswagen that are used to make the cars.

Service businesses are those organisations that provide a service to individual customers or clients, or another business. This could be a firm of accountants or a cleaning company.

A manufacturing organisation will find it relatively easy to identify the cost of the products that it makes and sells by identifying the materials, labour and overheads that relate to them. A service organisation will find this more difficult, as the majority of its costs will relate to staff time and expertise and the overheads to run the business. Consequently, the cost information available within a service organisation may not be as defined.

There are a number of qualities that differentiate a service business from a manufacturing business. These qualities can be summarised as:

- **intangibility** – a service does not provide a physical product, ie it cannot be seen, touched, tasted, or smelled
- **inseparability** – a service cannot be separated from its consumption by customer, ie it is usually consumed at the same time as it is provided
- **perishability**– any unused service cannot be stored for future use
- **variability** – a service will be tailored to the needs of an individual customer

FUNDING SOURCES

An organisation that wants to invest in its future growth may need to raise additional finance. The way in which it raises these funds depends on what type of organisation it is. Public sector organisations normally rely on the Government for funding, whilst charities, and not-for-profit organisations will carry out fundraising, or rely on donations to raise finance. Public and private limited companies will normally raise funds for investment from their owners or using long-term debt.

We will now look at different ways in which a business can raise additional funds.

borrowing

Businesses may raise additional funds by borrowing money. This is usually done through a bank loan. If a business decides to take out a loan, it will be expected to repay the amount it has borrowed, plus interest, to the lender over an agreed period of time.

For example, a business may take out a loan of £150,000, at an interest rate of 5% over a five-year period. Each month of the five years the business will pay the bank £2,831 so that by the end of the loan term it will have been completely repaid.

Borrowing is normally used for longer-term investment, and the repayment term should be matched to the life of the asset that the business intends to use the funds for. Let's say in the example above, the loan is taken out by the business to buy four new delivery vehicles that it expects to use for five years – the term of the loan will then match the life of the assets.

Businesses should avoid using loans for short-term funding. If a business has a short-term requirement for funds, it may wish to use an overdraft facility with its bank. This must be pre-agreed to avoid high interest and/or bank charges.

new capital

New capital can be introduced to a business by issuing further share capital. In a private company this will either be issued to the existing shareholders, or privately offered to a new investor(s). In a public limited company, a new share issue will be made on a stock exchange.

Capital is a long-term source of finance, and is normally used to invest in business growth. The key disadvantage of issuing new capital to raise funds is that it will dilute the ownership of the existing shareholders. However, a key advantage is that, unlike using borrowing to raise funds, the business will not have to pay interest on the amount invested, and is not required to repay the shareholders if they later decide they do not wish to invest in the business. Instead, the shareholders will need to sell their shares privately, or on a stock exchange.

retained profit

When shareholders invest in a business, they will normally expect some of the profits that the business generates to be distributed as dividends. However, a business may wish to retain some of its profits to reinvest in the business. Provided the shareholders agree to this, retained profits can be a less expensive way of investing in business growth. As long as the business continues to be profitable, shareholders will be rewarded by future growth in the value of their investment, and, potentially, higher dividends in the future.

working capital

Working capital is the difference between a business's current assets and current liabilities, ie cash + inventories + receivables – payables. Working capital circulates round the business as things are bought and sold, and payment is made and received, so the amount of working capital changes on a daily basis. The important thing for a business is that the working capital cycle ensures that the business has sufficient funds to pay its payables (suppliers) on time.

Working capital may be a suitable method of short-term funding, for example to pay a VAT bill, or to cover staff bonuses, but should only be used if the business has sufficient working capital that it will not affect the day-to-day operations of the business.

Working capital should not be used as a longer-term source of funding.

BUSINESS STAKEHOLDERS

A stakeholder is a person or organisation that has an 'interest' in another organisation.

The stakeholders in a business fall into two categories: internal stakeholders, including directors, employees and other departments in the business; and external stakeholders, which are businesses and individuals outside the organisation. The stakeholders in a business will have various information needs.

Customers who buy goods and services will want to ensure that the business produces good quality products and services at reasonable prices. They will mostly deal with the sales department and the finance department. They will need price lists, statements showing how much they owe, and details of how they make payment. In return for all of this, the customer will pay its invoices on time and will remain loyal to the business by continuing to trade with it.

Suppliers who sell goods and services to the business will been keen for the business to continue to trade with them. They will interact with the purchasing department and the finance department. They will provide invoices and statements and will expect to be paid on time. If a business has a good working relationship with its suppliers, they will ensure that they supply good quality products and services at reasonable prices.

Finance providers, such as banks and leasing companies, will lend money to the business. They may expect the directors to show them the financial statements of the business before providing funds, but will then mostly deal with the finance department, to ensure that payments are made on time and for the correct amount.

Owners, or shareholders, will be interested in how much profit the business makes. They are provided with information about the financial performance of the business in the annual report. If the business is a private limited company, the owners may have regular communication with the directors and managers.

Businesses will interact with HMRC which is a **government** department. They will be expected to calculate and pay corporation tax, VAT, income tax and national insurance.

Employees of the business are key internal stakeholders. They will want to know how well the business is performing as this will affect the security of their jobs and their pay. Employees will expect the business to provide them with the necessary training to allow them to do their jobs, together with an opportunity to develop and progress through the organisation. In return, the employees will continue to use their knowledge and skills in the business, remaining loyal to it and being less likely to leave and pursue a career elsewhere.

The way in which businesses operate will be affected by **regulatory bodies** that require them to comply with legislation and regulation. An example would be a manufacturing business that is expected to comply with health and safety regulations.

Businesses, or the individuals who work for them, may be members of **professional bodies.** This membership will give customers and clients confidence to do business with them. However, the profession body will expect the business to comply with its rules and regulations and maintain its standards. For example, a UK travel agency will normally be a member of the Association of British Travel Agents (ABTA). The fact that the business is a member will encourage potential customers to book with that travel agent as they will feel confident should anything go wrong with their travel plans.

A qualified accountant will be a member of a professional accounting body and will be expected to comply with its ethical code. They will also be expected to complete continuing professional development (CPD) to ensure that they are maintaining their accounting knowledge and expertise. The professional accounting body will have the power to discipline its members should they fail to comply or if they bring the profession into disrepute.

The **general public** will expect businesses to operate in the public interest in a safe and sustainable way and to make a positive contribution to the local community.

STAKEHOLDERS' ATTITUDE TO RISK

We have seen that it is important for businesses to be aware of the needs of its stakeholders and their impact on the business. We must also be aware of the stakeholders' attitude to risk. This means the level of risk that stakeholders are prepared to accept and what they will do if they feel that the level of risk is unacceptably high. Some stakeholders will try to avoid risk at all costs and will accept a lower return or pay higher prices if this will minimise the risk (**risk averse**). Other stakeholders will actively seek out riskier options if this will increase the likelihood of a higher return (**risk seeking**). There are also some that fall somewhere in the middle and are prepared to accept some risk and this will not be a prime factor in their decision-making process (**risk neutral**).

How much risk a stakeholder will accept is affected by their:

risk appetite – the level of risk they are prepared to accept to achieve their objectives

risk tolerance – as the names suggests, this is how much risk they are able to withstand (ie tolerate)

risk threshold – the level up to which risk is acceptable, this could be quantified as an amount of money that could be lost if a project fails

If we return to some of the stakeholders we identified earlier, we can consider what their attitude of risk is likely to be.

Customers are likely to be risk averse. They will want the goods and services that they buy to be of good quality and for the supply to be reliable. Possible circumstances where a customer might be willing to accept a higher level of risk would be if they were offered a significant discount, or in a situation where goods that they need are scarce and they have to source them from a different, untested, business.

Suppliers will only want to deal with reliable businesses that they are confident will pay for the goods that they order and receive. Consequently, suppliers are also likely to be risk averse.

Finance providers, such as banks and leasing companies, are notoriously risk averse. Before lending money they will want to ensure that the business they are lending to will be able to afford the repayments and that they will be made on time.

Owners, or shareholders, are generally interested in maximising their investment. They will want to invest in a business that generates a good profit so that they receive dividends and/or the value of their investment grows. This means that they have a reasonable appetite for risk, but will normally have a threshold above which they are not prepared to risk losing their investment.

Chapter Summary

- Organisations that are run for profit include: sole trader, partnership, limited liability partnership, and private limited company, public limited company.
- Not for profit organisations include: charites and public sector organisations.
- Sole trader and partnership businesses are cheap and easy to form, but self-employed individuals are fully liable for the entire debt of the business.
- Limited liability partnerships and private and public limited companies are more complex to form, but provide limited liability to members and shareholders for their investment in the business.
- Sole trader businesses often have less scope for expansion when compared with partnerships which may have increased capital and partners who are able to specialise in particular areas of the business.
- Limited companies are governed by the Companies Act 2006.
- Not-for-profit organisations include charities which are governed by the Charity Commission and the Charities Act 2011.
- It is important for all organisations to meet the required deadlines for the preparation of their financial statements.
- Common features of business organisations include: structure, common objectives and team working, co-operation, responsibility, authority, and division of work.
- Manufacturing businesses are those that make and sell products, whilst service businesses provide a service.
- Businesses have a variety of funding methods available to them including, new capital, retained profit, borrowing and working capital. It is important that the business matches the funding method to what it is being used for.
- Key stakeholders of a business include: customers, suppliers, finance providers, owners (or shareholders), Government, employees, professional bodies and the general public. Each stakeholder will have different requirements of the business and different attitudes to risk.

Key Terms

sole trader	an individual in business
partnership	a group of individuals working together as partners in business
incorporated	a business formed into a legal corporation
limited liability partnership (LLP)	an incorporated form of partnership, which is a separate legal entity, where members are able to limit their personal liability for the debts of the business
limited company	an incorporated business, which is a separate legal entity, owned by shareholders and run by directors. The shares of public limited companies are traded on a stock exchange, whilst those of a private limited company are not
charity	an organisation, run by trustees, which uses its resources to fund charitable activities under its control
public sector	organisations, funded by central and local government, that provide public services in the UK
companies act 2006	legislation governing limited companies in the UK
manufacturing business	an organisation that actually make and sell products
service business	an organisation that provides a service to individual customers or clients, or another business
stakeholder	a person or organisation that has an 'interest' in another organisation
risk appetite	the level of risk a stakeholder is prepared to accept to achieve their objectives
risk tolerance	how much risk a stakeholder can tolerate, or withstand
risk threshold	the level up to which risk is acceptable; this may be quantified as an amount of money that could be lost if a project fails

Activities

1.1 Which of the following are characteristics of a sole trader?

Select **all** correct options.

(a) The owner is independent and can run the business as they wish without consulting others	
(b) The owner has limited liability	
(c) The financial statements are made up of a statement of profit or loss and a statement of financial position	
(d) The sole trader must make an annual return to Companies House	
(e) The investment in the business by the owner is known as capital	

1.2 Which of the following will normally be included in a partnership agreement?

Select **all** correct options.

(a) The way in which profit will be shared	
(b) Details of partners' salaries	
(c) The location of the partnership's offices	
(d) The rate of interest allowed on partners' capital	
(e) The rate of interest charged on partners' drawings	

1.3 What is the following the definition for?

'The difference between the value of a business as a whole, and the net value of its separate assets and liabilities.'

1.4 **(a)** Explain what is meant by incorporation.

(b) Give two advantages and two disadvantages of incorporation.

1.5 **(a)** Define a charity.

(b) What are the main rules that govern charities?

1.6 The directors of Jaybridge Ltd are considering several requirements it has for funding.

Select the most appropriate funding source each of the following, using each option only once.

	Loan	**Working capital**	**Retained earnings**
Expansion of the business by opening a distribution centre in Scotland.			
Purchase of a new machine for production line C which is expected to cost £220,000 and last for eight years.			
Payment of the business' corporation tax liability.			

1.7 Identify whether each of the these is an internal or external stakeholder?

	Internal stakeholder	**External stakeholder**
Directors		
Customers		
Suppliers		
Finance Providers eg banks		
Owners		
General public		
Employees		
The Government		

1.8 Complete the following sentence by selecting the correct word for the options available.

'Risk [ ] is how much risk a stakeholder is able to withstand, whereas risk [ ] is the level of risk a stakeholder is prepared to accept to achieve their objectives. Risk [ ] is the level up to which risk is acceptable – often measured as amount of money that could be lost.'

Options: threshold, appetite, tolerance.

2 Organisational structure and governance

this chapter covers...

At the start of this chapter we will look at three ways in which an organisation might be structured: functional, divisional and matrix. Some organisations will have a tall structure with a long change of command and narrow span of control, whereas others will have a flat structure with fewer levels of management and a wider span of control.

The next part of the chapter focuses on the governance within a business which provides a framework for managing the organisation. This will include corporate, financial, and legal governance and the impact the structure of the organisation will have on its governance.

We will then take a detailed look at the role of the finance function and how it contributes to the operation of the other, key functions in a business.

Finally, we will investigate business risk and the way in which this risk is evaluated and then managed. This will include using a risk matrix to assess individual risks and then the TARA model to manage the risk.

ORGANISATIONAL STRUCTURE

Business can be structured in a number of different ways. The size and nature of a business will affect the way in which it is structured. Three of the common organisational structures are:

- functional
- divisional
- matrix

A **functional** structure divides the business into specialised functions or skills such as production, sales and marketing, finance, and IT. It is one of the most common organisational structures as it groups individuals with similar knowledge and expertise together. Work can be carried out quickly and efficiently and staff in the function will develop their skills through training from more experienced team members.

Bringing members of staff with the same knowledge and skills together creates a pool of expertise so that other staff in the organisation know where to go if they need information relating to sales, IT, finance, or any other function in the business.

The diagram below is an example of a functional organisation structure.

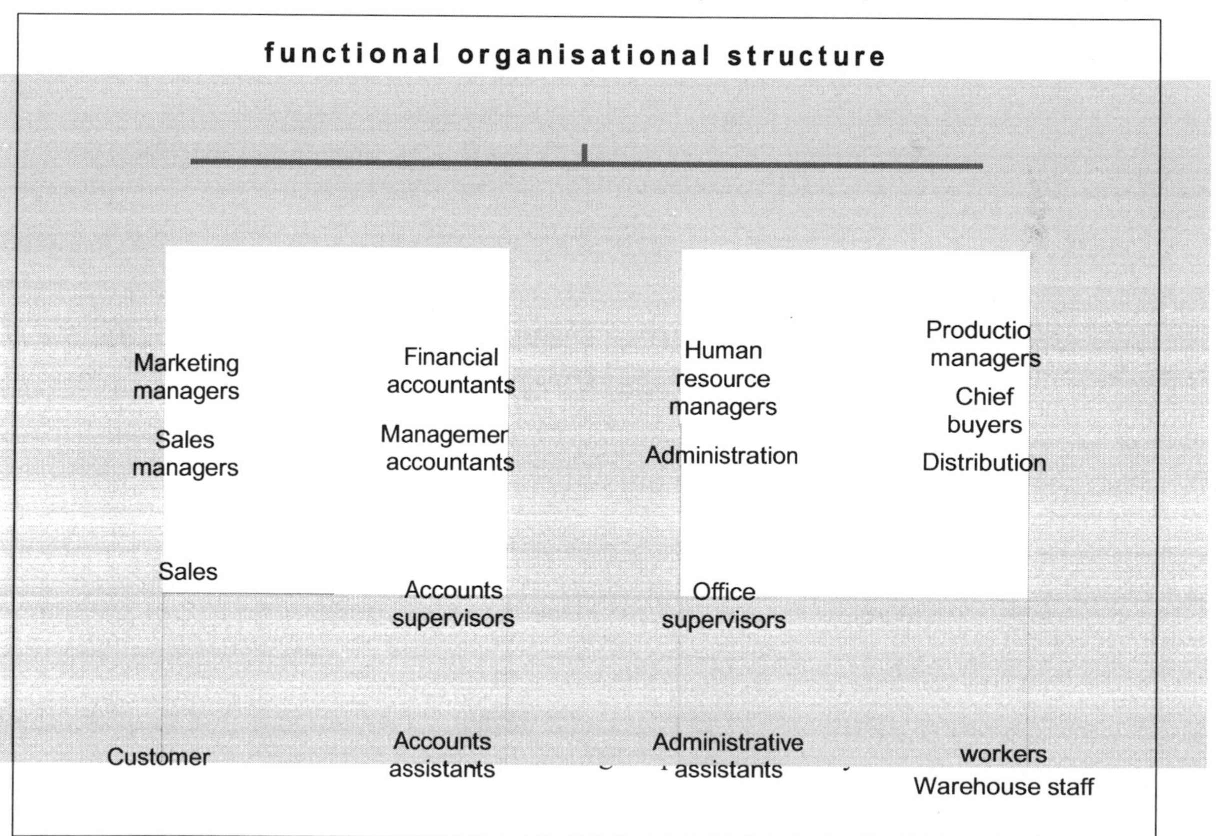

Larger businesses may have a **divisional** structure with a number of different teams that each focus on an individual product or service, or on a geographical area. For example, a firm of solicitors may have divisions specialising in property, family, tax, corporate law and litigation, and a multinational manufacturing business may have divisions for UK, Europe, USA, Australia, and the Far East.

Each division will have all the necessary resources and functions that it needs to support the product or service, or the area which it is covering. These divisions will typically have a director at the top and will be more autonomous than departments organised by function. Divisions will normally manage their own hiring, budgeting, marketing, and finance. A well organised divisional structure will promote a good team spirit and staff will become experts in their own product, service, or area. However, businesses that organise themselves in this way must be careful to avoid unhealthy competition between divisions which could lead to one division trying to 'outdo' another to the detriment of the organisation.

The diagram below is an example of a divisional structure.

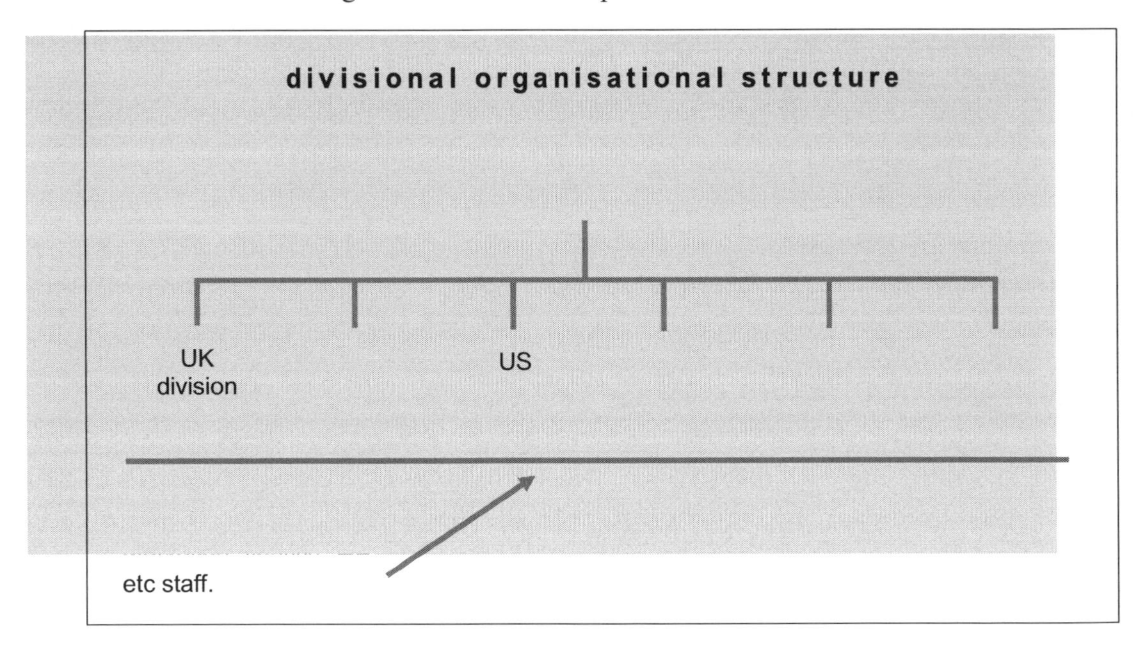

If a business is organised in a **matrix** structure this means that, as well as working in their own departments, individuals will work across teams and projects. A business that is developing a new product may set up a project team that includes members from product design, production, marketing, finance, and human resources. This team will work together on the project until it is completed before returning to their functional team.

The next diagram is an example of a matrix organisational structure.

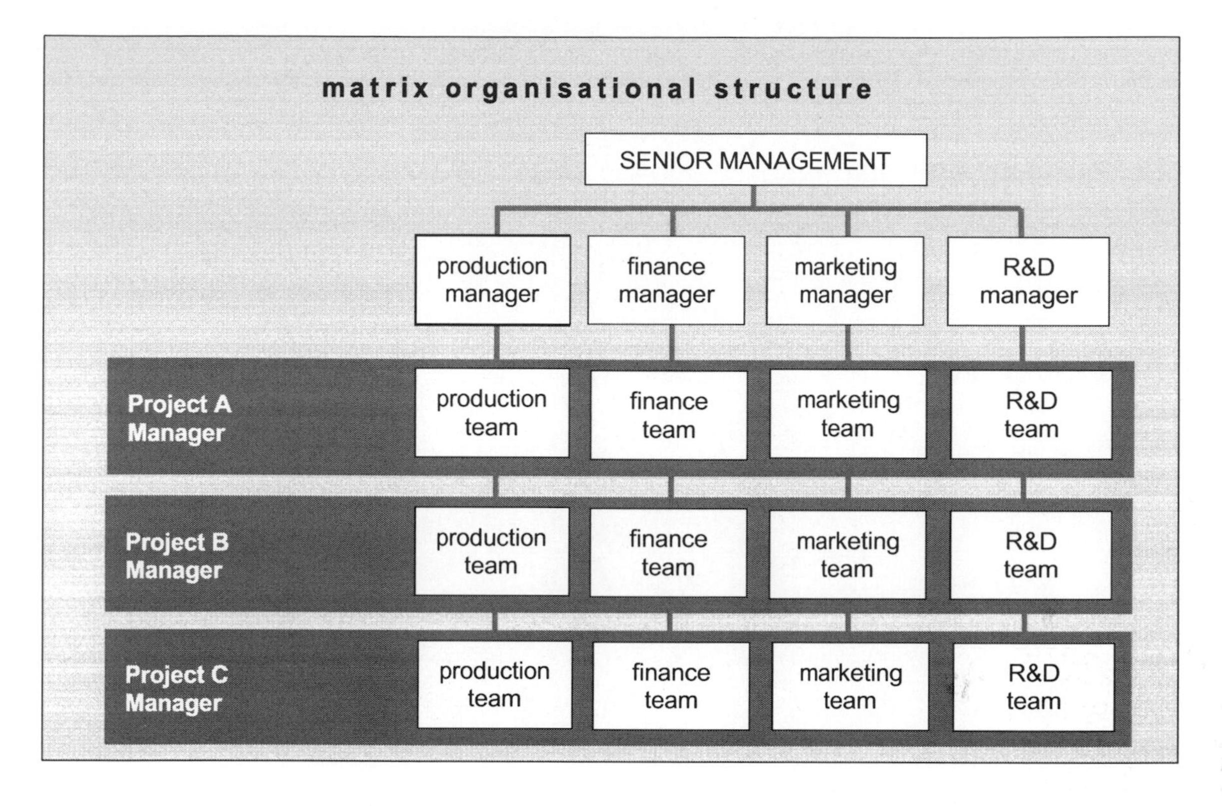

span of control

The span of control of the managers within an organisation refers to the number of individuals that they are responsible for. This will vary depending on:

- the size of the organisation– a manager in a smaller business will have a wider span of control
- the type of work that the individuals do – it is easier to manage a larger group of individuals that complete straightforward repetitive tasks than a smaller group with diverse and complex roles
- the location of the staff – if all the individuals a manager is responsible for are located together the span of control can be wider

tall organisational structure

A **tall organisational structure** will typically be organised by function. The chain of command in these types of business will have several layers of management. This type of structure means that there are clear reporting lines, and that the manager has a narrow span of control. Decision-making often takes longer in an organisation with a tall structure, as information must pass between several layers of management.

The diagram below shows what a tall organisational structure might look like.

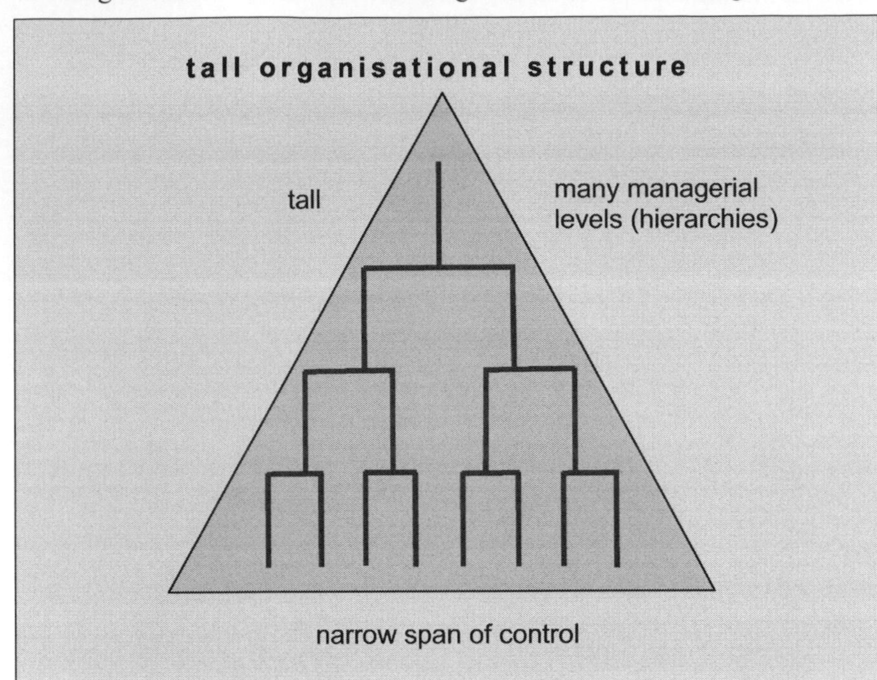

flat organisational structure

A **flat organisational structure** has fewer levels of management. This typically means that there is wider span of control. An advantage of a flat organisational structure is that decisions can be made more efficiently as information can pass up and down the chain of command quickly. However, it can mean that staff 'stagnate' in their roles as there are fewer opportunities to move up the managerial scale.

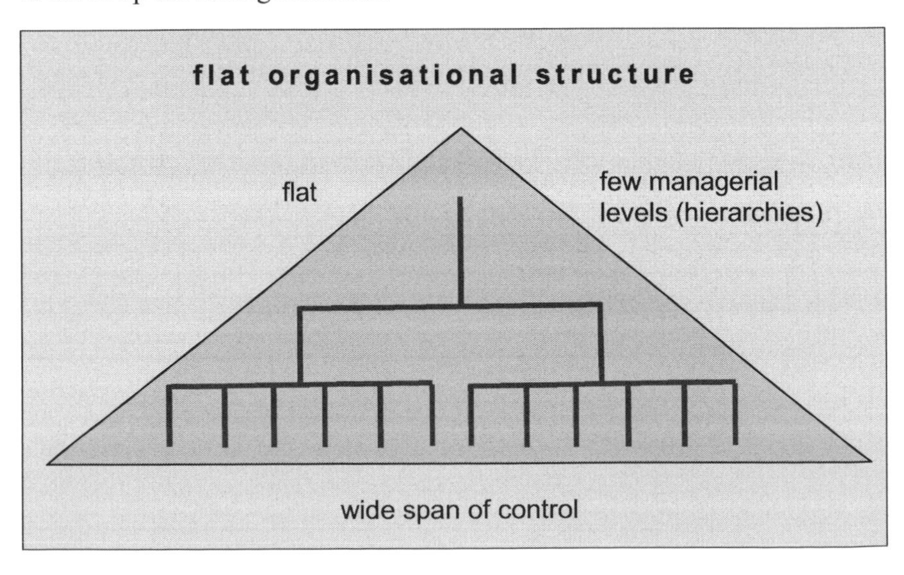

GOVERNANCE

what is governance?

The Chartered Governance Institute (CGI) defines **governance** as:

> *'A system that provides a framework for managing organisations. It identifies who can make decisions, who has the authority to act on behalf of the organisation and who is accountable for how an organisation and its people behave and perform.'*

governance in a business context

A business with good governance will have delegated the authority for decision-making to the appropriate people and will have a structure in place to support this. To ensure effective governance a business will have controls in place to ensure that an individual cannot go beyond their scope of authority. Good governance enables the board of directors, together with the management, to run a business legally, ethically, sustainably, and successfully, for the benefit of all stakeholders, not just the shareholders. This includes employees, customers and clients, suppliers, lenders, and the general public.

As part of effective governance a business will have to think about:

- **corporate governance** – although shareholders 'own' a business, it is the board of directors, appointed by the shareholders, that are responsible for the governance of the business. They must have systems in place to direct and control the way in which the business is operated. This will include setting the business's strategic aims and objectives and providing the necessary leadership to put them into effect.

- **financial governance** – this focuses on how the business collects, manages, and controls financial information. It allows the business to monitor the operation of the business and promptly identify where there may be a financial risk. In extreme cases this could be fraud or money laundering. However, it may simply relate to the systems and structures in place that ensure amounts that are owed to the business are collected on time and that amounts owed to suppliers are paid when they fall due.

- **legal governance** – it may seem obvious, but a business must ensure that it complies with the necessary legislation and regulation. Legal governance ensures that this happens by implementing appropriate levels of authorisation together with internal documented processes that individuals must follow to ensure compliance.

centralised and decentralised control

We have already identified that authorisation to make decisions is a key element of governance. However, the extent to which the control over this decision-making is centralised also plays a key part.

Centralised control means that decision-making rests with the higher tiers of management in the business. This may be the owner(s) in a smaller business, or the board of directors in a larger business. Decisions in this type of organisation are imposed on staff who will be expected to implement them rather than contribute to the decision-making process.

This type of control structure means that the higher the level someone is in the business, the more influence they have on the direction in which the business goes. It also means that they will be distanced from the 'coal face' ie they will not have much involvement in the actual activities of the business. A centralised structure is sometimes referred to as a 'top-down' structure and can be less flexible than a decentralised approach.

Decentralised control means that authority for making decisions is given to lower levels of management in the business. This may be departmental managers, branch managers or even team leaders. These 'lower level' managers will not need to check every decision they make with the board of directors or senior management team. Instead they will be able to work with their team members to address issues and take on board suggestions their team makes. This 'bottom-up' approach often leads to a more collaborative working atmosphere.

The key advantages of decentralised control are that senior management can focus on the key decisions of the business, and its strategy, and leave the day-to-day decisions to team and departmental managers who can take decisions quickly. However, there are also downsides to this – lower level managers may not have the necessary experience to make 'good' decisions or may make decisions that are good for their team rather than for the business as a whole. It may also lead to a disconnection between the senior managers of the organisation and its staff which could ultimately lead to a loss of control.

impact of organisational structure and size on governance

We have looked at tall and flat organisational structures and the span of control. But how will this impact the governance of an organisation? We will briefly look at each one.

It is more likely that a **larger business** will have a tall structure organised into departments. This will mean there are lots of levels of management, and hence levels of authority. The span of control in a tall organisation tends to be narrow.

A **smaller business** will often be headed up by one or two owners with a large span of control. The business is likely to have a flat organisational with few levels of management.

Obviously, many businesses will have a mix of these characteristics, so the way in which they operate, and their governance, will be slightly different.

levels of management in an organisation

The final way in which we will look at the governance of an organisation is in terms of the levels of management and the types of decisions that they are responsible for.

Strategic or corporate level – starting at the top of the organisation, this is where strategic decisions are made that affect the whole organisation; these decisions tend to be long-term. Should the business open another branch? Should it develop a new product? Should it start trading overseas?

Managerial level – this is the middle level of an organisation's management. Here the decisions relate to the way that the business should go about achieving its goals. Which product should it produce? Should it reduce the price of a product to remain competitive?

Operational level – decisions made at this level tend to be shorter-term and relate to the practical day-to-day operation of the business. Do staff need to work overtime? When should raw materials be requested from stores? How many items do we need delivered from a supplier this week?

What is important with these different levels of planning and decision-making in an organisation is that they work together and support each other for the good of the organisation as a whole. For example, at the strategic level of an organisation the decision may be made to develop a new product. This will need to be supported at the managerial level with input on what characteristics the new product should have to appeal to the target market. At the operational level of the business, plans will need to be in place to ensure there are sufficient, competent staff to make the new product.

THE ROLE OF THE FINANCE FUNCTION

A business will have a variety of functions which contribute to the way in which it operates. Each function has a different role to play but all will interact with the finance function to a greater or less extent. Other than the finance function, the key functions in a business are:

- operations/production
- sales and marketing
- human resources (HR)
- information technology (IT)
- distribution and logistics

Before looking at the role of the finance function in contributing towards the operation of these other business functions, we will remind ourselves of the role of each one and the contribution it makes to the business.

function	role in business	contribution to business
operations/ production	responsible for all the activities which are involved in the production of a product or service *for example, the transformation of raw materials into finished goods*	■ ensuring that production can be run as efficiently as possible ■ ensuring a fair price is paid for purchases
sales and marketing	responsible for the selling and promotion of products and services	■ ensuring customers are made aware of products and services ■ ensuring that the needs of customers are met ■ sourcing new customers and markets
human resources (HR)	responsible for the management of the workforce including: ■ recruitment of staff ■ training ■ performance appraisal ■ remuneration, holiday and sickness entitlements ■ termination of employment	■ ensuring all employment rules and regulations are met ■ ensuring a positive working environment ■ ensuring that good staff are retained
information technology (IT)	responsible for all computer-based information systems, including setting up and maintaining: ■ organisation's website ■ emails systems ■ software applications ■ computer hardware ■ sourcing new relevant technologies ■ maintaining adequate system and data security	■ ensuring that all systems are working correctly ■ ensuring that computer issues are dealt with promptly to minimise disruption to the operation of the business ■ ensuring that the needs of staff are met
distribution and logistics	responsible for all the activities which are required to deliver a product or service to the final client or customer, including: ■ receiving, storing, and handling raw materials ■ storing, distributing, and delivering finished products and services	■ ensuring the movement of raw materials and finished goods is performed effectively and efficiently ■ ensuring that all goods within warehouses are stored safely with the minimum chance of damage or obsolescence, and are easy to locate

So how does the finance function contribute to the operation of these individual functions? Let's look at each one in turn.

OPERATIONS/PRODUCTION

Operations/Production is the heart of the business and what it does. This may be producing goods for sale, such as Sony producing televisions, or providing a service, for example a large accountancy firm such as PwC preparing accounts for its clients. The finance function will need to carry out certain key roles and provide financial information to allow operations/production to function effectively. Some of these are detailed below.

setting up credit accounts with suppliers and agreeing terms

Most businesses will have someone, or a department, who is responsible for purchasing. Whoever this is that is responsible for creating commercial relationships with suppliers, they will also need input from finance. This may include agreeing prices, negotiating credit terms, and agreeing discounts. The finance function will be expected to contribute to these negotiations by advising on the maximum price the business can pay to maintain margins, the effect credit terms will have on the cash flow of the business, and what discounts they might expect from comparable businesses.

A copy of all documentation that relates to inventory purchases and issues should be provided to the finance department. This will include orders, delivery notes, goods received notes and invoices. Finance will have responsibly for matching these documents and liaising with the production department if there are any issues.

Finance will also be responsible maintaining the financial relationship with the supplier, including paying amounts as they become due.

inventory control

For a business to operate effectively it must have sufficient inventory of raw materials to produce the right products at the right time. The finance function will work with the operations function, or purchasing department in a larger business, to ensure that sufficient inventory is available to maintain production. This will include monitoring the receipts of inventory and issues to production, as well as highlighting when further inventory needs to be ordered.

Finance must also monitor inventory of finished goods to ensure that customer orders can be fulfilled within agreed timescales.

As part of its role, the finance function will also carry out regular inventory counts to ensure that physical inventory agrees with inventory records. This will help to minimise the risk of theft going unnoticed, resulting in financial loss to the business, and the risk that customers order cannot be fulfilled.

budgeting

The finance function will be heavily involved in setting budgets. The main aim of most businesses is to make a profit, and in order to do this the full cost of its products must be established so that the business ensures the prices it charges will generate a profit.

Finance will also monitor the actual results of the operations function against the budget and identify any variances. These variances, good or bad, can then be promptly investigated and the causes resolved before they have a significant effect on the profitability of the business.

SALES AND MARKETING

Sales and marketing deal with the customers, or clients, of the business. They will be responsible for marketing the products or services and negotiating the sales. The finance function will work with sales and marketing in the following areas.

pricing

Finance will need to be involved in calculating the prices to be charged for products to ensure that all costs are covered. To some extent the prices that are charged will be affected by what the market is willing to pay. However, it is important that products are sold at a price that will generate a profit for the business, and finance must be part of the pricing process.

The finance department will also need to be involved in setting discount levels that the sales team can offer customers to make sure that the business still remains profitable after the discounts have been applied.

setting rates for services

Where a business provides a service rather than manufacturing a product, the finance function will need to be involved in the calculation of rates to be charged. For example, a firm of accountants will have to set hourly rates to charge its clients. These rates will need to cover all the overhead (running) costs of the business, the salaries of the staff plus an element of profit. There will need to be different rates depending on the seniority of each member of staff, and their qualifications and experience, together with the complexity of the work.

Some service businesses will charge for a specific service, for example a cleaning company may quote to clean all the carpets in a client's offices. This will be a fixed price to the client, regardless of the amount of time it takes.

Again, the finance function will need to be involved in setting this price to ensure that all costs are covered.

budgeting

As with finance's input into budgeting for the production function, there will also be a need to set budgets within sales and marketing. The sales budget will need to include sales volumes and prices and take into account the effect of discounts. A discounted price may reduce sales revenue but may also increase the sales volume.

performance indicators

The finance function will be involved in setting performance indicators against which the sales and marketing department will be monitored. This may be monitoring the sales revenue against target for areas of the business, comparing sales for different individual members of the sales team or assessing the take up rate for marketing campaigns. It may also be setting budgets for each product, branch or sales team, and then monitoring actual performance against these.

Whatever the key performance indicators (KPIs) are for an individual business, it is important that finance is involved in setting targets and monitoring the actual results against them.

HUMAN RESOURCES (HR)

The human resources, or HR, function of a business is responsible for its people and their welfare and wellbeing. At first glance it might appear that finance and HR will have limited interaction. However, there will be several areas of HR's work which will require input from finance.

recruitment costs

HR will be keen to recruit high quality staff that are a good fit to the role and the business. In addition to paying new staff members an appropriate amount there will also be costs associated with the recruitment, so these costs must be factored into the cost budgets of the business.

staff training and development

It is important that staff keep their skills up-to-date to ensure that they can continue to carry out their role efficiently and effectively. Regular and relevant staff training will ensure that this is achieved. However, this training will come at a cost, so it is important that HR justifies spending on staff training and development, and that it is included in the budgets for the departments that the staff work for.

pay and benefits

Salaries and benefits must be competitive to ensure that staff are motivated to do a good job and to remain with the business. Staff must also be rewarded for their achievements, whether this is through bonuses or commission, or with an increase in pay. All this costs money, so the finance and HR functions must work together to ensure that the business can afford its budgeted cost of pay and benefits and that they are properly included in the budget.

When a new employee joins the business, HR must ensure that it provides the finance function with details of the employee's start date, rate of pay, and overtime rates, to ensure that it is properly reflected in the budget. HR must also ensure that the finance function communicates overtime hours worked to the HR function so that the two functions can decide whether more staff are needed.

INFORMATION TECHNOLOGY (IT)

The information technology, or IT, function is responsible for all aspects of the information systems of the business including both the hardware, ie computers and networks, and the software, such as the computerised accounting system and the email system, the business uses. Below are some examples of how finance will interact with the IT function.

investment in IT

Businesses will have limited resources to invest in capital projects. New IT systems will often require a significant investment. Finance will normally be expected to carry out an investment appraisal on this investment, including a cost-benefit analysis, to ensure that the system meets the investment criteria of the business.

data security

The IT department and the finance department should work together to ensure that the way in which data is held by the business complies with data protection regulations and remains private and secure. This will include data that is directly used by finance including customer data relating to sales and receivables, supplier data for purchases and payables, and personal staff data which is held for payroll. It will also include sensitive information about products and sales which must be kept secure from competitors.

performance indicators

Like many other functions in the business, IT will wish to monitor its success, or failure, against relevant performance indicators. Where these performance indicators are financial, finance will need to be involved in setting them.

DISTRIBUTION AND LOGISTICS

The distribution and logistics function is a key element of the business's supply chain. The distribution element facilitates the actual delivery of the product or service, while the logistics element is concerned with the organisation, storage and control over inventory, as well as managing the distribution. Given that finance is normally involved in the management of inventory, it would seem logical that there will be some interaction between the two functions.

inventory management

The finance function will work with distribution and logistics to ensure that there is sufficient inventory 'in the right place at the right time'. This will involve calculating reorder levels and lead times, and analysing usage in different parts of the business. It will also be able to advise on the costs of holding inventory, such as warehousing, risk of damage and the cost of tying up funds in inventory.

exporting and importing

If the business is considering whether to import or export goods and services, the finance function should be part of the decision-making process. It will be able to provide advice on the tax implications of trading overseas.

performance indicators

As we have seen for the other functions of the business, distribution and logistics will wish to monitor its success, or failure, against relevant performance indicators. Finance will need to be involved in setting these indicators and monitoring actual performance against them.

RISK

The term **risk** immediately brings with it the idea of danger, or the possibility of failure. Risk can be defined as:

'The possibility of something bad happening.'

In simple terms, risk focuses on negative or undesirable outcomes of decisions that are made. This might be the risk of an accident if you go skiing, or the risk of losing money if you make a bad investment decision.

But is risk always a bad thing? The risk of a business not being able to operate if there is a fire at its premises is certainly a bad thing, but what about the risk of investment in new plant and machinery? There is certainly the risk of the machinery costing a lot of money and not generating a decent return. But there is also the possibility that the investment in the new machinery might prove to be successful, and that the business makes more profit. This can be seen as the 'upside' of risk.

difference between risk and uncertainty

We have said that risk is the possibility of something happening that has not been planned. The decision-maker in a risky situation will know that there is more than one potential outcome of their decision and will have assessed each possible outcome before deciding to take the risk. **Uncertainty** refers to situations where the decision-maker either does not know the possible outcomes and/or the probability that they will occur.

How does uncertainty and risk affect business decisions? Read the following example that illustrates this difference.

example

Fruity Fizz Ltd makes carbonated drinks using fresh fruit juice and sparkling spring water. It has done some market research and has found that its customers would like to be able to buy its most popular flavours, Bursting Berry Crush, in larger bottles.

The shareholders of the business have said they would like the business to be more environmentally friendly.

The business is considering producing two litre bottles of the product. It has not yet decided whether to replace its bottles with bottles made from 100% recycled plastic, as this will increase the price of the product.

The business knows that Bursting Berry Crush is popular, but the **uncertainty** for Fruity Fizz Ltd in this situation is how many customers will buy the new two litre bottles of the product.

The business faces a **risk** that if it doesn't move to the recycled bottles, its shareholders may withdraw their investment in the business.

The key thing to do when faced with risk and uncertainty is to gather as much information as possible before making a decision on how to minimise uncertainty and assessing the risk.

business risk

But what does risk mean in a business context? Well let's start with a definition of business risk:

> *'A business's vulnerability to factors that could decrease its profits or cause the business to fail.'*

Business risk affects a business because of the products or services it produces and the way in which it operates. It can be further analysed into the types of risk that are detailed below.

strategic risk

Strategic risks are those that arise from the fundamental decisions the directors of the business make about the business's objectives, or strategies. An example of a strategic risk would be for a car manufacturing business to move production of one of its models overseas. This may be a positive move for the business but could result in risks associate with exchange rates, working conditions in different country or changes in the duties on imports and exports.

financial risk

Financial risk for a business comes from a change in the financial conditions in which it operates. This might be a change in interest rates that increases the cost of borrowings, or a deterioration in the credit rating of one of its customers. If a business heavily relies on loans (ie debt) it is referred to as being highly geared. An increase in interest rates will increase the repayments that need to be made by a highly geared business.

A business that offers credit terms to its customers will need to ensure that these customers are able to pay when their invoices are due. Most businesses expect to receive credit from their suppliers, but non-payment by customers is hugely expensive for a business. Consequently it is very important to reduce the risk of non-payment by regularly monitoring the credit rating of customers.

operational risk

An operational risk is a risk that arises from the way in which an organisation operates its business functions. It is a very broad concept which focuses on risks arising from the people, systems and processes and the ethical attitude of the organisation. Examples of operational risk are:

- **process risk** – there will be risks of loss inherent to the processes of a business. Most organisations will have internal controls built into their systems and processes. For example, most companies carry out a bank reconciliation on a regular basis to ensure that the cash book reflects what is actually held in the bank account once timing differences have been taken into account. If this control was not carried out, the risk that money could be fraudulently taken from the business without detection is significantly increased.

- **people risk** – this is the risk from issues caused by the people who work for an organisation. References should be sought when recruiting a new member of staff to confirm their qualifications and experience. Failure to do this increases the risk of employing someone who is not competent, or is even dishonest. People risk is also the risk from over-reliance on key members of staff. If a manager leaves a business to join a competitor, this is an example of operational risk as the business will lose their skills and expertise.

- **systems risk** – most organisations are heavily dependent on computer systems in all aspects of their operations. Unless these systems have strong controls built in, there are increased risks that the systems could be used to process fraudulent transactions. An example of this would be a payroll system. A lack of controls over access to the payroll system could result in fictitious employees being set up on the system and money being fraudulently paid to the person who set them up.
- **legal and regulatory risk** – this is the risk of loss resulting from an organisation failing to comply with legislation and/or regulations. This could be risks relating to health and safety regulations, or breaches of regulations relevant to the industry that the business operates in, resulting in the risk of fines.
- **event risk** – other categories of operational risks are event risks which may be present due to an external factor or event that affects the business. The causes of these event risks can be:
  - **physical event risks** – the risk of fire or flood which could damage documents or assets, or could interrupt business, are examples of physical risks.
  - **social event risks** – as the public is becoming increasingly socially aware, a business that uses inexpensive labour in certain parts of the world could be exposed to a social event risk if this was reported in a negative fashion as 'slave labour.'
  - **political event risks** – when governments make political decisions such as increasing rates of taxation or introducing environmental legislation, this will have an effect on organisations. These are examples of political risks.
  - **economic event risks** – if the Bank of England raises interest rates, this has an impact on the interest rates charged by lenders. This would be an example of an economic event risk for a business that has to pay interest on loans.

cyber risk

The increased use of technology in all aspects of business operations has meant that cyber risk for most businesses has increased. PwC defines cyber risk as:

> *'Any risk associated with financial loss, disruption or damage to the reputation of an organisation from failure, unauthorized or erroneous use of its information systems.'*

Cyber risks most commonly come from outside the organisation. Some examples of cyber risk are:

- **phishing** – an attacker sends a message to a person within the business which attempts to trick them into opening the email or an attachment. Once opened, this will release malware or ransomware into the system, or will identify information that will allow the attacker to access, or withhold access to, the organisation's network and data.

- **malware** – this is malicious software that is often inserted into computers when attachments on phishing emails are opened, or links are clicked. The malware breaches information systems by finding the weaknesses in the business's network. Malware can include viruses, keyloggers, spyware, worms, or ransomware.
- **ransomware** – this is a form of malware that locks a user out of their own information systems. It then asks for a 'ransom' to be paid to the attacker. Failure to make the payment may lead the attacker to retaliate by posting the business's confidential data online.
- **distributed denial-of-service attack (DDoS)** – this bombards an organisation's central server with huge numbers of data requests simultaneously. This then causes the system to freeze up, and effectively holds the business hostage until the attacker's demands are met.
- **spyware** – if this gets into an organisation's system, it allows the attacker to spy on its operations and gather information without been seen.
- **keylogging** – this is similar to spyware, and it records every keystroke made by the users of the system. This can then be recreated by the hacker to identify passwords and other sensitive information.
- **password attack** – this occurs when a hacker tries to steal a user's password. Hackers rely on users selecting short, easy to 'guess' passwords, and use automated programmes to generate a large number of combinations of common words and numbers in the hope that they will 'guess' the right password.
- **browser hijacking** – the attacker will change the default homepage or search engine in the user's web browser without their permission, using a malicious programme. This then allows the hijacker to feed the user with unwanted advertising and popups and to steal information using malware.

reputational risk

Something that threatens the good name of a business, or its reputation, is known as a reputational risk. This can result from a number of different factors, the direct actions of the business, the actions of one or more of its employees, or the actions of a third party that is linked to the business such as a partner in a joint venture or a supplier. Damage to the reputation of a business can have a significant detrimental effect on the business, causing loss of sales and profit, employees to resign and reluctance on the part of suppliers, customers, and investors to be associated with the business.

An example of this is the damage to the reputation of the coffee chain Starbucks, which was hit by allegations of (legally) avoiding tax in the UK.

To avoid reputational risk damage, organisations must have good codes of conduct, strong governance and be transparent in their dealings with customers, suppliers, employees, and all other external parties. In addition to this, the organisation needs to be socially responsible and environmentally conscious.

RISK MANAGEMENT

Once a business has identified the risks that we have looked at in the previous section, it is important to have a process for managing these risks. The first step is to evaluate each risk by deciding the **likelihood** of the risk actually happening, and the **impact** on the business if it does, ie how bad will the effect be if the risk actually materialises?

evaluating risk

Many organisations will use a risk map, or **risk matrix**, to assess risk. This is simply a table or chart which plots the impact of the risk on one axis and the likelihood of it materialising on the other. Risks can then be grade by multiplying impact and likelihood.

The diagram below shows a risk matrix which grades impact and likelihood each from 1–4. The lowest risk is a project that is graded 1, ie low impact and very unlikely, with the highest risk being graded 16, which is high impact and very likely to materialise. In this example the risks that are graded the highest are the ones that will need to be addressed as the highest priority.

Impact					
	4	4	8	12	16
	3	3	6	9	12
	2	2	4	6	8
	1	1	2	3	4
		1	2	3	4
		Likelihood			

managing risk

Once risks have been identified and evaluated, the business must decide how the individual risks can be managed. The **TARA framework** is used to do this. TARA is a mnemonic for the four possible actions that can be taken to address each risk. These are explained below.

- **Transfer** – there are certain situations where risk can be wholly or partly transferred to a third party. This means that if the risk materialises, rather than having an adverse effect on the organisation, the third party will bear most, or all, of the loss. The best example of this is insurance: if a business takes out buildings and contents insurance, the risk of loss from a fire or flood is transferred to the insurance company. The business may end up having to pay a small excess, depending on the details of the policy, but this is likely to be substantially less than the cost of any damage should a fire or flood occur.
- **Avoid** – once a risk has been identified, an organisation may decide to avoid the risk completely. This is a difficult strategy to adopt as some risks are unavoidable unless the business withdraws completely from an opportunity. Avoidance of risk should only be considered when risks are highly likely and would have a significant adverse impact on the business if they were to materialise.
- **Reduce** – in some ways this would seem the most obvious approach to take. It involves proactively taking steps to reduce the possibility of the risk materialising and minimising the effect if it does. An example of reducing risk would be to send staff members on regular training courses to ensure that they have the necessary skills to operate machinery.
- **Accept** – the final option available is to accept that the risk might happen and make a conscious decision to deal with it if and when it does. Acceptance of risk tends to be the strategy used for risks that are unlikely to occur and which would not have a significant adverse effect on the business. An example of a risk that might be accepted is the risk of bad weather postponing a sporting event.

The TARA approach to managing risk can be plotted on a **risk map** like this:

		Impact/consequence on business	
Likelihood		Low	High
	High	Reduce the risk	Avoid the risk
	Low	Accept the risk	Transfer the risk

Chapter Summary

- There are three main organisational structures: functional, divisional and matrix.

- The span of control of managers in an organisation will depend on its size, the type of work that the individuals in the organisation do, and the location of the staff.

- A tall organisational structure will typically be organised by function and will have a long chain of command, whereas a flat organisational structure will have fewer levels of management so that information can pass quickly up and down the management chain, leading to quicker decision-making.

- In order to operate efficiently and effectively and achieve its objectives, an organisation must have strong governance. This will provide a framework for managing the business and will identify who can make decisions. This will include corporate governance from the board of directors who have been appointed by the shareholders, financial governance which focuses on how the business collects, manages, and controls financial information, and legal governance which ensures that the business complies with the necessary legislation and regulation.

- The control within a business may be centralised which means that decision-making lies with the higher tiers of management, or decentralised where authority for making decisions is given to lower levels of management in the business.

- There are three key strategic levels in most organisations which will affect the way they are controlled. At the top of the organisation is the strategic, or corporate, level where key 'strategic' decisions are made that tend to be longer term. Next there is the managerial level where decisions that relate to the way in which the business is run are made. The final level is operational where shorter term decisions are made relating to the practical day-to-day running of the business.

- The finance function interacts with all other key functions within a business, giving advice, and providing key financial information to inform decision-making, budgeting and performance indicators against which the functions are monitored.

- Businesses need to able to differentiate between risk (the possibility of something happening that has not been planned) and uncertainty (where the decision maker does not know what will happen).

- Operational risk arises from the way in which the functions of a business operate. This includes cyber risks associated with financial loss, and disruption or damage as a result of unauthorised access to the organisation's system and data. It also includes reputational risk that threatens the good name of the business.

- Once a business risk has been identified, it will need to be assessed in terms of the likelihood of it happening and the impact it will have if it does. The combination of these two factors can be combined using a risk map, or risk matrix, to see how serious a risk is.

- A business can choose four options as to how to deal with a risk:
  - Transfer it to a third party, eg an insurance company
  - Avoid the risk completely, eg by withdrawing completely from a business situation
  - Reduce the possibility of the risk materialising and minimise the effect if it does, eg by sending staff on training courses
  - Accept the fact that the risk might materialise and decide to do something about it if it does, eg accept that rain may postpone a rugby game

Key Terms

functional structure — a structure that divides the business into specialised functions or skills such as production, sales and marketing, finance, and IT

divisional structure — a structure that divides the business into a number of different teams that each focus on an individual product or service, or on a geographical area

matrix structure — a structure where as well as working in their own departments within a business, individuals will work across teams and projects

span of control — the number of individuals that a manager is responsible for

tall organisational structure — a business structure which has many layers of management and a narrow span of control

flat organisational structure — a business structure which has few layers of management and a wide span of control

governance — a system that provides a framework for managing organisations. It identifies who can make decisions, who has the authority to act on behalf of the organisation and who is accountable for how an organisation and its people behave and perform

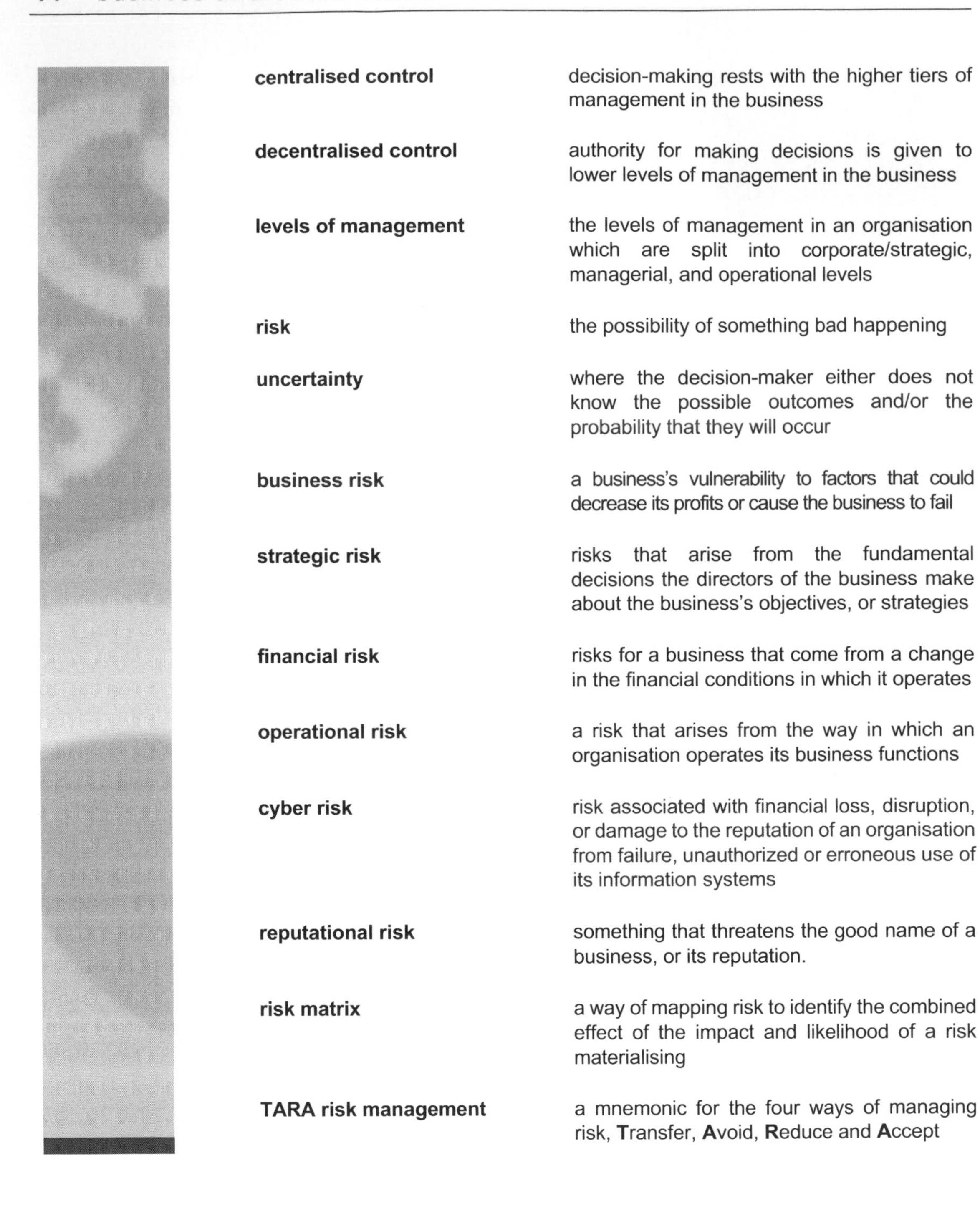

centralised control
decision-making rests with the higher tiers of management in the business

decentralised control
authority for making decisions is given to lower levels of management in the business

levels of management
the levels of management in an organisation which are split into corporate/strategic, managerial, and operational levels

risk
the possibility of something bad happening

uncertainty
where the decision-maker either does not know the possible outcomes and/or the probability that they will occur

business risk
a business's vulnerability to factors that could decrease its profits or cause the business to fail

strategic risk
risks that arise from the fundamental decisions the directors of the business make about the business's objectives, or strategies

financial risk
risks for a business that come from a change in the financial conditions in which it operates

operational risk
a risk that arises from the way in which an organisation operates its business functions

cyber risk
risk associated with financial loss, disruption, or damage to the reputation of an organisation from failure, unauthorized or erroneous use of its information systems

reputational risk
something that threatens the good name of a business, or its reputation.

risk matrix
a way of mapping risk to identify the combined effect of the impact and likelihood of a risk materialising

TARA risk management
a mnemonic for the four ways of managing risk, **T**ransfer, **A**void, **R**educe and **A**ccept

Activities

2.1 Decide which organisational structure is best for each of the following businesses.

	Functional	Divisional	Matrix
Dessus Ltd, an accountancy practice with individual teams that are responsible for audit, taxation, accounts preparation and consultancy services.			
Fabulous Phones and Tablets Ltd, a mobile phone business that sells exclusively on the internet, with teams for sales and marketing, finance, production, administration, and human resources, that all report to the board of directors.			
Pharmacular plc, a pharmaceutical company that has autonomous businesses in different countries all over the world that report to the managing company.			
Jenious Ltd, an engineering business that has a number of project teams that are developing new products.			

2.2 Complete the following sentences by selecting the correct options to fill the gaps.

A manager who works in a business with a **flat/tall** organisational structure is usually responsible for a larger number of employees and is said to have a **narrow/wide** span of control.

A manager who is responsible for a smaller number of individuals is said to have a **narrow/wide** span of control and will usually work in a **flat/tall** organisational structure.

2.3 Decide whether each of these options is a feature of a business with centralised or decentralised control.

	Centralised control	**Decentralised control**
Decisions are made at higher levels of the organisation's management.		
Senior management will be distanced from the day-to-day running of the business.		
Authority for decision-making is given to lower levels of management.		
This 'bottom-up' structure often leads to a more collaborative working atmosphere.		
This 'top-down structure' has less flexibility.		

2.4 The system that directs and controls the way in which a business is operated is which of the following?

Select **one** option.

(a) Centralised control	
(b) Corporate governance	
(c) Companies Act	
(d) Corporate goals	

2.5 Identify the type of cyber risk in each of the following situations by selecting from these options (use each option once):

Phishing, Malware, Ransomware, Keylogging, Spyware, Distributed denial-of-service attack (DDoS), Password attack, Browser hijacking

Type of cyber risk	Option
An attack that locks the user out of their information system and asks for money to be paid to the attacker to prevent further disruption.	
This allows the attacker to watch the operations of the business without being seen by the user.	
An email stating that the user's bank details have been compromised, with a link asking them to input their existing password so the bank can supply them with a new one.	
The attacker uses automatic software to generate huge numbers of word and number combinations in the hope that they will 'guess' the user's password.	
If this type of malware gets into a computer, it can record every keystroke made by users. This then allows the hacker to identify passwords and access sensitive information.	
The user's default homepage or search engine changes so that the attacker can feed the user with unwanted pop-ups and advertising.	
The general term for malicious software, often inserted into computer via phishing emails, that can introduce viruses, keyloggers, spyware, worms, or ransomware.	
This type of cyber-attack overwhelms the organisation's computer systems with a huge number of data requests simultaneously. This then causes the system to freeze up.	

2.6 A threat to the good name of a business is known as which of these?

Select **one** option.

(a)	Legal and regulatory risk	
(b)	Reputational risk	
(c)	Operational risk	
(d)	Financial risk	

2.7 Which of the following might create a strategic risk to a business?

Select **one** option.

(a)	Failure to comply with health and safety regulations	
(b)	An increase in the interest rate on a business loan	
(c)	Management deciding to introduce a new product to the market without carrying out any market research	
(d)	Employing staff without the necessary qualifications or experience	

2.8 What are the two factors that a business should consider when grading a risk using a risk matrix?

Select **two** options.

(a)	Legality	
(b)	Impact	
(c)	Scope	
(d)	Likelihood	

2.9 The TARA Framework is commonly used to manage risk with the decision being whether to transfer, avoid, reduce, or accept the risk. For each of the following situations, decide which of these risk management techniques is being used.

A music festival that takes place in the summer regardless of whether it rains or not.	
A freight business insures all the cargo on its ships against damage or loss at sea.	
A business ceasing clothing production overseas due to the risk to its reputation of using child labour.	
Regular staff training in a business where there is a risk of wastage of raw materials if the staff do not operate the machines effectively.	

3 The external and internal environment

this chapter covers...

In this chapter we will look at PESTLE analysis as a way of analysing how political, economic, social, technological, legal, and environmental factors affect the way in which a business operates.

We will then consider the micro-economic environment in which a business operates, starting with the concept of supply and demand. When we look at demand, we will consider normal goods, inferior goods, necessity goods, substitute products, and complementary products. We will cover the factors that cause an actual shift in the supply and demand curves, compared with movement up or down the curves themselves.

We will also cover the price mechanism, and the way in which the forces of supply and demand operate to reach the equilibrium price.

The next section of the chapter will focus on factors that affect competition in the micro-economic aspect of the market, including product features that differentiate a product (or not), the number of sellers and buyers, barriers to entry, location of the business, its customers and the resources it needs to access, and availability of information.

PESTLE ANALYSIS

The way in which a business operates is constantly affected by external factors that the business cannot control. Therefore, the business must assess these external factors carefully, to ensure that it takes the necessary action to minimise any negative effects and maximise any positive effects that they have on the business's success.

PESTLE is an analysis technique that is often used to help a business to understand the impact of external factors on its operation. PESTLE is an acronym made up of the first letters of six key types of factor. External factors can have a positive or a negative effect on the business – some may even have both. It is very important to identify these factors and how important they are to the business.

P	Political
E	Economic
S	Social
T	Technological
L	Legal
E	Environmental

political factors

Political factors relate to the extent to which the Government influences the economy. Several aspects of government policies and decision-making will affect the way in which a business operates. If a business is considering operating overseas, or trading with a business in another country, the political stability of the Government in that country, and any local regulations, will have an impact on the way in which it does this. We will now look at some specific political factors that affect the environment in which businesses operate.

government policy

Government policy will influence the way in which a business operates. For example, some governments will be keen to encourage overseas investment by businesses that locate their operations in their country and will offer them tax breaks, ie reduced taxation, to encourage them. Other governments may have policies that make it more difficult for businesses to operate in their country.

taxation

The Government can increase or decrease rates of **taxation.** This may be corporation tax that is paid by businesses on their profit; VAT, which is charged on products and services that the business buys or sells; or income tax which is paid by individuals, sole traders and employees of the business. If corporation tax is increased, this will reduce the profit of the business. An increase in the rate of VAT will increase the selling price charged to customers which may have a negative impact on the volume of sales. An increase in income tax will mean that sole traders have less income after tax and individuals will have lower disposable income which may have an adverse effect on sales. Conversely, if the rates of any of these taxations reduces, this will have the opposite effect, with profits and disposable income increasing.

imports and exports

Tariffs may be imposed by governments on **imports and exports**. Tariffs are a form of tax and are a common feature for a business that trades internationally. Governments often impose tariffs on imports to reduce the amount of goods that are imported into the country. They do this to protect domestic producers against being 'undercut' by cheaper imports. They may also do it protect consumers in the country against risks from cheap imported goods that may contain components, or ingredients, that could cause harm.

Similarly, a business may wish to export its goods or services and be faced by tariffs and duties in the country to which it wants to export.

public spending

Expenditure in the public sector by the Government is known as **public spending**. The Government decides how much of the money collected in taxation should be allocated to the various areas of the public sector, and, therefore, how much they have to spend. Many businesses will provide goods and services to the public sector and consequently will be affected by the level of public spending.

The following example illustrates a political factor that might affect a business and what the business might do to reduce the threat this poses.

political factor – Jenus Ltd

the effect of a new tariff

As well as trading in the UK, Jenus Ltd exports its products overseas. The government of one of the countries that it exports to has recently announced that it will be imposing a 30% tariff on imports from the UK. Jenus Ltd has realised that this will make its products uncompetitive in that country and its customers are likely to purchase from domestic suppliers instead. This will have a significant effect on its revenue and profitability.

action to minimise the effect of this factor

There are two things that Jenus Ltd can do in this situation:

1 Assess the effect of the import tariff and reduce its prices to try and continue to be competitive.

trading relationships with customers in these countries.

economic factors

The **macro-economy** refers to the economy as a whole and will have a direct impact on the way in which a business operates. The financial state of the economy of a country, or even at a global level, is a key factor that affects consumer demand, growth of the business, and its profitability. We will now look at some of the key economic factors that may be relevant to a PESTLE analysis carried out by a business.

interest rates

The **interest rate** is the price at which a business, or an individual, can borrow money, or the return they will get on money that they save. A business that has finance in the form of bank borrowing will see an increase in its costs if interest rates rise, as it will have to make higher repayments. When interest rates are high, businesses are also less likely to take out new borrowing and so will invest less in growing the business. Higher interest rates mean that consumers will save more money and consequently spend less money on goods and services.

When interest rates are low, this will encourage businesses to borrow more to invest in the business. Consumers are less likely to save and more likely to spend their money on goods and services.

exchange rates

The **exchange rate** between the UK pound and other currencies will go up and down. A fall in the rate of exchange, which is sometimes called a weakening of the pound, means that the amount of the other currency that £1 is worth is falling. For example, if the exchange rate was £1:US$1.45 and it fell to £1:US$1.30, this means that one pound now is worth 15 cents less than it was previously.

A weak pound means that anything that is produced in the UK and sold abroad will be cheaper for the buyer. However, it also means that a business in the UK that has to buy raw materials from abroad will get less for its money and so will have to pay more for it. This will increase the production costs which may be passed on to customers as higher prices.

What we do have to remember is that a strong pound will have the opposite effect. Any raw materials bought from abroad will cost a UK business less as it gets more for its money. It will also mean that goods that are produced in the UK and sold abroad will cost the buyer more. This could mean that the UK business has to reduce the price to ensure that it doesn't lose the business.

changes in disposable income

Disposable income is the money that people have to spend after taxes and essential living costs have been deducted. In periods when economic growth is increasing, the economy is able to produce more goods and services, more jobs will be created and there will be higher levels of employment. This all means that the level of disposable income will rise. This will be good for businesses as people will spend their additional disposable income on goods and services.

Of course, there are also periods when economic growth is decreasing. This is known as a recession. During these periods unemployment will increase, resulting in people having less disposable income to spend on goods and services.

business cycles

The amount of goods and services that are produced in the economy does not rise at a constant rate over time. We generally see a regular rise and fall, or cycle of change in business activity. This is known as the **business cycle** or sometimes the economic or trade cycle. The four elements of the business cycle are:

- **boom** – this is when the economy is growing, unemployment is low and consumer demand is high. Businesses are making high levels of profit and the Government is collecting high levels of taxes – a win-win
- **downturn** – the boom cannot last forever, inflation starts to rise and also interest rates, resulting in businesses getting more nervous. Basically, the economy begins to slow down
- **recession** – if the economy slows so much that it actually starts to shrink, then this is known as a recession. In this period of the business cycle unemployment will rise and businesses may start to struggle as demand for their products and services decreases.
- **recovery** – when there has been a period of recession, interest rates are likely to be lowered to try to stimulate the economy. This may prompt businesses to make investment and start to grow which will create new jobs; unemployment will fall; disposable income will increase and with it, consumer spending.

It is important for business to be able to adapt the way it operates for each stage of the business cycle.

inflation

Inflation is the percentage rise in prices over time. When there is inflation, it means that money does not buy as much as it did previously. For example, if the inflation rate for the cost of butter is 5% over a year, it means that consumers will need to spend 5% more on butter than they did a year ago. A small level of inflation (around 2%) is generally considered to be okay, as it means that customers will buy sooner rather than leaving it until later in case prices fall.

However, businesses do not want high levels of inflation as this will cause rapid price increases and discourage consumers from buying anything more than the essentials. This will have a negative impact on businesses that produce luxury, or non-essential, items.

But what causes inflation? Well, two of the key drivers are **demand-pull** and **cost-push**.

- **demand-pull inflation** – when demand for products and services increases, and businesses cannot meet this demand, this drives the price up. This is known as demand-pull inflation This increased excessive demand normally occurs in an expanding economy. An increase in government spending or growth in trade overseas will also contribute to demand-pull inflation.
- **cost-push inflation** – when the supply of goods and services decreases because of an increase in production costs, this will result in cost-push inflation. This increase in production costs may be due to scarcity of raw materials or labour pushing the price up, or an increase in taxes by the Government. Whatever the cause of the increase in production costs, this will inevitably have to be passed on to consumers in the form of price increases.

The next example illustrates an economic factor that might affect a business and what the business might do to reduce the threat this poses.

economic factor – Fine Furnishings Ltd

the effect of an increase in interest rates

Fine Furnishings Ltd is a business that produces high quality, bespoke furniture in the UK. Interest rates have been increasing which has resulted in the disposable income of its potential customers decreasing. This has resulted in a small, but significant, drop in sales for the business, and the sales director is concerned that this trend will continue.

action to minimise the effect of this factor

Fine Furnishing Ltd could consider designing and producing more affordable furniture which its potential customers are more likely to buy. The business will have to decide whether to replace its existing range or to extend the range.

social factors

As the names suggests, social factors that affect the operation of a business relate to the society in which the business operates. This will include cultural and demographic aspects such as:

- income levels
- language and culture
- religion
- education

- family structure
- age
- occupations

These factors will affect the businesses on a local level as well as a national and international level. For example, a business that requires a highly skilled workforce may decide to locate itself in an area with high levels of educational attainment. Equally, a retail business with multiple locations may decide to adjust the range of items it sells in specific branches to reflect the local community.

Businesses must carefully monitor **demographic changes**, ie the change in the structure of the population, so that they continue to meet its wants and needs. This may be an increase in the overall size of the population which will increase demand for products and services, or it may be an increase in a specific segment of the population which has specific tastes and spending power. For example, as people live longer in the UK this means that there is an ageing population. Generally, this older generation has a higher disposable income and are more likely to spend money on holidays, new cars and home improvements.

Another social factor is the shift in **trends**. Over the last 20 years people have become much more health conscious; gym memberships have increased as have healthy meal options such as organic, low-fat and low-sugar foods. Twenty years ago, the idea of buying a takeaway coffee on the way to work would have been met with surprise, but now it is very much considered the norm. Again, businesses must be aware of trends and monitor them to ensure that they adapt their business to maintain their market share and remain relevant and competitive.

We have already seen that **unemployment** can be a consequence of a reduction in economic growth. However, this can also be a social factor. If a business is located in an area of high unemployment there will be a larger population to draw its workforce from. But if a business relies on the local population to buy its products or services and there is high unemployment, this means that the business will have to adapt. This might be by reducing prices, or by offering a more basic range rather than the more expensive luxury ranges.

The example on the next page illustrates a social factor that a business might face and the ways in which it might address it.

social factor – Johnstone & Sons

the effect of a change in customer tastes

Johnstone & Sons is a long established family business that produces traditional, old-fashioned confectionery. The business has a loyal customer base, but research it has carried out has established that customer tastes are changing, and whilst people are buying their confectionery as treats, increasingly they are looking for healthier, more natural snacks. The owners of Johnstone & Sons are concerned that sales of their products will continue to fall due to this change in customer tastes.

action to minimise the effect of this factor

There are two things that Johnstone & Sons could consider in this situation:

1. Introduce new products that include healthier ingredients, such as nuts, seeds, and dried fruit, which would appeal to a more heath conscious customer base.
2. Reduce the sugar content in some of its products – although there is a risk that this may affect the taste.

technological factors

'T' in a PESTLE analysis represents technological influences on the business. In recent years, technological innovation has been a huge factor in the way in which businesses operate and can affect an individual business, a whole industry or even all industries. **Changes in technology** can have both positive and negative effects on a business.

Examples of the positive impact that changes in technology can have are:

- easier access to market through website sales and internet marketing
- computer aided design (CAD) reducing the time it takes between the idea for a new product and its production
- automated production lines which reduce labour costs and increase productivity
- Improved safety due to automation of processes
- Electronic point of sales systems (EPOS) which monitor inventory from the warehouse to the checkout, and provide instant up-to-date data on inventory levels and consumer spending habits
- more choice for consumers and information on products via the internet

But negative impacts that technological changes can have on businesses include:

- products becoming obsolete more quickly meaning inventory of older versions need to be sold more cheaply or written off
- more choice for consumers and information on products via the internet mean they can easily switch from one supplier to another

- the introduction of automated processes may mean redundancies which will cost the business money and cause staff unrest

Technology can also have an **impact on the structure** of a business. Global communication has meant that many businesses have decided to locate their support departments, such as customer services and even finance, overseas. By locating these department overseas, businesses can see a significant reduction in costs. However, before deciding to do this a business must ensure that the staff it recruits are well trained so that customers do not see a reduction in the quality of service that they receive.

Businesses may also decide to outsource elements of their production processes to other business in the UK, or overseas. Technology allows them to remotely monitor production which reduces the risk of quality issues and/or delays in supply previously associated with outsourcing.

The next example illustrates a technological factor that affects a business and the way in which it can be addressed:

technological factor – Trendy Threads

the opportunity created by new technology

Trendy Threads is a business that produces rucksacks and kitbags which are popular with the parents of school age children who buy these durable bags for their children to use for school.

The business has been looking into replacing some of the existing machinery on its production line with digitally-controlled machines. It has found that the machines it wants to buy have new technology that would allow Trendy Threads to personalise some of the bags and rucksacks that it produces, by adding names of schools, sports clubs, or businesses.

action to maximise the opportunity of this technological factor

If Trendy Threads decides to buy the new digitally-controlled machines, it could offer an option to personalise some of its products. For example, reading book bags for primary schools, sports bags for clubs and associations eg football or netball clubs or dance schools. They would be able to produce smaller batches of these products with colour options and charge a premium on the price to reflect the fact that they have ben personalised.

legal factors

Businesses are required to comply with the laws and regulations of the countries in which they operate and/or sell their goods and services. The relevant laws and regulations that affect a business will depend on what the business actually does, but can include:

- health and safety law – this will particularly affect production departments within businesses, as they must comply with this legislation in order to keep their workforce safe. But it will also be relevant to working conditions for office workers within the business, and to workers overseas.

- employment law – businesses cannot simply 'hire and fire' employees. They must ensure that employees are treated fairly which may include working conditions, flexible working, or the right to maternity/paternity leave.
- discrimination law – The Equality Act (2010) protects employees with 'protected characteristics' – including age, disability, sex, race, religion, marital status and pregnancy – against discrimination.
- national minimum wage regulations – businesses must ensure that they pay all employees in accordance with the national minimum wage regulations in the UK. If they employ workers overseas, they must also ensure that they pay a fair wage for the country in which they work.
- consumer protection – many businesses need to devote significant amounts of time to producing detailed information about their products and services so that consumers are clear what they are buying.
- import/export law – any business that imports into the UK will need to comply with its import laws and tariffs. Equally, any UK business that exports will be required to comply with the import laws of the counties where it is selling its goods or services. Since Brexit, this is particularly relevant in the UK.

Having ensured that it complies with the current legislation and regulations, the business must also be aware that these may change. For example, the national minimum wage increases each year. Also new laws or regulations may come into force which relate to the business and with which it must comply. For example, in the last decade all of the countries that make up the UK have made it a legal requirement for retail businesses to charge their customers for plastic carrier bags. These businesses have had to adapt their working practices to comply with this.

The situation in the scenario below is an example of a legal factor that affects a supermarket business.

legal factor – Firmfare Ltd

the effect of an increase in the national minimum wage

Firmfare Ltd runs a chain of supermarkets across the UK and employs over 20,000 members of staff on the shop floor of its stores. A significant number of these employees are paid the national minimum wage.

The Government increased the national minimum wage annually at a higher rate than inflation for over several years, which is having an adverse effect on Firmfare Ltd's profit margin. The business has been looking for ways to reduce its staff costs.

action to address this legal factor

Firmfare Ltd could consider introducing self-service till points in its stores. This would allow the business to reduce its workforce, as it would need fewer members of staff to supervise these tills. However, the business would have to be careful that the risk of shoplifting did not increase, or that customers were dissatisfied with the new arrangement so that they moved their shopping to a different supermarket.

environmental factors

The final letter of a PESTLE analysis is another 'E', but this time it represents environmental factors that affect a business. Scientists spend a lot of time assessing the way in which people and animals affect the environment. Global warming and the erosion of the ozone layer continue to be serious threats to the planet with deforestation, burning fossil fuels, air pollution and increases in population all contributing to this issue.

Environmental factors create two types of issue for businesses:

- the direct impacts of **environmental change**, including climate change, changes in the weather, increased pollution, and availability of non-renewable resources such as oil and gas and pollution, may all affect the way in which certain businesses operate. Farming has been forced to change its methods to take account of changing weather patterns, while energy companies have spent huge amounts of money researching renewable energy options.
- the need for the business to act **sustainably**. This may be because the business is motivated to protect the environment and consequently take steps to ensure they act sustainably. Or it may be because of customer expectations to act sustainably. If a business is not seen to be 'green' – ie environmentally friendly – then customers may decide to take their business elsewhere. We will look at sustainability in more detail later in Chapter 4.

The example below highlights an environmental factor that might affect a business.

environmental factor – Beanzz

minimising the use of plastic and increasing recycling

Beanzz is a successful coffee shop business in the UK, with branches on the high street of most tc and cities. Traditionally it has sold its hot drinks in plastic lined paper cups, which are not recycla with plastic lids, and its cold drinks in clear plastic cups.

A government initiative has meant that the business must now reduce its use of plastic and en that more of its packaging is recyclable. The continued concerns about sustainability have also m that customers are more likely to buy from businesses that they believe to be actively protecting environment.

action to address this environmental factor

Beanzz may consider ways to encourage its customers to bring their own reusable coffee cups. could be by reducing the cost of the coffee for these customers, or by introducing a loyalty sch whereby customers collect points each time they bring their own cup which can be exchanged for drinks.

The business should also investigate alternative cups that can be recycled for customers who ch not to bring their own cups.

summary

PESTLE analysis is a useful way in which an organisation can assess external factors that affect it. Although these factors are outside its control it allows the business to identify ways in which it can adapt to minimise any risks and maximise any opportunities.

MICRO-ECONOMIC ENVIRONMENT

The micro-economic environment looks at the factors that affect how prices are set between buyers and sellers for good and services. The key factors are supply and demand.

the concept of supply and demand

The theory of **supply and demand** explains the interaction between sellers and buyers. It identifies the relationship between the price of a product or service and the inclination of individuals to buy or sell it. It would seem logical that if the price increases individuals are inclined to supply more but demand less. However, it is not as simple as that, and the laws of supply and demand, and what determines them, are actually separate and interact to arrive at the price and volume of goods and services.

demand

Demand is the quantity of a good or service which consumers want and are willing and able to pay for. Generally, the more that people earn, the more they buy. This means that the demand for most goods and services goes up as income rises and down as income falls. These goods are known as **normal goods**. However, there are also **inferior goods** for which demand decreases as income rises. These tend to be cheaper goods that people can afford when their income is lower. However, once their income starts to rise, they will choose to move on to more attractive and more expensive alternatives. For example, people on a lower income may buy cheap, 'own brand', coffee, but when their income rises, they will purchase more expensive, branded coffee instead.

Of course, there are certain goods that are a necessity. A necessary, or **necessity good,** is a type of normal good that consumers will buy regardless of whether their income changes. Examples of necessity goods are utilities including power and water, communication such as mobile phones, and medicines. Because these goods are a necessity, they are less sensitive to changes in income or price.

Two, or more, goods or services are classed as **substitute products** if they carry out the same purpose for the consumer. For example, Coca Cola and Pepsi are substitute products. If the price of one of the two products rises this will increase demand for the other, and vice versa. So, if the price of Pepsi was to increase this would mean that demand for Coca Cola would rise. Of course, there are always exceptions to this – some people will be prepared to pay more if they prefer the characteristics of one of the two substitutes. In the case of the cola, this might be the taste, or the look of the product packaging.

Complements are goods that must be used together – think vehicles and fuel, or a games console and games. If two goods are complements, a rise in the price of one will cause a fall in the demand for the other, and vice versa.

demand curve

We have already touched on the fact that demand for a product or service will be affected by a number of factors, but the most important of these in most cases is price. For most products demand will increase or **expand**, as the price falls and decrease, or **contract,** as the price rises. This relationship can be shown on a graph as a demand curve, which shows the relationship between the price of a good and the quantity of that good that people are willing and able to buy at that price.

The two graphs below are examples of demand curves.

demand curve examples

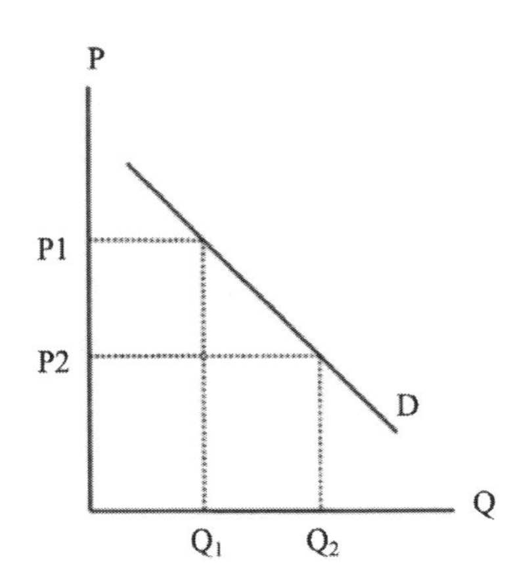

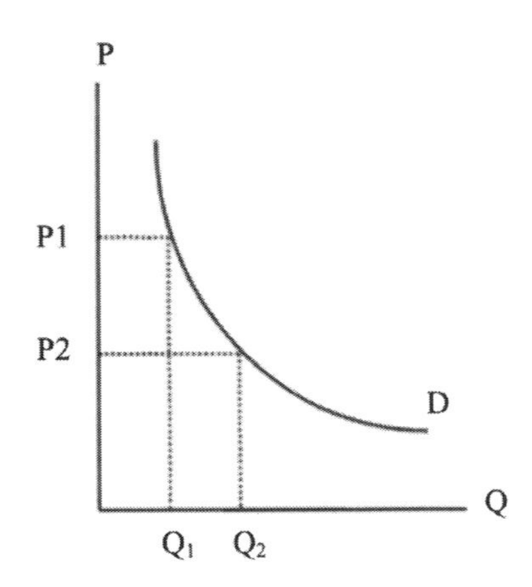

On the graph of a demand curve D is demand, P is price and Q is quantity.

Price is always shown on the vertical axis, and quantity on the horizonal axis. On each of the two graphs above it shows that a reduction in price from P1 to P2 results in a rise in demand from Q1 to Q2. The first graph shows that the relationship between price and quantity is a straight line, but even if this is the case, it is still referred to as the demand 'curve'.

supply

Supply is the quantity of a good or service which suppliers are willing and able to produce in a given period. Like demand, price is one of the most important factors affecting the decision about how much to supply.

supply curve

Although the quantity supplied depends on price, unlike demand, as the price increases supply also increases. If we think about this, it is logical as suppliers will be keen to sell more of a product if the price goes up. Consequently, the **supply curve** is always sloping upwards.

The two graphs below are examples of supply curves.

supply curve examples

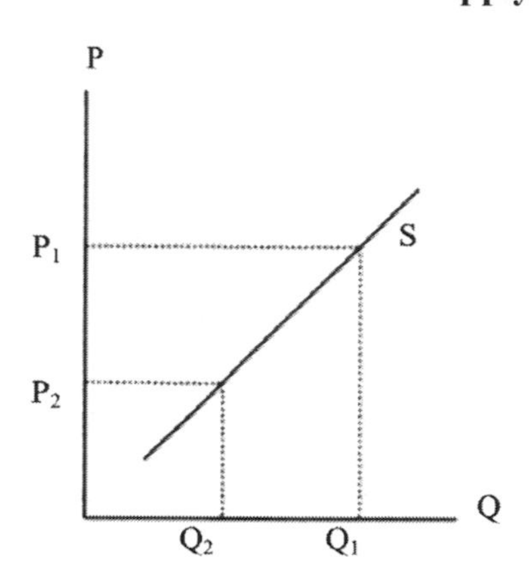

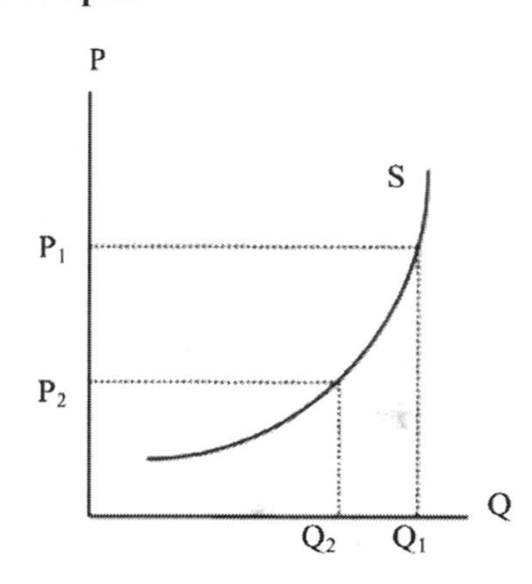

On the graph of a supply curve S is supply, P is price and Q is quantity.

As with the demand curve, price is always shown on the vertical axis, and quantity on the horizonal axis. On each of the two supply curve graphs above it shows that an increase in price from P2 to P1 results in a rise in supply from Q2 to Q1. As we saw with demand curves, it is possible for a supply curve to be a straight line, but even if this is the case it is still referred to as the supply 'curve'.

the price mechanism

Looking at demand and supply separately we can see that consumers generally want to pay as low a price as possible, whilst suppliers want to charge as much as possible. So, at some point, there will have to be a compromise between the two. If we bring the demand and supply curves for a product together then the point at which the two curves meet will determine the price.

This meeting of supply and demand may not be instant because the price of the product will affect both supply and demand, and demand and supply will affect the price. But once it settles down, and supply and demand have adjusted, then the **equilibrium price** will be reached. Basically, the market has found a **price mechanism** through the forces of supply and demand, to determine the price of goods.

The graph on the next page shows the equilibrium price where the supply and demand curve bisect.

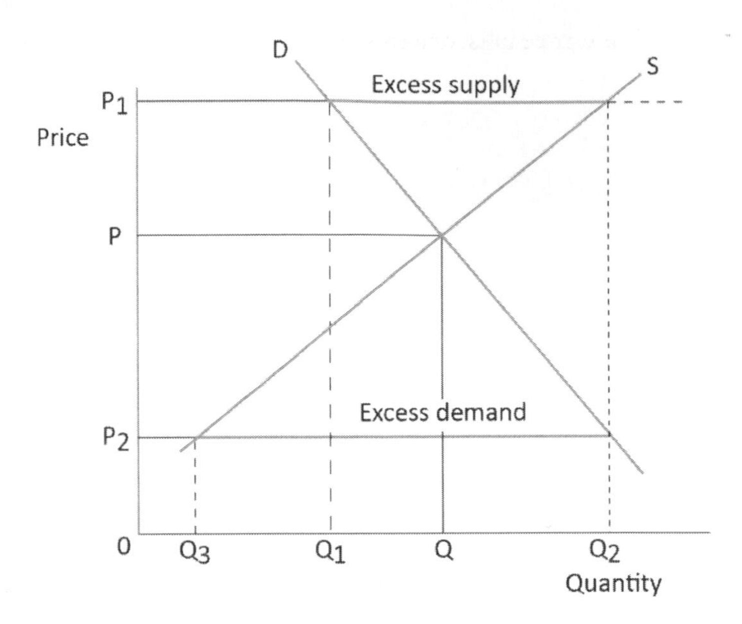

In the graph we can see that **equilibrium** is where the two 'curves' bisect ie at price P and quantity Q. At price P1 (higher than the equilibrium price), demand from consumers will reduce to Q1, resulting in excess supply. At price P2 (lower than the equilibrium price), demand will increase to Q2 which is substantially higher than the quantity available at that price, Q3. This will result in excess demand, which in turn, will lead to shortages.

In the short term these changes in price and demand will lead to a shortage or an excess of goods, but suppliers and customers will reassess the situation and a new equilibrium will be reached.

shift along the demand curve and shift in the demand curve

As we have seen, a change in the price of a good or service will result in a movement **along** the demand curve. A change in anything else will actually cause the demand curve itself to shift.

If there is an increase, or rise, in demand for a good or service, this will result in the demand curve shifting to the right – effectively, demand will increase at the same price. For example, if a celebrity chef uses a specific ingredient in a recipe, everyone wants this ingredient. So the demand increases without any change to the price. The demand curve them moves to the right.

If, on the other hand, the demand for a product decreases – maybe because the price of a substitute product has decreased – the whole demand curve will shift to the left.

In the diagram below we can see that an increase, or shift, in demand at the same price, P, moves the whole demand curve to the right from D1 to D2. Conversely, there will be an **expansion** in demand **along** the demand curve if the price falls, or a **contraction** in demand **along** the demand curve if the price rises.

shift in the demand curve

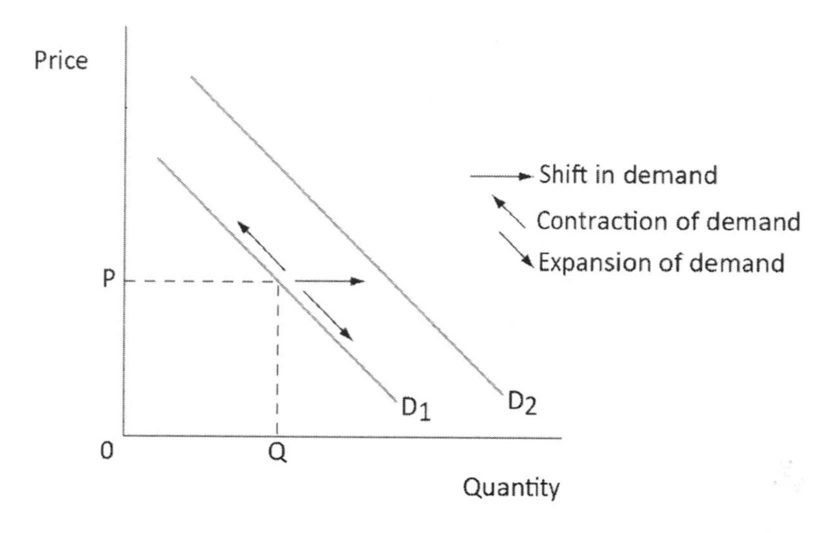

shifts along the supply curve and shift in the supply curve

If the price of a good changes, then there will be a movement along the supply curve – if the price increases, supply increases, if the price decreases, supply decreases. However, if something other than price, for example the cost of production, changes the level of supply, this will result in a shift in the whole supply curve.

If there is a scarcity of raw material that is used to make a product this can cause the cost of raw material to increase. If this happens, profit will reduce and the producer may decide to focus its efforts on other, more profitable products. This will lead to a reduced supply and the supply curve will actually shift to the left.

If there is a change in the cost of production so that it decreases – maybe because the production process has been automated and the cost of machinery is cheaper than the cost of labour – this will result in the supply curve shifting to the right.

In the diagram below we can see a decrease in supply at price P moves the whole supply curve left, from S2 to S1. Conversely, if supply at price P increases from S1 to S2, the supply curve shifts right.

shift in the supply curve

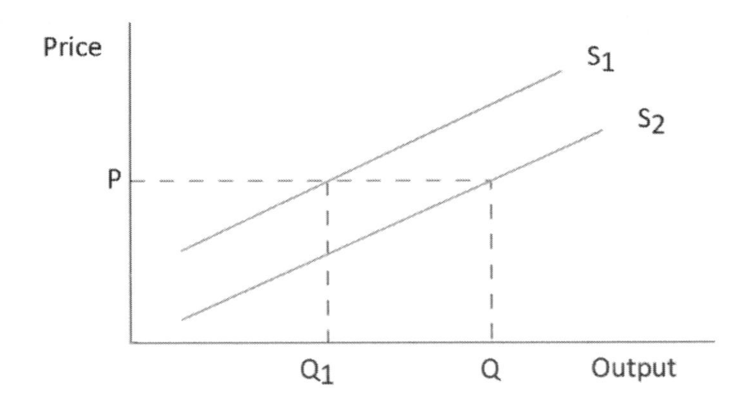

competition

It is generally the case that the more competition there is in the market for a product or service, the better it is for the consumer. In a market with lots of suppliers they will all be attempting to attract customers with competitive pricing and high quality goods and services. However, if there are few competitors in the market there is a danger of complacency on the part of suppliers, leading to higher prices and lower quality.

In the next section we will consider some of the factors that affect competition in the micro-economic environment.

product features

The thing that will make a consumer choose one product over other, similar, products will be if it has a particular feature, or features, that other products do not have. This may be the taste of Heinz tomato ketchup compared with other ketchups, the design of Nike trainers compared with other brands, or the ethical credentials of the Cooperative bank compared with other banks. Price may also be a feature that differentiates products, for example the popularity of low cost supermarkets in the UK which target consumers for whom price is a key feature.

The more that a supplier is able to **differentiate** its product, the fewer competitors it will face in the market. However, for undifferentiated products such as toothpaste, flour, or milk there will be much higher levels of competition.

number of sellers and buyers

Given what we have said so far about competition, it is fairly obvious that if there are more sellers this will result in a more competitive market. However, what happens if the converse is true and there are only a few, or even just one, seller in a particular market? A market with one major supplier who controls most, if not all, of the market is known as a **monopoly**. This generally occurs in markets that are difficult to enter and where there are no close substitutes for the product, and generally results in higher prices. For this reason legislation has meant that there are fewer monopolies in recent years. However, an example of a monopoly is a pharmaceutical company that has produced a drug to treat a particular medical condition. Development of such a drug will have required significant spending on research, testing and approval, meaning other suppliers are unlikely to have produced a similar drug.

The number of buyers in a market will also affect competition. In a market where there are few buyers for a product, the suppliers will need to be competitive to ensure that the consumers buy from them. This may be by reducing prices or improving quality. An example of this would be dairy farmers. There are many farms in the UK that produce milk; however, most of the milk produced is sold to the big supermarkets. The supermarkets can dictate the price that they pay to the farmers as there is no significant alternative market for them if they don't sell to the supermarkets.

barriers to entry

In economic terms, a barrier to entry can be defined as:

'The costs, or other obstacles, that prevent, or deter, new competitors from easily entering the market for a product or service.'

There are a number of barriers to entry that might affect a business entering a particular market, and therefore the level of competition in that market. These include:

- **legal barriers** – businesses may be required to obtain licenses from the Government before they are allowed to operate in a particular market eg pharmaceauticals. There may also be standards and regulations that the business must adhere to before it can start trading. An example of this would be health and safety and food hygiene requirements for a new restaurant.

- **set-up costs** – the initial costs of setting up a business before it has even started trading can be prohibitive. This will include premises, marketing, capital expenditure, purchases of inventory, costs of employing staff, etc, all of which must be funded before the business starts to trade

- **brand loyalty** – entering an established market will be difficult for a business, as customers will have an existing favourite brand in the market. Imagine a new burger chain entering the market – even if its products tasted the same as those of McDonalds and Burger King, the business will find it almost impossible to penetrate the market and change a customer's brand loyalty.

- **expertise** – when a business owner is setting up a new business, they are likely to have had some previous expertise in the industry. The owner of a new shop is likely to have worked in retail previously, and a restaurant owner will probably have worked in other restaurants before starting their own. But in industries there can be a significant knowledge barrier, for example a new computer software business, where the owner will either need to have the technical knowledge and expertise or sufficient funds to hire someone who has.

location

In certain markets the location of raw materials and customers will influence the level of competition and the location of a business. Some examples of this are:

- frozen food producers need to locate their processing plants close to where the crops are grown, or fish are caught, to ensure freshness
- retailers need to be located close to their customers, or in locations with good transport links and parking
- distribution companies need to be centrally located close to good transport links to ensure that they can deliver quickly and efficiently to their customers
- businesses in the technology industry need to be located where they can recruit staff with the appropriate skills.

availability of information

When we are considering the effect of availability of information on competition in a market, we are referring to how difficult it is for consumers to find and compare prices of products. If it is easy, and the information is readily available, the level of competition increases. However, if the opposite is true, and pricing information is not easily available, competition will decrease.

For example, in a street where there are a number of cafés which all have menus in their windows, it will be easy for customers to compare the prices and decide where to have lunch, and pick the most competitively priced option that fits their needs, However, if none of the cafés display menus, and customers have to go inside each café to see what is on offer before they can decide where to go, they probably won't do this as it is too time consuming. This will lead to less competition.

Chapter Summary

- PESTLE is an analysis technique that is often used to help a business to understand the impact of external factors on its operation. PESTLE is an acronym made up of the first letters of six key types of factors:

  Political factors: these are factors such as government policy, taxation, imports and export, and public spending

  Economic factors: these include interest rates, exchange rates, changes in disposable income, business cycles, and inflation

  Social factors: including cultural and demographic factors, trends, and unemployment

  Technological factors: changes in technology can have a positive and negative effect on businesses eg increased automation can lead to greater efficiencies but can also result in redundancies

  Legal factors: businesses must comply with laws and regulations such as health and safety, employment law, and minimum wage requirements

  Environmental factors: environmental changes, such as increased pollution and climate change may have an impact on the way a business operates. Sustainability will also have a significant impact; businesses will be motivated to protect the environment and also to be seen to be 'green'.

- The economic concept of supply and demand explains the interaction between sellers and buyers, and identifies the relationship between the price of a product or service and the inclination of individuals to buy or sell it.

- Demand for a product can be plotted on a demand curve with price on the vertical axis and quantity on the horizontal axis. A change in the price of a product will cause a shift along the demand curve: a shift to the left if the price increases as demand decreases, and a shift to the right if the price decreases causing demand to increase.

- If there is a change in demand for the product or service, this will cause the actual demand curve to shift - right if it is an increase in demand and left if demand decreases.

- Supply of a product can be plotted on a supply curve with price on the vertical axis and quantity on the horizonal axis. A change in the price of a product will cause a shift along the supply curve; an increase in price will cause a contraction in demand, so moving left along the supply curve, whilst a decrease in price will cause an expansion in demand, moving right along the supply curve.

- If there is a change in the level of supply of a product or service, for example a decrease in supply due to scarce raw materials or labour, this will cause the actual supply curve to shift – up and left if supply reduces and down and right if it increases.

- The forces of supply and demand will come to an equilibrium price where the supply and demand curves bisect.
- Competition in the market will be affected by product features ie how differentiated a product is, the number of buyers and sellers in the market, barriers to entry, location, and availability of information.

Key Terms

PESTLE analysis — an analysis technique that is often used to help a business to understand the impact of external factors on its operation, split into political, economic, social, technological, legal and environmental factors

public spending — government expenditure by the public sector

macro-economy — the economy for the whole country rather than individual markets

interest rate — the price at which a business, or an individual, can borrow money, or the return they will get on money that they save

exchange rate — the value of one currency if it is converted into the currency of another country, eg £1: US$1.40

disposable income — money that individuals have to spend after taxes and essential living costs have been deducted

business (trade) cycle — a regular rise and fall in business activity split into boom, downturn, recession, and recovery

inflation — the percentage rise in prices over time. Demand-pull inflation occurs when businesses cannot keep up with demand, whereas cost-push inflation occurs when the supply of goods and services decreases because of an increase in production costs

demographic changes — the change in the structure of the population which could include age, income levels, education, or culture

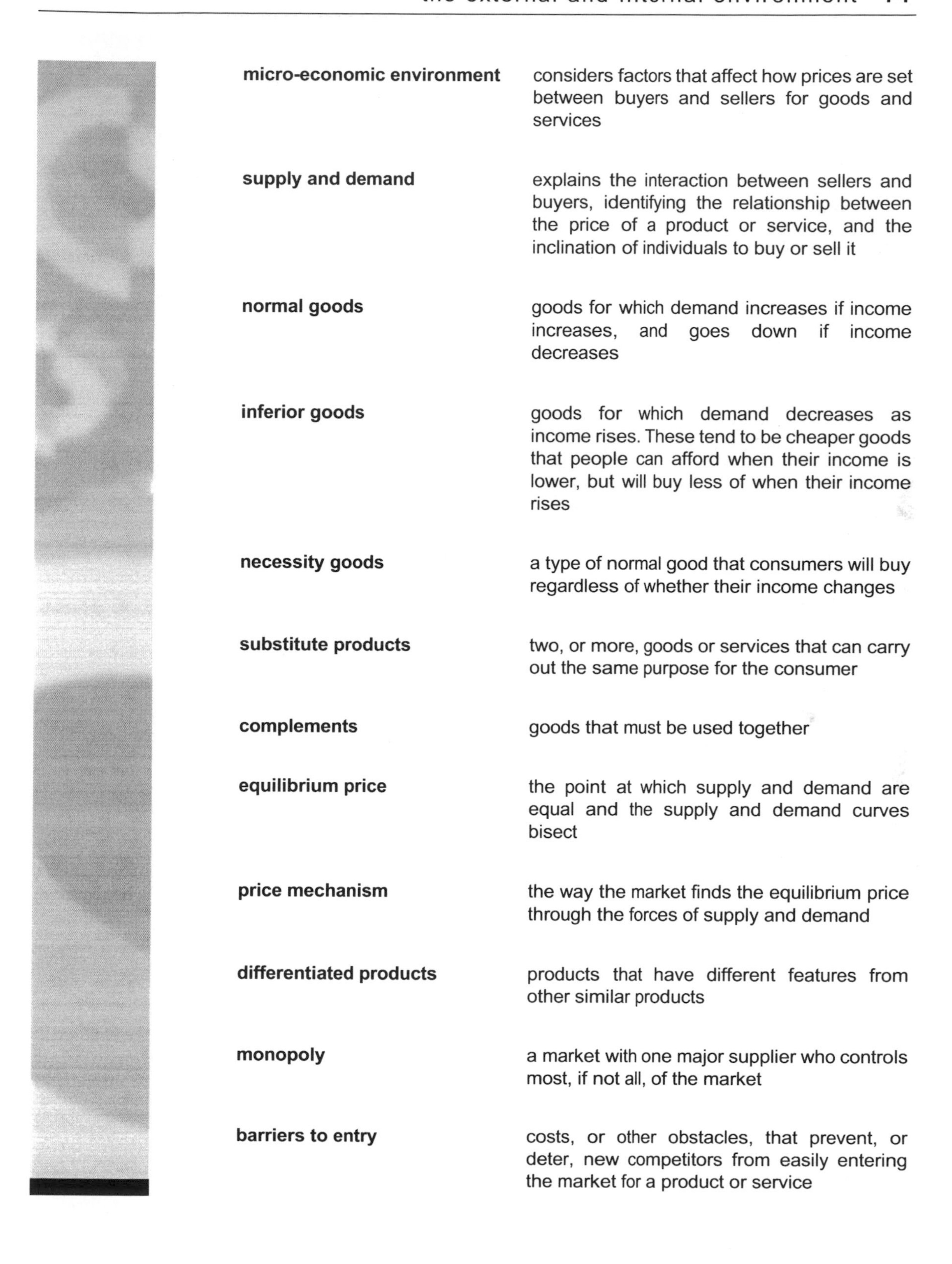

micro-economic environment	considers factors that affect how prices are set between buyers and sellers for goods and services
supply and demand	explains the interaction between sellers and buyers, identifying the relationship between the price of a product or service, and the inclination of individuals to buy or sell it
normal goods	goods for which demand increases if income increases, and goes down if income decreases
inferior goods	goods for which demand decreases as income rises. These tend to be cheaper goods that people can afford when their income is lower, but will buy less of when their income rises
necessity goods	a type of normal good that consumers will buy regardless of whether their income changes
substitute products	two, or more, goods or services that can carry out the same purpose for the consumer
complements	goods that must be used together
equilibrium price	the point at which supply and demand are equal and the supply and demand curves bisect
price mechanism	the way the market finds the equilibrium price through the forces of supply and demand
differentiated products	products that have different features from other similar products
monopoly	a market with one major supplier who controls most, if not all, of the market
barriers to entry	costs, or other obstacles, that prevent, or deter, new competitors from easily entering the market for a product or service

Activities

3.1 Which of these is not one of the six categories included in a PESTLE analysis?

Select **one** option.

(a) Economic	
(b) Environmental	
(c) Efficiency	
(d) Social	

3.2 Which of these is not a Political factor in a PESTLE analysis?

Select **one** option.

(a) Public spending	
(b) Government policy	
(c) Taxation	
(d) Currency exchange rates	

3.3 Which of these is a Legal factor in a PESTLE analysis?

Select **one** option.

(a) Currency exchange rates	
(b) Inflation	
(c) Unemployment	
(d) National minimum wage regulations	

3.4 You have carried out a PESTLE analysis for Fred's Freight, a family-owned road haulage and delivery business. You have been asked to complete a table showing which PESTLE category certain issues you have identified fall into.

Identify the PESTLE category for each of the issues in the table below. Use each category only once.

	Political	**Economic**	**Social**	**Techno-logical**	**Legal**	**Environ-mental**
The minimum wage rate is due to rise in April of next year by more than the rate of inflation.						
More people working from home has led to an increase in the number of deliveries.						
The business is considering updating its website which has not changed for several years.						
The Government has a new subsidised scheme to help pay for people to get their heavy goods vehicle driving license.						
Most of the business's vehicles have been bought using loans and bank interest rates have increased over the last 18 months.						
The business is considering replacing all its small delivery vans with electric vans.						

3.5 Scenario

Rose & Bumble is a business that imports handmade, leather handbags and wallets into the UK from several overseas countries. Since Brexit the cost of importing has increased significantly and there have been delays in the delivery of products due to border control issues.

Currency exchange rates have been quite volatile in recent months which has meant that it is difficult for the business to predict the actual cost of the products it is buying.

Rose & Bumble has a head office and a small warehouse in South London. Although it has a website, it does not sell direct to the public and only sells wholesale to small independent shops in the UK. It does not have any retail premises of its own.

When the goods arrive from abroad, they are unpacked, and all the packaging is disposed of as it is not all recyclable and Rose & Bumble markets itself as being green. The products are then re-packaged in Rose & Bumble recycled and recyclable, branded packaging before being delivered to its customers. Rose & Bumble uses a delivery company to send its products to retailers, which currently uses a fleet of diesel delivery vehicles.

A member of staff who is due to come back from maternity leave has requested flexible part-time working to fit in with their childcare arrangements. Although legally obliged to offer flexible working, the business will find it very difficult to accommodate this.

The business has been tracking visits to its website and is increasingly seeing individuals visiting who want to buy directly from Rose & Bumble rather than having to find a local retailer.

The recent change in government has led to increased rates of income tax and corporation tax. This has meant that household income has fallen, and the profits of the business have reduced.

Market research that has been published recently has shown that customers are increasingly looking for vegan leather products rather than purchasing genuine leather goods.

Rose & Bumble prides itself on selling handmade goods which it believes is a key selling point for its products. However, it has recently been to a trade fair where some other suppliers in the same market have displayed goods that are machine-made which are of similar quality but considerably cheaper.

Identify one issue for each of the six PESTLE categories, explain how this may impact the activities of Rose & Bumble, and what action the business can take to reduce the impact.

Issue	**Action**
Political	

Economic	
Social	
Technological	

Legal	
Environmental	

3.6 List the four elements of the business (trade) cycle.

1	
2	
3	
4	

3.7 Identify what is defined by each of the statements below by selecting from the following options (use each one once):

Necessity goods, Substitute products, Normal goods, Inferior goods

Definition	**Option**
Goods that consumers will buy regardless of whether their income changes.	
Cheaper goods for which demand generally decreases as income rises.	
Two, or more, goods or services that can carry out the same purpose for the consumer.	
Goods for which demand increases when income increases and goes down if income decreases.	

3.8 Which of the following may cause a shift to the right in the demand curve of a normal good?

Select **one** option.

(a) A decrease in the price of a substitute good	
(b) An increase in the price of a substitute product	
(c) An increase in the cost of raw materials	
(d) A decrease in the cost of raw materials	

3.9 The following three products are available in the market:

- Aye is a normal good
- Bee is a complementary product for Aye
- Cee is a substitute for Aye

Which of the following will happen if the price of Bee increases?

Select **one** option.

(a) An increase in demand for Aye	
(b) A decrease in demand for Aye	
(c) An increase in demand for Bee	
(d) No change in demand for Aye	

3.10 The following three products are available in the market:

- Aye is a normal good
- Bee is a complementary product for Aye
- Cee is a substitute for Aye

Which of the following will happen if the price of Cee increases?

(a) An increase in demand for Aye	
(b) A decrease in demand for Aye	
(c) No change in demand for Aye	

3.11 Complete the following sentences by selecting the correct options to fill the gaps.

The forces of supply and demand determine **an equilibrium price/a price mechanism** to reach **an equilibrium price/a price mechanism**. This is the point on a graph where the supply curve and the demand curve bisect.

4 Sustainability

this chapter covers...

This chapter will look at the need for organisations to operate in a sustainable manner and to protect sustainable development. The chapter goes on to explain the three aspects of sustainable performance:

- *economic/financial*
- *ecological/environmental*
- *social*

The last part of the chapter will focus on the responsibility of professional accountants to uphold the principles of sustainability throughout all aspects of their work.

AN INTRODUCTION TO SUSTAINABILITY

what is sustainability?

One definition of sustainability is *'the ability to last'*. Over recent years the UK Government has placed increased emphasis on the importance of 'green' policies for organisations and individuals. This ranges from encouraging recycling by households and businesses, to the Government's own commitment to reduce the country's carbon emissions. These green policies protect the environment, save energy and ultimately benefit society as a whole.

However, it is not simply 'being green' that supports sustainability and sustainable development. Organisations must ensure the responsible, long-term management of the resources that they use. In addition to the environmental impact of management decisions, sustainability also involves economic and social issues.

the Brundtland report

In 1983 the United Nations (UN) set up the World Commission on Environment and Development (WCED), chaired by Gro Harlem Brundtland, a former Norwegian Prime Minister. This organisation aimed to bring together the international community to pursue a common goal to support sustainability by identifying sustainability problems worldwide, raising awareness of them, and suggesting and implementing solutions. The problem was that for too many years, businesses worldwide had been able to operate without restriction; their only goal being to generate profit. One of the consequences of this need for 'profit at all costs' approach was increased environmental damage.

In 1987 the **Brundtland commission**, as WCED became known, published its report 'Our Common Future.' This report defined sustainable development as:

> *'development that meets the needs of the present without compromising the ability of future generations to meet their own needs.'*

The report then went on to highlight three key components of sustainable development:

- economic growth
- environmental protection
- social equality

In the next section we will look at each of these three objectives of sustainable development in more detail.

the triple bottom line

The three elements of sustainable development that were identified by the Brundtland committee are sometimes also referred to as the **triple bottom line**. Economic growth, environmental protection and social equality may also be abbreviated to 'profit, planet and people' – an easy way to remember these three key objectives. These are explained in more detail below.

economic growth and sustainability

In order for sustainable development to happen, the resources to allow it must be available. **Economic growth** provides these resources. It relates to:

- individual countries; the growth in the economy of a country should lead to an overall increase in the wealth of that country which then benefits its population as a whole
- individual organisations; profit generated by organisations will increase the wealth of the owners and employees

One key principle to remember is that sustainable growth relies on all three factors, not simply the generation of profit. Hence economic growth should not be pursued at the expense of the two other factors. In recent years the spotlight has been on sustainability; consequently, organisations now realise that cost-cutting can no longer be the number one business priority, and transferring production and services to lower-cost countries such as Bangladesh, China and Mexico brings with it hidden social and environmental costs. These include cheap labour and poor working conditions, excessive use of hydrocarbons (for example, coal power) which adversely affects the ozone layer, and results in huge deforestation.

environmental protection and sustainability

The green policies of an organisation are those most commonly associated with sustainability. The **protection of the environment** is key to conserving the world's resources with organisations keen to highlight their 'green' credentials. You may have heard the phrase 'reduce, re-use, recycle'. Some examples of environmentally friendly policies that contribute to sustainability are:

- supermarkets charging customers for plastic shopping bags to encourage them to bring their own 'bags for life', thereby reducing the number of plastic bags that end up in landfill
- recycling paper, metal and certain plastics and also using recycled office supplies such as printer paper and printer ink cartridges
- promoting car-sharing schemes, 'cycle to work' incentives and the use of low-emission, or electric, company vehicles, all reduce the 'carbon footprint' of a business and its employees

- only trading with suppliers that have certified green policies eg companies that make toilet tissue will ensure their paper suppliers replace the trees they use with new trees
- encouraging staff to reduce energy usage by turning off lights, only filling and boiling kettles with the required amount of water

Although the primary objective of an organisation's 'green' policies is to protect the environment by reducing waste and using fewer resources, the organisation itself may also benefit. Using less energy and other consumables will actually save the organisation money as it will spend less on expensive resources.

social equality and sustainability

This objective of sustainability focuses on the social well-being of people. Social equality extends beyond ensuring that employees are happy and well treated in the workplace. An organisation should consider the social equality of the local community and also society as a whole. We do not have to look far to see evidence of worldwide social inequality. International news reports regularly highlight the extreme poverty and poor living conditions in certain parts of the world.

Organisations can promote social responsibility both locally and in a worldwide context in a number of ways. Some examples are listed below:

- making charitable donations which help and support the socially underprivileged
- only trading with overseas suppliers that can provide evidence of reasonable pay and decent working conditions for its staff
- supporting local initiatives to get people who are out of work back into work
- sponsoring local sports events that 'give something back' to the local community

CORPORATE SOCIAL RESPONSIBILITY

Increasingly, large organisations are publishing **corporate social responsibility (CSR)** reports. These reports detail how the organisation takes responsibility for supporting sustainable development through its policies and procedures. It also identifies to what extent it has achieved its CSR objectives.

There is mounting pressure on businesses to be transparent in the way in which they operate and a growing number of organisations are choosing to voluntarily report on their CSR. While there is no legal requirement to produce a CSR report, businesses are realising that the public and investors are keen to see their attitude to sustainability. If an organisation can show progress towards achieving its CSR goals, the public will look more favourably on the business which will enhance its reputation as an ethical organisation.

CSR initiatives that a business may adopt include:

- reducing CO2 emission from its premises
- trading with organisations with a proven track record of good staff working conditions
- supporting charitable fundraising activities (eg matching amounts of fundraising that staff members have raised)
- making regular donations to charity
- setting recycling targets for the organisation
- promoting car-sharing schemes and 'cycle to work' initiatives
- using local suppliers where possible

When a business is reporting on sustainability it should strike the right balance of positive and negative information. Positive information will include measurement of how the organisation has met its sustainability goals. Negative reporting will show where it has failed to reach its CSR targets or has only partially achieved its goals. Although there is a risk that reporting negative results could damage the organisation's reputation, companies are expected to report on their sustainability practices 'warts and all'. If CSR reporting is too positive there is a risk that management will be perceived as overplaying their 'green credentials'. A business that uses CSR reporting simply as a public relations exercise won't fool anyone!

THE RESPONSIBILITY OF ACCOUNTANTS TO UPHOLD SUSTAINABILITY

We have seen the importance of sustainability and sustainable development to the way in which organisations operate. We will now look at the responsibilities of finance professionals in upholding the principles of sustainability.

public interest duty

Professional accountants have public interest duties to protect society as a whole. Consequently, they must consider the economic, social and environmental aspects of their work in order to support sustainability and sustainable development. This should include:

- ensuring the long-term responsible management of resources used by their organisation

- contributing to the running of their organisation in a sustainable manner
- assessing and minimising the risks to the organisation, and to society as a whole, of not acting sustainably

An accountant will be involved in the production of a significant amount of information that will be used by a wide range of stakeholders including shareholders, banks, customers, suppliers and employees. The accountant's ethical duty of integrity means that when preparing this information, they must be transparent, ie not hide anything, and must ensure that this information is not misleading to its potential users.

Professional accountants within a business are also often involved in the introduction of corporate social responsibility (CSR) policies and in reporting the success (or failure) of the business in complying with these objectives. As responsible, professionally qualified individuals they should have the skills and knowledge to report accurately on the way in which the organisation has achieved its sustainability aims and objectives.

promoting an ethics-based culture

The need to operate sustainably and to promote sustainable development goes hand-in-hand with the need to operate ethically. Sustainability inherently relies on the management of an organisation acting in an ethical manner. Professional accountants must act ethically in all aspects of their working life and in addition to this, should actively encourage and promote an ethics-based culture that discourages unethical or illegal practices, including money laundering, terrorist financing, fraud, theft, bribery, non-compliance with applicable regulations, bullying and decision-making that does not consider the longer term. In the long-term these factors may have an impact on a business's continued operation as well as potentially having an impact on society and the environment. This should be both within the organisation that the accountant works for and for accountants in practice, when they are dealing with clients.

promoting sustainability

Accountants should promote sustainable development within the organisation they work for. An accountant in practice should also encourage clients to support sustainable development. However, accountants must also remain objective, which means that they should give equal consideration to all relevant issues before making a decision. This need for objectivity is still important when an accountant is promoting sustainability in the organisation. The accountant should not necessarily support sustainability initiatives simply because something fulfils CSR objectives: they should consider what other effects the introduction of this initiative will have on the effective operation of the business.

reputational risk

As we have seen earlier in this chapter, the attitude of a business to sustainability can have a significant impact on its reputation with its wider stakeholders. This can be investors, employees, customers and suppliers. Failure to act sustainably can have an adverse effect on the reputation of the business. However, sustainable development will have a positive effect on the organisation's reputation as ethical and sustainably aware.

consider the triple bottom line

The Brundtland report identifies the three key objectives for sustainability, often referred to as the 'triple bottom line'. These are:

- economic growth
- environmental protection
- social equality

Accountants are frequently involved in providing information for management decision-making. Historically this information has focused on the success of the business measured primarily on profitability and growth of the organisation. However, in recent years there has been a shift in reporting so that not only financial measures are used to assess success. The sustainability initiatives that the business has introduced and the extent to which it has managed to achieve them is also considered a measure of success. Consequently, professional accountants must ensure that the triple bottom line is considered as part of their reporting on the performance of the business and that sustainable development is activity encouraged.

This means that in addition to promoting economic/financial aspects when measuring an organisation's income, expenses, assets and liabilities, accountants should also promote social and environmental aspects. For example, an accountant may be asked to provide information about how to reduce costs by buying raw materials from overseas. When the accountant does this, they should also report on whether the production of these raw materials overseas is done responsibly, with good pay and working conditions for the employees that produce it.

promoting sustainable practices

Accountants must also promote sustainable practices through the organisation in relation to each of the following:

- products and services – eg ensuring that the products or services supplied by the organisations are produced from sustainably resourced materials and that suppliers' staff have fair pay and decent working conditions
- customers – eg businesses should supply to their customers in a sustainable manner, through efficient delivery methods, and fair long-term pricing strategies

- employees – eg encouraging staff to take appropriate qualifications and providing them with good working conditions
- the workplace – eg implementing green policies relating to recycling and conservation of energy and then monitoring the participation of staff in the schemes as a measure of their success
- the supply chain – eg encouraging their organisation or clients to source supplies from suppliers with an ethical approach to sustainability
- business functions and processes – accountants should constantly review the way in which the business operates to ensure that it continues to be operating in a responsible way that supports and encourages sustainability and sustainable development

raising awareness of social responsibility

The professional accounting bodies in the UK include sustainability as part of the assessments and examination for students wishing to qualify with them; this Unit is an example of this. Qualified professional accountants are expected to promote the need for corporate social responsibility (CSR) and to encourage employers and clients to assess the impact of their decisions and actions on sustainable development in the future. For example, this may be through ethical buying decisions or encouraging recycling initiatives.

Chapter Summary

- The need for sustainability and sustainable development was highlighted by the Brundtland report which was published in 1987 and defined sustainable development as:

  'development that meets the needs of the present without compromising the ability of future generations to meet their own needs.'

- The three aspects of sustainability are:
  - economic/financial
  - ecological/environmental
  - social

- These three objectives are often known as the 'triple bottom line'.

- Some organisations now publish corporate social responsibility (CSR) reports that show the extent to which they have met their sustainability targets and objectives.

- Professional accountants have a responsibility to uphold sustainability in the workplace.

- Accountants' public interest duty to protect society as a whole means that they must consider the economic, social and environmental aspect of their work to support sustainability.

- Accountants should promote an ethics-based culture.

- It is important for professional accountants to remain objective when championing sustainability.

- An organisation's attitude to sustainability will have a direct effect on the reputation of the organisation.

- Accountants must take into account the triple bottom line of social, environmental and ethical factors when measuring the performance of an organisation and when assisting decision-making.

- Professional accountants should promote sustainable practices and raise awareness of social responsibility in their workplace.

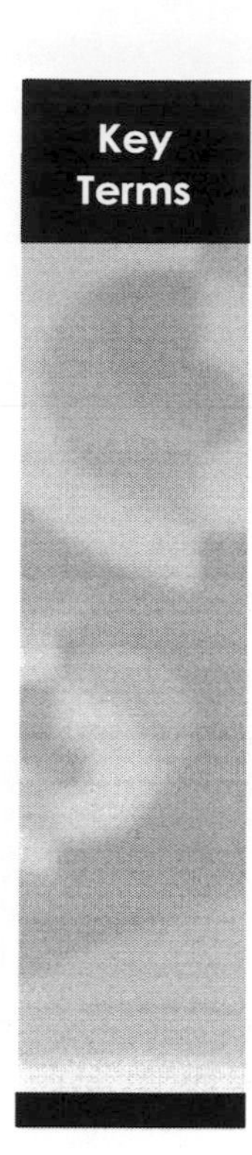

sustainable development	development that meets the needs of the present without compromising the ability of future generations to meet their own needs
Brundtland report	a report entitled 'Our Common Future' issued by a commission of the United Nations which aimed to pursue a common goal to support sustainability worldwide
triple bottom line	the three components of sustainable development: economic growth, environmental protection and social equality
corporate social responsibility (CSR)	objectives and policies adopted by an organisation to support sustainability and sustainable development
public interest	the welfare of the general public in which the whole of society has a stake
reputational risk	a risk of loss resulting from damage to an organisation's reputation which could be as a result of a poor attitude to sustainable development

Activities

4.1 The UN Brundtland report identifies three key objectives of sustainability and sustainable development.

(a) State these three objectives and give one example of how a business can support each one.

1	Objective: Example
2	Objective: Example
3	Objective: Example

(b) State the definition of sustainable development as set out in the Brundtland report.

4.2 Organisations publish reports detailing their success in supporting and promoting sustainability.

(a) What are these reports called?

(b) Organisations in the UK are not legally obliged to produce these reports. Give a reason why a business might decide to report on how well they have met their sustainability targets.

4.3 Mitchell is an accountant who works in the Accounts Department of Alecon Ltd, a business that manufactures sportswear which it supplies to high street retailers. He has been asked by the management of Alecon Ltd to review three ways of reducing costs and assess whether they are appropriate. Alecon Ltd has a policy of taking a sustainable approach to business wherever possible.

Look at the list of possible cost cutting methods below, and for each one explain what sustainability issues the business may have to consider.

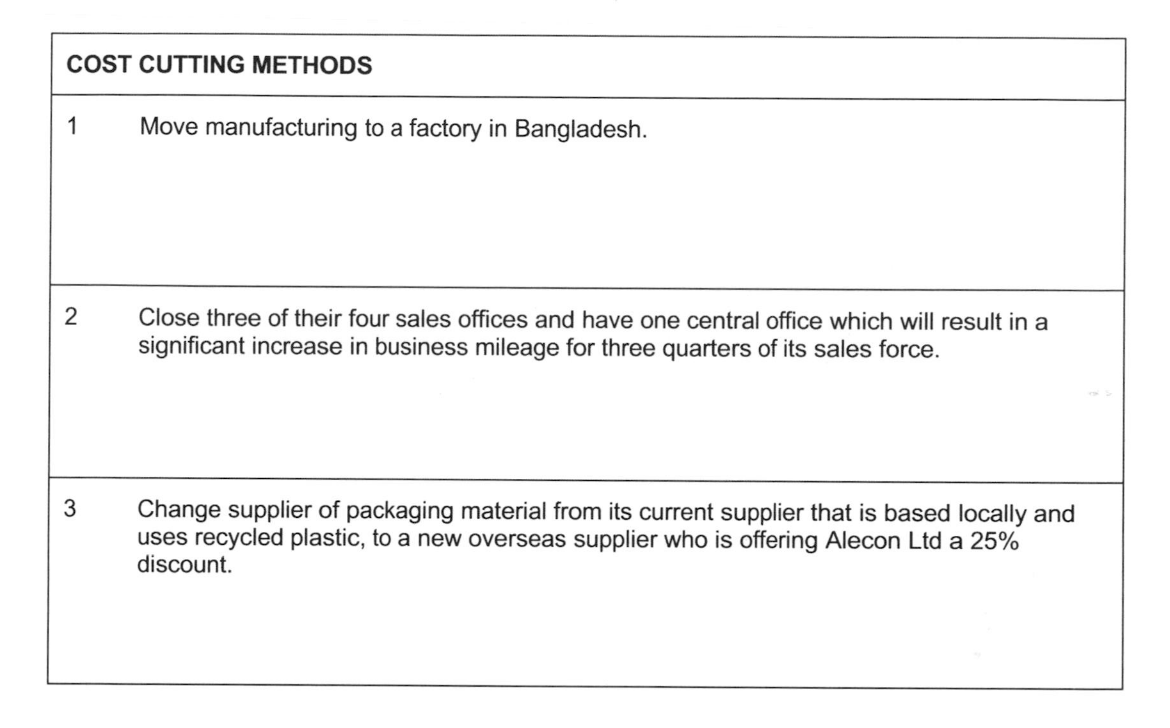

COST CUTTING METHODS	
1	Move manufacturing to a factory in Bangladesh.
2	Close three of their four sales offices and have one central office which will result in a significant increase in business mileage for three quarters of its sales force.
3	Change supplier of packaging material from its current supplier that is based locally and uses recycled plastic, to a new overseas supplier who is offering Alecon Ltd a 25% discount.

4.4 Explain what is meant by the term 'reputational risk' and how this is, potentially, affected by an organisation's attitude to corporate social responsibility.

4.5 You are the most recently qualified member of staff at Delta & Co, a medium sized firm of accountants in Blistertown which has a total of 128 members of staff. Simon, the senior partner, has asked you to produce a document that explains to members of staff the key areas where they should encourage sustainability and sustainable development with their clients.

You should identify at least four points to include in this document.

ENCOURAGING SUSTAINABILITY

5 Principles of professional ethics

this chapter covers...

The aim of this chapter is to explain the principles of professional ethics. We will look at what 'professional ethics' means and describe and explain the fundamental ethical principles that members of the accounting profession should follow. These principles are covered in the 'Code of Professional Ethics' published by AAT, which, like all professional accounting bodies' codes of ethics, is based on the IFAC ethical code.

Specific areas covered include:

- *the fundamental principles of professional ethics*
- *the people to whom these ethical principles apply*
- *the reasons why professional ethics are necessary*

The chapter also explains what is meant by professional scepticism and the importance for an accountant to consider this when exercising their professional judgement. It will also look at professional scepticism as a way of protecting the accountant from accusations of fraud or bribery.

AN INTRODUCTION TO PROFESSIONAL ETHICS

what are ethics?

First, a definition:

> *'The professional ethics of an organisation are the moral principles or standards that govern the conduct of the members of that organisation.'*

You may have heard people refer to the fact that a person, or an organisation, has done something that is 'unethical', or that they themselves wouldn't do something because it was unethical. For example, you would consider it unethical for a doctor to give information to a newspaper about the treatment given to a celebrity patient without the patient's consent.

So why do we feel that this is unethical on the part of the doctor? In this case the doctor would have broken patient confidentiality – ie released information that is 'secret' and 'private' to that patient – and the doctor's actions would be considered unethical because of this.

Members of professional bodies are expected to maintain the standards of their organisation. As part of this they are expected to behave in a professional and ethical manner. Within the published rules and guidelines of most professional organisations there will be specific sections covering professional ethics. If you have online access, try doing a search on the phrase 'professional ethics for accountants' to appreciate how important the topic is.

professional ethics and the accounting profession

In the example above the doctor will be governed by the specific standards of the medical profession in the country in which they practise. However, as trainee accountants you are interested in the standards that affect you in your training and when you are qualified. As a professional body AAT has published the **Code of Professional Ethics** which has been designed to help its members maintain the high standard of professionalism that is expected of them. Like all professional accounting bodies, the AAT Code is based on the International Ethics Standards Board for Accountants (IESBA)'s Code of Ethics. IESBA is the independent standard-setting board responsible for setting global ethical standards for accountants and is part of the International Federation of Accountants (IFAC).

It is important to remember that compliance with the ethical code is a professional obligation rather than a legal obligation.

Decisions made by members of the accounting profession in their professional life can have real ethical implications. The Code is designed to help AAT members with these decisions. Specifically, it states that it:

- sets out the expected standard of professional behaviour
- helps protect the public interest
- helps to maintain AAT's good reputation

In the same way members of other professional accounting bodies will be governed by their own ethical code.

to whom does the AAT Code apply?

The AAT Code of Professional Ethics applies to all fellow, full, affiliate and student members of AAT. When applying for student membership the student signs a declaration agreeing to abide by the relevant regulations and policies of AAT. Therefore, as student members you are required to uphold the high professional standards of the accounting profession even before you have qualified and become a full member.

Some members of the accounting profession, when they become qualified, will decide to set themselves up in practice rather than continuing to be employed. Whilst the general ethical principles within the accountancy profession will be the same for members whether they are employed in business or in practice, there are a number of different legal and ethical issues that are specific to each group of members.

The AAT has recognised this and has separated the Code into three consecutive parts:

- Part A applies to **all members**
- Part B represents additional guidance which applies specifically to **members in practice** (ie one who works in an accounting practice that provides accounting and other services to clients)
- Part C applies specifically to **members in business**

do you need to know the Code in detail?

You are not expected to have a detailed knowledge of the content of the AAT Code of Professional Ethics for your assessment. However, you are expected to have a clear understanding of professional ethics and be aware that the AAT Code and the ethical codes of other accounting bodies in the UK are based on the IESBA Code of Ethics.

FUNDAMENTAL ETHICAL PRINCIPLES

A professional accountant is required to comply with the five fundamental principles. Each of these is explained below, with practical examples. It is important to realise that many of the issues regarding professional ethics cannot be looked at on their own but should be seen collectively. Where ethical issues arise, a number of the fundamental principles may be involved in any one particular case.

These fundamental principles can be remembered using the letters PPCIO, which also stands for 'Popular People Chat in Offices'.

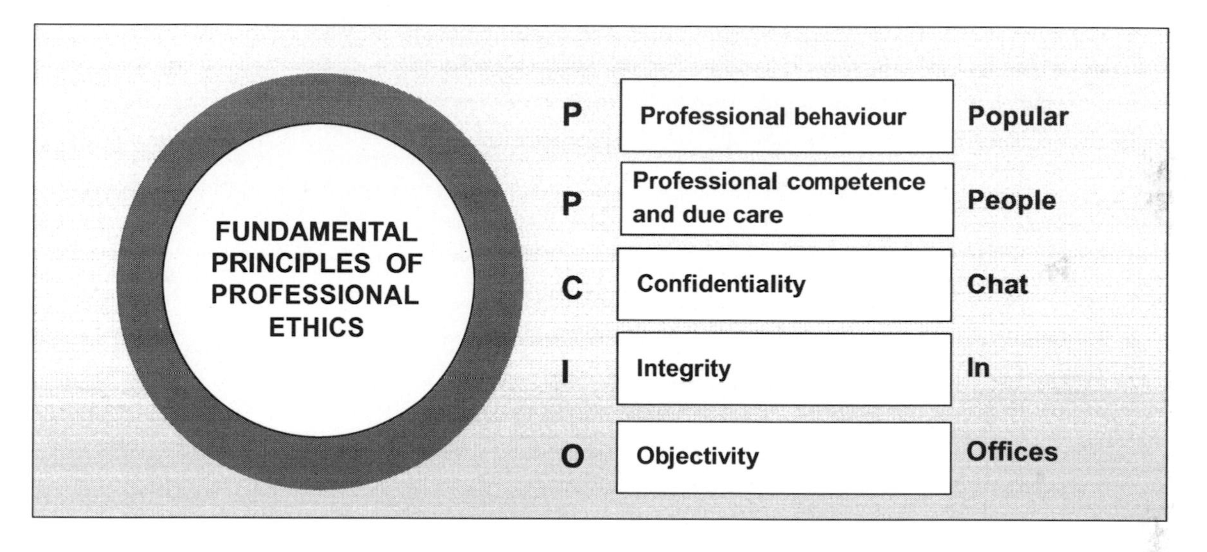

In the next sections we will look at each of these principles in a bit more detail.

INTEGRITY

Integrity is the quality of being honest and having strong moral principles that you refuse to compromise. An accountant should be straightforward and honest in all professional and business relationships and when carrying out professional work. Failing to act with integrity may mean that the accountant is directly or indirectly associated with misleading information. This could ultimately call into question their honesty and lead to users of the information such as clients, colleagues or even the general public no longer trusting the individual accountant or the accountancy profession as a whole.

There are also three key ethical values that contribute to the fundamental ethical principle of integrity: honesty, transparency and fairness. These are defined on the next page.

- **honesty** – being truthful and trustworthy
- **transparency** – operating in a way that is easy for others to see what is being done or said
- **fairness** – acting reasonably and without bias

A professional accountant must ensure that they act at all times with integrity, honesty, transparency and fairness whether they are dealing with clients, suppliers or colleagues.

The following situation is an example of where the integrity of an accountant might be tested.

example

a question of integrity

It is the end of the financial year and the Managing Director has told the Chief Accountant that he wants to maximise the profit for the year. He has asked the Chief Accountant not to set up an allowance for doubtful receivables of £60,000 against an outstanding amount that the Chief Accountant knows is unlikely to ever be paid as the customer has recently gone into liquidation.

Clearly in this situation the accountant is faced with a difficult decision. He is employed by the company and consequently has a duty to the Managing Director. However, he knows that in order for the accounts to show the true position, the receivable should be provided against. In order to maintain his integrity in this situation the Chief Accountant should explain to the Managing Director that he is not prepared to ignore the doubtful receivable and that in his opinion it should be provided for in the accounts.

OBJECTIVITY

A person who is **objective** is someone who bases their opinions and decisions on real facts and is not influenced by personal beliefs or feelings. Accountants should always be objective. In addition, when they are faced with a **conflict of interest**, it is their duty not to let their own self-interest – or the interests of the firm that employs them – affect the professional decision that they make. This means that any decisions that are made should be based on real facts and should not be influenced by personal beliefs or feelings.

The ethical code says that an accountant must not allow bias, conflict of interest or undue influence of others to override their professional or business judgement. Essentially, they must always act fairly and sensitively and without bias.

An example where the objectivity of an accountant could be affected by a conflict of interest is illustrated on the next page.

example

a conflict of interest

Jill Saunders is in practice and has been the accountant for Stallone Ltd, a local firm of house builders, for a number of years. The company has two options for its next building project and the directors have asked Jill to draw up a business plan incorporating these options. The directors' preferred option involves purchasing a plot of land directly behind Jill's house and building 20 three- and four-bedroom houses. Currently Jill has unspoilt views from her house. There is clearly a conflict of interest here. Jill does not want the houses to be built behind her house as this will spoil her view and reduce the value of her house. Consequently, Jill can no longer be objective in these circumstances.

It is very important that Jill informs the directors of Stallone Ltd as soon as possible of this conflict of interest so that they are then able to make a decision as to whether they wish her to continue to prepare the business plan.

So, to remain objective accountants need to be free from conflicts of interest. This means that they must not allow their own self-interest, or that of the organisation that they work for, to influence any decision that they make.

independence

The principle of objectivity goes hand-in-hand with the need for independence. A definition of independence is *'freedom from control or influence of others'*. Often objectivity and independence are used interchangeably to mean the same thing.

An accountant must always carry out their work in an independent way and regardless of any external pressure. There may be people who try to put pressure on an accountant, or even make threats to try to ensure that the accountant's work is performed to best suit their needs. In order to act in a professional and ethical manner the accountant must not be influenced by this pressure and must remain independent, thereby protecting their fundamental principle of objectivity.

example

a question of independence

Amerdeep Johal works for a firm of accountants and is currently preparing the year-end accounts for ABP Supplies, a local company owned by two brothers Andrew and Brian Potter. Amerdeep has calculated a draft profit figure for the year of £56,000 compared with £127,000 in the previous year. During a meeting with the two brothers Andrew says that he is not happy with this profit figure as he has a meeting with the bank at the end of the week to discuss a loan and he knows they will be unhappy with such a large drop in profit. He asks Amerdeep if there is any way that he could 'improve' the profit figure.

Amerdeep explains that this would not be appropriate as the accounts would no longer give an accurate picture of the financial state of affairs of the business. Andrew replies that he will need to speak to the partner in the firm that Amerdeep works for who is a close friend of his and if this is not resolved he may consider changing the firm of accountants that ABP Supplies uses.

In this situation Amerdeep is being pressured by Andrew. Firstly, he will feel personal pressure as Andrew has threatened to speak to Amerdeep's boss. Secondly, he has threatened to take his business elsewhere which will have an impact on the firm that Amerdeep works for. In order to remain independent Amerdeep should not allow these pressures to influence him. He must stick to his principles and, provided his boss has the same ethical principles, Amerdeep should be confident that he will support him and will not expect Amerdeep to change his opinion.

appearing to be objective

In addition to maintaining objectivity and independence, an accountant must ensure that they are **seen to be** objective. This means that any reasonable person who comes into contact with the accountant must be confident that they always behave independently and have avoided doing anything that may bring that objectivity into question.

The following example highlights a situation that may affect the **appearance of objectivity** of a professional accountant.

example

appearance of objectivity

Ashton and Groves is a small firm of accountants in Broom Town. One of the partners, Jemima Ashton, is married to Frank, who owns a local car dealership, Ashton Motors. For many years Ashton Motors have used Edwards & Co, another firm of accountants in the town, to prepare their year-end accounts. But Jim Edwards has just retired and Edwards & Co have ceased to operate.

Frank has suggested that the obvious solution would be for Ashton and Groves to take on the preparation of Ashton Motors accounts. But would this be appropriate?

The answer is no. Jemima, one of the Ashton & Groves partners, is clearly linked to the car dealership because she is married to Frank, its owner. Even if she had no involvement in the preparation of the accounts for Ashton Motors, her close personal relationship with Frank means that any outsider could quite justifiably question the independence and objectivity of Ashton and Groves.

PROFESSIONAL COMPETENCE AND DUE CARE

The ethical code states that a member must act with **'professional competence and due care'** to maintain professional knowledge and skill at the level required to ensure that a client or employer receives competent professional service based on current developments in practice, legislation and techniques. A member shall act diligently and in accordance with applicable technical and professional standards when providing professional services.

Professional Competence means professional accountants have a duty to keep themselves up-to-date with developments in the accounting profession, including relevant (international) accounting or auditing standards, and also regulatory and statutory requirements. The way in which they are expected to do this is by completing continuing professional development (CPD) on a regular basis, by reading current information on technical developments in the profession or attending relevant training courses.

The influence of international accounting standards is a specific example of the need for professional accountants to update their technical knowledge through training courses run by their own professional bodies. Failure by an accountant to maintain their CPD may mean that their technical knowledge is not up-to-date, leading to errors in the work they carry out. Failure to carry out CPD may also result in disciplinary action by the accountant's professional body.

Ideally, professional accountants should only take on new assignments for which they already have the necessary professional and technical skills. However, in certain circumstances, they may take on new work for which they will need some additional help or advice, as in the following example.

example

VAT expertise

One of your firm's clients has asked you to provide specific advice on the VAT implications of a new product imported from overseas. Although you have come across VAT as part of your accounting studies, it is not something with which you feel particularly comfortable. So, what options are open to you in this situation?

1 You could decline the assignment on the basis that you are not suitably competent to carry out the work involved

2 You could employ someone with the appropriate skills to complete the work you cannot do, or subcontract the parts of the assignment you are unable to undertake

3 You could arrange appropriate training for yourself to enable you to carry out the VAT work that the client has requested

In each of the three options above, as a professional accountant you are ensuring that the work carried out is performed to the highest standards, either by someone else, or by you with additional training

Due Care means that when carrying out an assignment an accountant must always take the appropriate amount of care (ie '**due care**') to ensure that the quality of the work performed meets the high standards expected of the accounting profession. Due care and diligence that are referred to in the ethical code mean acting in accordance with the requirements of the task: carefully, thoroughly and on a timely basis. Each assignment must be assessed individually in relation to its importance to the client and the time allowed for its completion. Whilst the work should be completed as quickly as is reasonably possible this should not compromise its quality.

Accountants must take particular care where clients are totally unfamiliar with anything to do with accounting or taxation. In such circumstances, accountants must be very careful to ensure that they carry out their work to the required standard. In addition to this they must also ensure that they explain fully to the client the results of the work that they have performed and the implications that this may have for the client.

For example, if two sole traders who do not seem to know much about accounting or taxation approach a professional accountant for financial advice as to whether they should go into partnership together, the accountant must ensure that they make each of them fully aware of all the taxation and accounting implications involved.

CONFIDENTIALITY

duty of confidentiality

Information obtained during the course of an accountant's professional work should not be disclosed without proper and specific authority or unless there is a legal duty to do so.

Members of the accounting profession have a 'duty of confidentiality' which means that they have **an obligation to respect the confidentiality of information about a client's or employer's affairs which has been gained during their employment or during the course of their professional work**. In addition to ensuring that they themselves observe this duty of confidentiality, accountants must also make sure that any staff they supervise or manage also respect the principle of confidentiality.

Below is an example of a situation where an accountant must observe their duty of confidentiality.

example

a duty of confidentiality

Elliot Graves has been employed in the Accounts Department of Simons & Simons for a number of years and currently works as the Financial Accountant for the firm. On the train home from work on Friday evening he meets a friend and they start chatting. The conversation moves on to work and his friend asks Elliot how the job is going. He then goes on to ask how Simons & Simons is doing and specifically asks what kind of a financial year the company has had.

How should Elliot answer his friend's questions?

Elliot has a duty of confidentiality to his employers not to disclose any confidential information about the company that he works for. Elliot can answer his friend's first question as to whether his job is going well as this is a personal enquiry about Elliot himself. However, Elliot should explain to his friend that it is not appropriate for him to discuss confidential information about Simons & Simons financial results.

using confidential information

In addition to ensuring that they do not disclose confidential information, professional accountants must ensure that they do not use, or appear to use, any information that they have access to for their own personal advantage or for the advantage of a third party, eg colleague, friend or family member.

We will now look in more detail at what this actually means. The point is illustrated in the following example.

example

a question of advice

Lubna Mirza is employed by a small firm of accountants and has been working on the year-end accounts of one of its largest clients, Richards Ltd. During the time that she spends at the client's premises Lubna learns that the company is currently in talks to take over another local company which is owned by a close friend of hers. The owner of Richards Ltd, James Richards, has mentioned that he would be willing to pay up to £250,000 for the firm, but only initially intends to offer £200,000.

Should Lubna tell her friend about James Richards' intentions? If not, would it be acceptable for her to give her friend advice about what offer to accept for her business?

Lubna has a duty of confidentiality to the client and so should not disclose any information she has obtained about Richards Ltd without specific authority from the company or unless she is legally obliged to do so. If she were to give her friend advice about what offer to accept, based on the information that she now knows, she would be using information that she had gained to benefit her friend (a third party), which is not acceptable.

Therefore, if Lubna's friend asks her for advice she should explain that Richards Ltd is one of her firm's clients and should suggest that the friend obtains independent specialist advice on how to value her business.

information. This is that accountants must not **appear** to use information that they have gained for their own personal advantage or that of a third party.

The point here is that even if the accountant is confident that they have not used confidential information for their own personal benefit or that of another, the accountant must also ensure that there is no possibility of anyone **thinking** that they have. It should not **appear** that the accountant has used confidential information inappropriately.

This is best illustrated with an example (shown on the next page), using the same scenario as the last example.

example

the danger of 'appearing' to pass on confidential information

We will now return to the example of Lubna Mirza that we looked at on the previous page. If Lubna follows the course of action recommended in the example she can be confident that she has not used confidential information about Richards Ltd to benefit her friend.

Suppose that James Richards has completed the takeover of Lubna's friend's business and has paid £230,000 for it. If he were then to find out that the owner of the business he had bought was a close personal friend of Lubna's, he could quite legitimately question whether Lubna had passed on the information to her friend about what his maximum offer would be.

What could Lubna do/have done to ensure that her duty of confidentiality was not called into question?

As soon as she knew that James was intending to make an offer to buy her friend's business Lubna should have informed James of her relationship with the owner. She should also have explained to him that she is fully aware of her duty of confidentiality regarding information that she gains about a client and will not pass on any information. This would get her out of the dangerous situation where she could have 'appeared' to have advised the owner – simply because James would not have known otherwise.

the ongoing duty of confidentiality

We have already established that an accountant has an obligation to respect the confidentiality of information about employers or clients during the time that they are employed or are working for the client. This duty of confidentiality extends to the period **after the relationship has ended**.

In practice this means that any information that the accountant gains in the course of the professional work they carry out for a client remains confidential – even after the accountant is no longer employed by the client.

Similarly, information regarding an accountant's employer remains confidential even when the accountant moves to another employer.

disclosure of confidential information

Having established that accountants have a duty of confidentiality, we will now look at the circumstances where confidential information can be disclosed. There are three main situations where it is acceptable to disclose confidential information. These are shown in the diagram below.

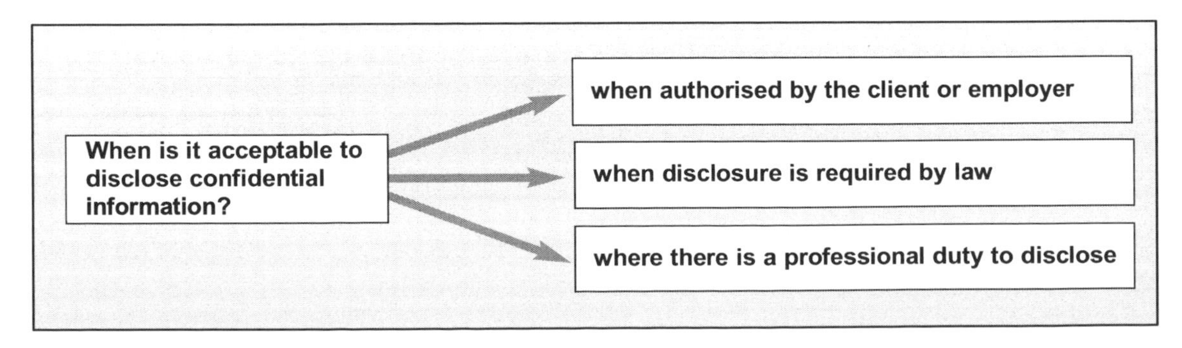

The example that follows highlights a common situation where a client authorises the accountant to disclose confidential information to a third party.

example

authority to disclose

You work for a firm of accountants and receive a telephone call from a local builders' merchants asking for financial information about one of your clients who has requested to trade with them on credit.

How should you deal with this call?

Financial information regarding your client is confidential. Therefore, you should not disclose any information about your client to the builders' merchants unless you have been authorised by the client to do so. You should contact your client to explain the situation and obtain specific authority to provide the financial information to the caller. Although verbal authority is acceptable, it would be better if this authority was given in writing.

When authority to disclose has been obtained from the client you can give the requested information to the builders' merchants. When doing this it is important to include a disclaimer making it clear that this is for the use of the builders' merchants only and is given purely to help them to make a decision about whether or not to supply goods on credit to your client. You should also explain that the information is given without any financial responsibility on the part of yourself or the firm for which you work.

This example illustrates that where a client has given permission, the accountant is then able to disclose confidential information. The main point here is that the accountant must get specific authority from the client before doing so.

disclosure required by law

In some circumstances the accountant will be faced with a legal requirement to disclose confidential information. This legal requirement to disclose confidential information can be divided into two main categories:

- where the information is required as evidence in a court of law
- where the law requires that information must be revealed to the relevant authorities in situations where the law has been broken

This is illustrated in the diagram below.

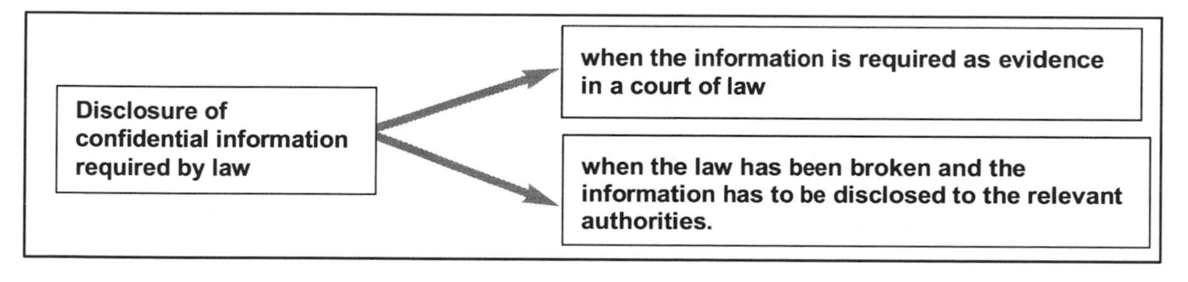

evidence in court

There may be circumstances where an accountant is required to provide evidence in a legal case in court. The accountant may receive a witness summons from the court and be required to:

- provide documents which will be used in court as evidence, and/or
- to appear in court in person to give evidence

Alternatively, the accountant might be the subject of a court order requiring them to disclose confidential information about the client.

In any of these circumstances the accountant has a legal obligation to comply with the request. As a consequence, the accountant must break their duty of confidentiality to the client or employer, even if the client or employer has refused to give permission for the evidence to be provided. The power of the law, through the witness summons or court order, is stronger and will prevail here.

The following example illustrates this point in practice.

example

a legal question of confidentiality

Rachael Thomas acts as the accountant for Rolls Ltd. One of Rolls Ltd's suppliers has taken the company to court for failure to pay for goods that have been supplied to it. There has been an ongoing dispute between Rolls Ltd and this supplier which has resulted in the non-payment by Rolls Ltd.

Rachael has been asked to provide copies of all documents relevant to this dispute, including invoices and correspondence, as evidence in the case. She has also been told that she may be required to appear in court as a witness to give evidence.

In these circumstances what steps should Rachael take before providing this information?

The information that Rachael has been asked to provide to the court is confidential. The first thing that she should do is to make her client, Rolls Ltd, aware that she expects to be called as a witness thereby giving Rolls Ltd the opportunity to give her authority to provide the information in court. If the company agrees then she is free to provide the relevant documents or evidence as requested.

If, despite being informed of Rachael's likely appearance in court, Rolls Ltd refuses to give authority for her to disclose then Rachael must wait until she receives a witness summons. When this occurs, she is legally required to comply with the summons and provide the relevant documentation, and if necessary, appear in court herself to give evidence.

disclosure where infringement of the law has occurred

Where a client or an employer has broken the law there may be a requirement for the accountant to disclose information to the relevant authorities that would otherwise be considered confidential.

A good example of this is in relation to money laundering.

A definition of money laundering is:

> *'to move illegally acquired cash through financial systems so that it appears to be legally acquired.'*

Basically, as the name 'money laundering' suggests, when the money has been gained through illegal activities it is seen as 'dirty money'. By using that money in legitimate trade or investment activities, this is like 'washing' or 'laundering' the money so that it then appears to be 'clean' and legally obtained.

Money laundering is covered in detail in Chapter 8, but it is clear that an accountant has to disclose confidential information about a client if they consider that the client has broken the law.

a professional duty to disclose

In certain circumstances, an accountant may have a **professional duty** to disclose confidential information. These circumstances are summarised below:

- to comply with the quality review of an IFAC (International Federation of Accountants) member body or other relevant professional body
- to respond to an inquiry by the professional accounting body or by a regulatory body of an ethical, investigatory or disciplinary nature
- to protect the professional interests of the accountant in legal proceedings
- to comply with technical standards and ethical requirements

Deciding whether to disclose confidential information where there is a professional duty to disclose is a particularly difficult and complex area. Accountants are, therefore, specifically advised to seek professional or legal advice before disclosing confidential information in these circumstances if they are in any doubt.

the decision to disclose

If an accountant makes the decision to disclose confidential information, there are three points which must be considered before making this disclosure. These points can be summarised as follows:

- the accountant must decide whether they know all the facts regarding the issue and has enough evidence to back up these facts. If they do not have enough evidence, then the accountant must use their professional judgement to decide to what extent (if any) the confidential information can be disclosed
- next, the accountant must decide who is the right person(s) to whom this information should be disclosed, and also how it should be communicated, for example by letter, report or verbally. This decision

should ensure that the person provided with the information has the necessary authority to act upon it

- finally, the accountant must consider whether they would face any legal consequences from disclosing confidential information, and if so, how serious these consequences could be

We can see that the accounting profession takes the subject of disclosure of confidential information very seriously and members must be very careful when deciding whether or not they should disclose.

In any circumstances where an accountant is unsure whether or not they should disclose confidential information, or where they are unclear as to how much they should disclose, they should consider taking legal advice from a solicitor or contact their accounting body's advice line. It is always better to get a second opinion if there is any doubt over the action that should be taken, rather than risk making the wrong decision.

data protection

When an accountant in practice works for a client, they will have access to a huge amount of information about the client. As we have discussed above, the accountant has a duty of confidentiality to the client regarding the disclosure of this information. In addition to this there are legal requirements set out in the data protection legislation. Sometimes, when an accountant is dealing with financial accounting information, they may be faced with a conflict between their compliance with the fundamental ethical principle of confidentiality and compliance with data protection laws. In these situations that accountant must comply with the Code of Ethics and maintain confidentiality unless they are legally required to disclose the information If there is any uncertainly the accountant should seek advice from an expert before disclosing confidential information.

PROFESSIONAL BEHAVIOUR

The final fundamental principle is that of **professional behaviour**.

As we have seen earlier in this chapter the accountancy profession is respected for the high standards that it requires of its members. The ethical code states that accountants should **'adopt professional behaviour to comply with relevant laws and regulations and avoid any action that brings our profession into disrepute'**. The whole of the ethical code sets out the required standards of behaviour that accountants should maintain and gives guidance on how to achieve them.

For example, a member of AAT who sends offensive or inappropriate emails from their place of work would be considered unprofessional. In addition, this could reflect badly on the firm that he works for and also on AAT.

A much more serious example of an accountant damaging the reputation of the accountancy profession would be if they gave professional advice to a client that the accountant knew failed to comply with relevant laws and regulations.

internal disciplinary procedures by an employer

Like any employee, if a professional accountant fails to adhere to the employer's organisational values or internal codes of practice, the employer may bring disciplinary procedures against them. These disciplinary procedures should be formally documented but will normally include some or all of the following stages.

- a verbal warning
- a written warning
- a disciplinary hearing
- the opportunity to appeal
- suspension from work
- dismissal

The extent of the disciplinary action that is taken will depend on the seriousness of the breach. For example, accepting a crate of wine from a client may result in the accountant receiving a verbal warning, particularly if it is the first time that they have done so. If, on the other hand, the accountant has committed an illegal act such as fraud this is likely to result in dismissal.

disciplinary action by professional accounting bodies

The **professional accounting bodies** in the UK expect their members to comply with the code of ethics and to uphold the high standards that are expected of the accounting profession. Failure by an accountant to comply with applicable regulations and codes of practice may result in the accountant being disciplined. Disciplinary action for misconduct can be taken by the individual accounting bodies and also by the Financial Reporting Council (FRC), which is the independent disciplinary body for accountants, accountancy firms and actuaries in the UK.

Misconduct falls into two main categories:

- bringing the accounting profession into disrepute
- acting in breach of the rules and regulations of the accountant's professional body

Individual accounting bodies in the UK have published disciplinary regulations, which set out the processes and sanctions that the accounting body will carry out if a member is guilty of misconduct. The procedures will involve a disciplinary investigation followed by a decision as to whether the accountant is guilty of misconduct. Depending on the severity of the misconduct the accountant could face any of the following penalties (listed in order of severity).

- be required to give a written undertaking to refrain from continuing or repeating the misconduct in question
- be fined a sum of money not exceeding a maximum figure set by the professional accounting body
- be reprimanded or severely reprimanded
- be declared ineligible for a practicing licence
- have their practicing licence withdrawn
- have their membership suspended
- be expelled from the professional accounting body

PROFESSIONAL SCEPTICISM

Accountants must ensure that they exercise a certain amount of **professional scepticism** when making professional judgements, particularly in relation to transactions recording and financial reporting.

Professional scepticism is an attitude that includes the following:

- a questioning mind, ie not taking what is said at face value but instead asking questions until satisfied that the information is correct
- being alert to conditions which may indicate possible misstatement due to error or fraud, ie using professional experience and training to identify signs that a mistake has been made either as a result of a genuine error or due to deliberate fraud
- making critical assessment of evidence that is provided

This doesn't mean that accountants should assume that everything they are being told by management is false or deliberately fraudulent. What it does mean is that where something is vague, or there isn't enough information to back it up, the accountant must investigate further until they are happy that the information is correct. Failure to do this may compromise the objectivity of the accountant and leave them open to accusations of bribery or fraud.

The next example illustrates how professional scepticism should be used in the workplace in relation to financial accounting.

example

exercising professional scepticism

Georgia works at Ross & Askew, a firm of accountants. She is working on the financial statements of a client, Anderson Ltd, and has reviewed the allowance for doubtful receivables. This has increased significantly since last year. On further investigation, Georgia finds that this was authorised and approved by the financial controller at Anderson Ltd. Georgia has also reviewed the receivables ledger at the year end. She has identified that the total balance is lower than last year, and there is no indication that there is any greater risk of amounts not being paid.

In this situation should Georgia accept the increase in the allowance for doubtful receivables on the basis that it has been approved by the financial controller?

Georgia should exercise professional scepticism in this situation, and not accept the increased allowance at face value simply because the financial controller has authorised it. Instead, she should discuss this matter with the client and confirm that she is happy that there is a valid reason for the increased allowance.

fraud and bribery

Fraud can be defined as:

> *'wrongful or criminal deception intended to result in financial or personal gain.'*

The **Fraud Act 2006** defines three classes of fraud:

- fraud by false representation – where a person makes any representation which they know to be misleading
- fraud by failing to disclose information – where a person fails to disclose any information to a third party which they have a legal duty to disclose
- fraud by abuse of position – where a person occupies a position where they are expected to safeguard the financial interest of another person, and abuses that position

The **Bribery Act 2010** covers the criminal law relating to bribery. A definition of **bribery** is:

> *'Giving or receiving something of value with the intention of influencing the recipient to do something favourable to the giver of the bribe.'*

A person that offers an inducement to another person for the improper performance of a function or activity is guilty of the offence of bribery. Equally a person who is willing to accept that inducement can also be prosecuted under the Bribery Act. The four key Bribery Act offences are:

- bribing another
- receiving a bribe

- bribing a foreign official
- failing to prevent bribery

The maximum penalty if a person is found guilty of the offence of bribery is 10 years imprisonment and/or an unlimited fine. There is also the potential for property to be confiscated.

An accountant must be very careful not to allow the actions of a client or an employer to compromise their objectivity. Professional scepticism is key for an accountant when exercising their professional judgement to ensure that there is no financial gain for their employer or for them, personally. If the accountant's objectivity is seen to have been affected, this could result in the accountant being accused of fraud or bribery.

Chapter Summary

- The professional ethics of an organisation are the moral principles or standards that govern the conduct of its members.
- Accounting bodies, including AAT, base their code of ethics on the ethical code of the IESBA.
- All accountants should adhere to the fundamental ethical principles of:
  - integrity
  - objectivity
  - professional competence and due care
  - confidentiality
  - professional behaviour
- When making decisions, an accountant must ensure that they remain independent of mind and only take into account issues and points that are relevant to the issues that they are addressing.
- In addition to independence of mind, the accountant must demonstrate independence in appearance. This means that they should avoid situations that could make a third party question the accountant's objectivity.
- Accountants have an obligation to respect the confidentiality of information about a client's or employer's affairs acquired in the course of professional work.
- Accountants must ensure that any staff who work for them also follow the principle of confidentiality.
- Confidential information should not be used, or appear to be used, for the personal advantage of an accountant or a third party.
- The duty of confidentiality continues after the end of the relationship between the accountant and the employer or client.
- Confidential information can be disclosed when a client or employer authorises the disclosure.
- If the law specifically requires it, confidential information about a client or employer can be disclosed.
- If an accountant has a professional duty to either comply with accounting standards, protect their professional interests in legal proceedings or respond to an inquiry by their professional body, confidential information may be disclosed.
- If an accountant requires advice on detailed ethical issues, they should contact their professional accounting body's advice line.
- The data protection legislation provides a framework to ensure personal information is handled properly.
- Failure to comply with an employer's organisational values or codes of practice can result in an accountant being disciplined by their employer or professional accounting body.

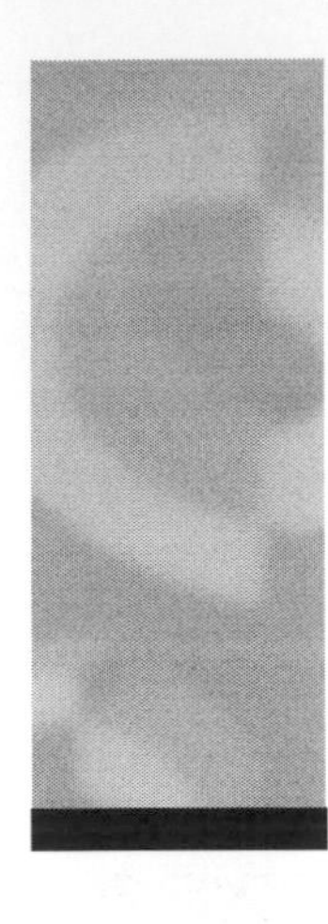

- Accountants should exercise professional scepticism by assessing information critically, with a questioning mind, and being alert to possible misstatements due to error or fraud.
- Accountants should use professional scepticism when exercising their professional judgment in relation to financial accounting
- The Fraud Act 2006 defines three types of fraud: fraud by false representation, fraud by failing to disclose information and fraud by abuse of position.
- The Bribery Act 2010 is the UK legislation covering the criminal offence of bribery.
- Where an accountant's objectivity is compromised, this may lead to accusations of bribery and fraud.

Key Terms

professional ethics — the moral principles or standards that govern the conduct of the members of an organisation

code of professional ethics — documents issued by the accounting bodies providing guidance to full and student members regarding professional ethics

integrity — accountants should be straightforward and honest in performing professional duties

honesty — being truthful and trustworthy

transparency — operating in a way that is easy for others to see what is being done or said

fairness — acting reasonably and without bias

objectivity — decisions should be made based on true facts and accountants must not let their own bias or prejudice, or pressure from others, affect decisions that they make

conflict of interest — this arises where the business or personal interests of an accountant may influence the accountant giving an objective opinion

independence of mind — only taking into account points that are relevant to decisions to be made or work that is being undertaken – this is very similar to objectivity

independence in appearance — ensuring that to a third party the actions taken by the accountant appear to be objective and free from the influence of others

professional competence and due care	accountants have a duty to ensure that they have the necessary skills to carry out any work that is assigned to them and that they always take sufficient care to ensure that the quality of their work meets the high standards expected of them
confidentiality	information obtained during the course of professional work should not be disclosed without proper and specific authority or unless there is a legal duty to do so
duty of confidentiality	the accountant's obligation to respect confidential information about the client's or employer's affairs
ongoing duty of confidentiality	the fact that the accountant's duty of confidentiality continues even after the end of the relationship between the accountant and the employer or client
authorised disclosure of confidential information	disclosure of confidential information by an accountant following authorisation by the client or employer
disclosure required by law	the legal requirement for an accountant to disclose financial information about a client or an employer
disciplinary action	processes and sanctions that a professional accounting body can carry out if a member is accused of non-compliance with its regulations and the code of ethics
professional scepticism	an attitude that includes a questioning mind, being alert to conditions which may indicate possible misstatement due to error or fraud, and a critical assessment of evidence
professional behaviour	accountants should maintain the good reputation of the profession and should not do anything to discredit the profession
bribery	giving or receiving something of value with the intention of influencing the recipient to do something favourable to the giver of the bribe
fraud	an intentional deception made for professional gain or to damage another individual

Activities

5.1 Professional accounting bodies in the UK base their ethical codes on the Code of Ethics issued by which global body?

5.2 The AAT Code of Professional Ethics applies to which categories of member in the following list?

Select **all** options that apply.

(a)	Full AAT members	
(b)	Student members of AAT	
(c)	AAT members who work in practice	
(d)	AAT members who are employed in industry	

5.3 There are five fundamental principles of professional ethics with which professional accountants must comply.

State these **five** fundamental principles.

5.4 Each of the following statements defines which fundamental ethical principle?

(a) *'Being honest and having strong moral principles that you refuse to compromise.'*

(b) *'Basing decisions on real facts rather than being influenced by personal beliefs or feelings.'*

5.5 Complete the following statement:

'A professional accountant who complies with the law and does not bring the accounting profession into disrepute is upholding the fundamental principle of [ ] .'

5.6 The duty of confidentiality to a client on the part of a professional accountant is only applicable for the duration of the assignment.

Is this statement **true** or **false**?

5.7 Robert, an accountant in practice, has been asked by Zeena, one of his clients, to provide her with some financial information about another client, James. James is one of Zeena's customers, with whom Zeena is currently in a legal dispute.

Explain whether Robert can provide Zeena with any information about his client, James, who is also her customer.

5.8 Findlay works for a firm of accountants in Moorbridge. He receives a letter from a local office supplies company asking for financial information about one of his clients which has requested credit terms with the company. Findlay is aware that the information it has requested is confidential.

What should Findlay do in these circumstances?

5.9 An accountant has a professional duty to disclose confidential information to protect their

[ ] interests in [ ]

Select the appropriate words from the selection below to fill the gaps in the sentence above.

personal	**taxation affairs**	**professional**
organisation's	**financial matters**	**legal proceedings**

5.10 Which of the following are characteristics of professional scepticism?

Select **all** options that apply.

(a)	A questioning mind	
(b)	Taking things at face value	
(c)	Being alert to conditions which may indicate possible misstatement due to error or fraud	
(d)	Making critical assessment of evidence that is provided	
(e)	Assuming that everything is false or deliberately fraudulent	

6 Threats and safeguards to fundamental ethical principles

this chapter covers...

This chapter focuses on circumstances that create threats to the fundamental ethical principles of a professional accountant in practice and an accountant in business. It then details the safeguards that can be put in place to eliminate these threats or reduce them to an acceptable level.

This chapter covers:

- *the difference between a principles-based and a rules-based approach to professional ethics*
- *threats to the fundamental ethical principles of professional accountants in practice and in business, ie self-interest threats, self-review threats, familiarity threats, intimidation threats and advocacy threats*
- *safeguards against these threats for accountants in practice*
- *safeguards against these threats for an employed accountant in business*
- *safeguards created by the accounting profession, legislation and regulation*

A CONCEPTUAL FRAMEWORK APPROACH

You will remember from the previous chapter the five fundamental principles of professional ethics:

- Integrity
- Objectivity
- Professional Competence and Due Care
- Professional Behaviour
- Confidentiality

The Code of Ethics sets out the fundamental ethical principles for members that provide a conceptual framework for dealing with ethical issues. In effect, the ethical principles are the concepts that an accountant should adopt when dealing with an ethical issue.

We have seen that these principles are general in nature and so cannot be applied rigidly in specific situations to solve ethical problems that accountants come across in their working lives. When ethical dilemmas occur, these principles should be considered together with the Code of Ethics. Accountants should use their professional judgement and consider the impact on their ability to comply with the five fundamental ethical principles before any decision is reached on ethical matters.

principles-based approach

The Code of Ethics says that accountants should take a principles-based approach to ethics which requires an accountant to identify, evaluate and address threats to their compliance with the fundamental principles rather than applying a set of rules exactly as stated, regardless of the circumstances (ie literally), which would be a rules-based approach. An example of a rules-based approach would be when you drive a car. You must follow 'the rules of the road' or you may cause an accident.

Put simply, this means that a professional accountant should evaluate anything that may prevent them following the fundamental ethical principles. If the principles are threatened then they should put safeguards in place to minimise the threat(s). We will look at threats and safeguards in the next section of this chapter.

The advantages of taking a principles-based approach are that it is applicable to all circumstances and because of the fact that an accountant should evaluate each individual situation, there is less chance of someone finding loopholes that will excuse unethical behaviour.

The difference between a principles-based approach and a rules-based approach can be seen in the example that now follows.

example

principles-based approach v rules-based approach

Your firm of accountants has recently been appointed to provide professional accounting services for James Roberts, who is a self-employed painter and decorator. When preparing James's end of year accounts, you realise that, early on in the year, the business's turnover has exceeded the annual limit for Valued Added Tax (VAT). This means that James should have registered for VAT and from that point should have been charging VAT on his services.

What should you do in this situation?

Taking a rules-based approach you would report James to HMRC for failing to register for VAT when his business had reached the VAT limit. This would arguably be a harsh course of action.

The preferred principles-based approach, on the other hand, would involve explaining to James that he must register for VAT immediately and should also make HM Revenue & Customs (HMRC) aware of the delay in registering that has occurred and the fact that he has not charged VAT on his services during the year as he should have done. Using this approach, you have identified the main issue – which is that James registers for VAT as soon as possible – and you have given James the necessary professional advice to allow him to do so.

acting ethically – not doing nothing

We have seen that an accountant must take a principles-based approach to professional ethics. They must evaluate anything that may affect whether the fundamental ethical principles can be followed. However, there may be circumstances where it might be easier to simply ignore the problem or do nothing about it. But is this ethical behaviour by the accountant? The answer is that in most cases, it is not. If an accountant believes there is an ethical problem, then they must take appropriate action in order to behave ethically.

The following example illustrates a situation where this might occur.

example

don't ignore the problem

Dustin is a management accountant who works in the accounts department of Vandex Ltd. Over lunch he is chatting with one of his colleagues, Lottie. Lottie explains that she has made an error on the firm's most recent VAT return that has resulted in Vandex Ltd underpaying HMRC by £2,000. She tells Dustin that 'no one seems to have noticed so I'm not going to do anything about it'. Dustin must now decide whether this situation is none of his business so he can ignore it or whether he should take some specific action.

In order to behave ethically Dustin cannot ignore what Lottie has said and do nothing about it, as this would be unethical. He must advise Lottie to report the issue to someone more senior in the accounts department and to correct the error on the next VAT return. If Lottie refuses to do this, he should report it himself.

We will see later in the book in Chapter 8 that accountants are expected to take specific action to behave ethically when they encounter potential money laundering; another situation where the accountant cannot ignore the problem or do nothing about it.

acting ethically – complying with the regulations

We have established that it may not be acceptable for an accountant to ignore a problem or do nothing about it. In addition to this, accountants cannot simply rely on complying with regulations as constituting ethical behaviour.

The example that follows shows how complying with regulations does not necessarily mean an accountant is behaving ethically.

example

maternity pay

Marina plc has an employee grading system from 1-8 with 1 being the lowest paid workers and 8 being director level. The business's Maternity Policy states that eligible employees graded 1-4 who go on maternity leave will receive minimum Statutory Maternity Pay (SMP) as required by The Employee Rights Act 1996. However, the directors of the business have said that employees graded 5 and above will receive significantly better benefits and a large bonus when they return to work after their maternity leave has ended.

The fact that the directors of Marina plc are favouring the higher-grade employees raises doubts about the ethical nature of the management and of its leadership culture. By simply complying with the SMP regulation they should not automatically be considered to be behaving ethically in relation to the business's employees.

A more ethical approach would be either to offer the minimum Statutory Maternity Benefit to all staff regardless of grade, or to offer improved benefits to all staff who go on maternity leave.

THREATS TO FUNDAMENTAL ETHICAL PRINCIPLES

There will be circumstances in a professional accountant's working life, whether they work in practice or are employed in a business, where they face threats to their fundamental ethical principles. These threats will differ depending on the circumstances and whether the accountant works in practice or in business. However, the accountant must take a conceptual framework, or principles-based, approach to these threats and consider each individual circumstance when deciding how to deal with the threats they face. We will now look at the types of threats faced by an accountant in practice and the safeguards that they can put in place to eliminate these threats or reduce them to an acceptable level. We will then look at the threats faced by a professional accountant employed in business and the safeguards that can help to eliminate these threats or reduce them to an acceptable level.

THREATS TO THE FUNDAMENTAL ETHICAL PRINCIPLES FOR ACCOUNTANTS IN PRACTICE

A professional accountant who works in practice will face a number of potential threats to their fundamental ethical principles. These threats are summarised in the diagram below.

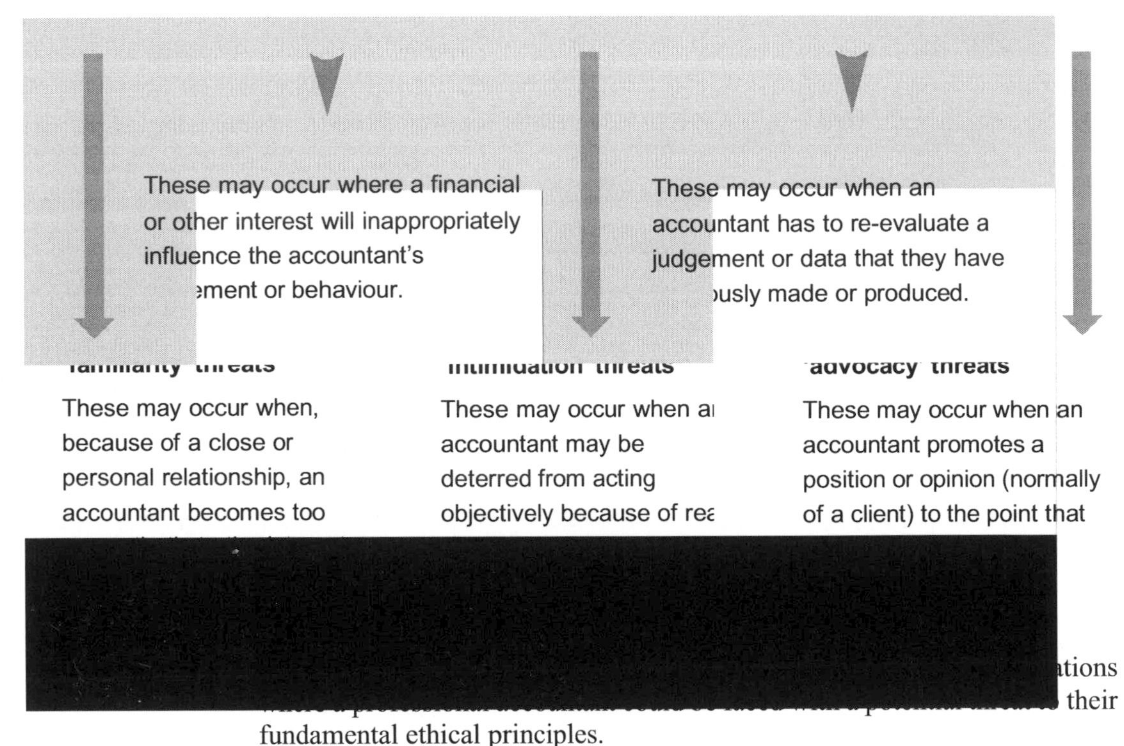

tions their fundamental ethical principles.

self-interest threats

Where an accountant has a financial involvement with a client or in the affairs of a client, or in the operation of the business that employs them, this may threaten their objectivity.

There are many examples of where the objectivity of a professional accountant may be threatened.

Set out below are several key areas where a financial involvement with a client or employer can arise. They are:

- direct or indirect financial interest in a client or employer
- loans to or from the client or any officer, director or principal shareholder of a client company or of an employer

- holding a financial interest in a joint venture with a client or employee(s) of a client
- when the receipt of fees from a client or group of connected clients represents a large proportion of the total gross fees of an accountant or the practice as a whole
- concern about losing a client
- potential employment with a client
- contingent fees relating to an assurance engagement
- discovering a significant error when reviewing previous work carried out by the accountant or a member of their staff

We will now explain these areas of financial involvement in more detail.

direct or indirect financial interest in a client or employer

If an accountant is a shareholder in a client company, they would be considered to have a direct financial interest in that client. In this case the accountant's objectivity would be threatened as they would have a financial interest in the performance of the client business which could affect their judgement when preparing accounts or providing financial or tax advice. This self-interest threat would also extend to shares in a client held by a close relative of the accountant, for example, the accountant's husband or wife. The following example illustrates a situation of a self-interest threat resulting from a financial interest in a client.

example

shares in a client

Julie Parker is an accountant who works as a sole-trader and has a number of local firms as clients. Her husband Simon and his business partner are considering buying shares in a local business and have been considering investing in one of Julie's clients, Doors & Windows Ltd. Simon discusses this proposal with Julie over dinner one evening.

What points should Julie raise with Simon?

If Simon and his partner were to buy shares in Doors & Windows Ltd this would create a self-interest threat to Julie's objectivity. The financial success of the company would have a direct impact on the value of the shares that Simon and his partner held. This in turn would affect the financial position of Julie and her husband.

Julie should explain to Simon that this would be a threat to her objectivity. In this situation Julie and Simon have two choices: either Simon can go ahead with his partner and buy the shares, in which case Julie should resign as accountant for Doors & Windows Ltd. Alternatively, Simon should not go ahead with the planned purchase of shares in Doors & Windows Ltd.

loans to or from the client

If a client made a loan to an accountant who provided the client with accounting, taxation or other services, this could again affect the objectivity of the accountant. In this situation the client has financial influence over the accountant because of the money that is owed.

The example below illustrates a situation where this form of self-interest threat may arise.

example

loan from a client

Peter Moss is a professional accountant who runs a small but successful accounting practice. Peter is keen to expand the firm, and during an informal chat with one of his clients, he explains that he is considering moving to larger premises and employing more staff. He also explains that he will need to arrange a substantial loan with the bank to allow him to do this. A few days later the client telephones Peter and states that he would be willing to lend Peter the money to finance his proposed business expansion.

Should Peter accept the offer?

Peter should not accept the offer of a loan from his client. This would immediately create a self-interest threat to Peter's independence and so his objectivity through a financial involvement with the client. Peter should thank his client for the offer of the loan and politely say 'no, thanks'.

The only other solution would be for Peter to say to the client that he is no longer able to act as his accountant – but this is hardly realistic.

financial interest in a joint venture with the client

A self-interest threat would also arise for an accountant if they were to enter into a joint venture with a client or with an employee of the client. For reasons similar to those highlighted above, there would be a financial relationship between the client and the professional accountant which could compromise their objectivity. We return to the example of the accountant Peter Moss to show how this threat could occur in practice.

example

the threat of a joint venture

A few days after Peter declined the loan from the client explained in the example above, he receives a further telephone call from the same client. The client says that he has been thinking about what Peter has said and believes he has a solution where he could help Peter with his business expansion without providing him with a loan. His suggestion is that he and Peter's firm embark on a joint venture to purchase the premises. Peter's firm would continue to provide accounting services to existing and new clients. In return for his investment the client would expect a share of Peter's profits but would not be lending any money to Peter.

Should Peter now accept the offer given that the circumstances have changed?

client.

substantial fee income from a single client

If the fees that an accountant receives from an individual client represent a large percentage of the total gross fee income for the accountant (or their practice) this could again cause a self-interest threat to the accountant's objectivity. As the fee income from the client is so significant in relation to the accountant's total fee income this may well mean that the accountant cannot afford to lose the client which in turn could mean that the client has

example

the threat of substantial fee income

Sanjay Patel is a professional accountant who runs a successful practice providing accounting and taxation services to around 150 clients. His largest client, Emerson Ltd currently accounts for about 9% of his total fee income. Although Sanjay currently only provides accounting services to Emerson Ltd, the Managing Director of Emerson has asked whether he would like to take on the taxation work for the business. Sanjay estimates the increased fees that this would generate would mean that Emerson Ltd would account for approximately 20% of his total fee income.

Should Sanjay agree to provide the additional taxation services to Emerson Ltd?

If Sanjay were to take on the taxation work, the total fee income from Emerson Ltd would represent a substantial proportion of Sanjay's total fee income. This could represent a self-interest threat for Sanjay as he could become economically reliant on Emerson Ltd. Therefore, in these circumstances, Sanjay should not accept the additional work that Emerson is offering him.

potential employment by a client

Inevitably when an accountant working in practice carries out an assignment for a client, the client will form an opinion of the ability of the accountant. In certain circumstances this may lead to the accountant being offered a job by the client. This could be as a financial accountant, a management accountant or in some other capacity. In this situation the potential employment of the accountant by the client could threaten their objectivity and professional behaviour when carrying out the assignment for the client. In order to protect their fundamental principles, the accountant should immediately put safeguards in place. This could be by informing more senior members of staff on the assignment that a job offer has been or will soon be made or asking to be removed from the engagement team.

self-review threats

There is a threat to the fundamental principles of an accountant if a circumstance arises where they have to review their own work. This could be because the accountant used to work for the client and has now moved on to work for an accounting practice. Alternatively, it could be because the accountant has moved from working for a practice into a role working for a client.

This type of threat to the objectivity of an accountant would also occur where the same situation applies to a close family member or colleague.

This self-review threat is illustrated in the following example.

example

a significant 'self-review' threat

Iris McDonald is a qualified accountant who worked for a number of years as Finance Manager for Catchett and Rank Ltd, a company that designs computer games.

After leaving the company, Iris was employed as a senior manager by Michael Croft & Co, a local firm of accountants. A year after joining, Iris became a full partner in the firm.

Shortly after this she received a telephone call from a director of her previous employer, Catchett and Rank Ltd. He congratulated her on becoming a partner and explained that they were looking for some new tax advisors and thought that Michael Croft & Co might be a good choice.

Should Iris agree on behalf of Michael Croft & Co to accept the assignment?

Iris must use her professional judgement to decide whether it would be appropriate to accept the assignment. It would appear likely that in this circumstance she will have to review work that she has carried out and therefore there is a self-review threat. If it is possible for other members of staff at Michael Croft & Co to carry out the work so that Iris is not directly involved then it may be possible to reduce this self-review threat to an acceptable level. However, Iris must consider how the situation would appear to a reasonable and informed third party, and whether they would consider her actions to be acceptable.

Other self-review threats to an accountant's fundamental principles:

- where an accountant discovers a significant error when reviewing work that they have previously carried out: they may decide not to highlight this error
- where an accountant is asked to report on the operation of financial systems after being involved in the design and implementation of these systems
- when an accountant performs a service for a client that directly affects the subject matter of the assurance engagement, for example when an accountant in practice prepares the depreciation calculation for a client and then is involved in the audit of the same client

If any of these self-review threats to an accountant's fundamental principles are present, the accountant should identify appropriate safeguards to eliminate the threats or reduce them to an acceptable level. This could be by ensuring that their work is thoroughly reviewed by another accountant in the practice.

finding significant errors

On occasions an accountant working in practice will have to review or refer to work that has previously been performed by themself or by a member of their staff. If they find a significant error in that work this could mean that they are faced with a difficult situation. Highlighting the error to the client could make the accountant or the member of staff appear incompetent. This could jeopardise the future relationship between the accountant and the client. This presents a self-interest threat to the accountant's objectivity and professional behaviour as the loss of the client would have a direct financial impact on the accountant's fee income. The alternative is not reporting the error to the client. This would threaten their fundamental principle of professional behaviour and also professional competence and due care.

Strong review procedures within the firm, together with a leadership culture that stresses the importance of compliance with the fundamental principles, will help to safeguard against this self-interest threat to the accountant's fundamental principles.

providing other services for clients

There may also be a threat to the fundamental ethical principles where professional accountants provide **consultancy services** to clients – eg management consultancy and tax advice – so they must take care that they:

- make recommendations
- do **not** make management decisions
- do **not** take responsibility for management decisions

In this situation accountants should also avoid reporting on management decisions which they have recommended. Professional accountants should be independent advisors and not managers.

familiarity threat

Where a professional accountant has a close or personal relationship with the client or a key member of the client's staff, this relationship may have a negative effect on the objectivity and the independence of the accountant. Because of this close or personal relationship, an accountant may become too sympathetic to that person's interests.

The following example highlights a situation where such a relationship exists and the effect it could have on the independence of an accountant.

example

the threat of a family relationship

Liz Robinson is a professional accountant who owns and runs a small firm of accountants toge with her business partner Tom Crusoe. She shares a house with her sister, Jo, who runs a succes training company. Up until now Jo has managed her own financial affairs, but her business is rap expanding and she can no longer manage the books herself. In addition, she has recently taken a substantial business loan from her bank and, as part of the agreement, they have requested reg independently prepared financial statements.

Jo asks Liz if she will take on her business as a client. Should Liz accept this assignment?

There is a close family relationship between the two sisters which is made even closer by the fact they share a house together. This close family relationship constitutes a familiarity threat to L objectivity; consequently, Liz should not agree to Jo's request and should instead recommend alternative accountant to her sister.

In addition to the threat identified in the example above, there are a number of other familiarity threats to an accountant's fundamental ethical principles. These include:

- where an accountant who was formerly a partner in the accounting practice is now a director, officer or employee at the client in a position of significant influence over the subject of the assignment
- where an accountant is offered gifts or preferential treatment from a client unless the value of the gift is clearly insignificant
- where there is a long association between a senior member of the assurance team and the client

In each of these circumstances the fact that there is a significant relationship between the accountant in practice and the client will pose a threat to their objectivity and potentially to their professional behaviour. Accepting a gift or preferential treatment from a client may influence the objectivity of the accountant, or equally important, it may appear to a person outside the accountant/client relationship that the accountant's objectivity is questionable.

As with all of the threats to an accountant's fundamental ethical principles, the accountant must ensure that they put sufficient safeguards in place to eliminate these threats or reduce them to an acceptable level.

intimidation threats

If an accountant takes on a client and a relationship develops in which the accountant is 'bullied' or put under pressure by the client – 'intimidated' in other words – then the objectivity of the accountant is under threat in a very real sense. As a result, the accountant's reporting could be biased in favour of the client. In cases such as these, the accountant should be changed. If a larger firm is involved, a stronger personality could be brought into the accounting team to counter the client's threat to this fundamental principle.

Examples of intimidation threats include:

- the threat to dismiss the accountant by the client
- the threat by a client not to award a contract to the accountant
- the threat of litigation
- the pressure to reduce the quality of work in order to reduce fees
- the pressure to agree with the client's judgment because they have more experience of the matter in question

advocacy threats

Advocacy means that you are seen to support the client's point of view publicly – even in a court of law.

In the context of a threat to the fundamental ethical principles of an accountant in practice, the advocacy threat is that the accountant could go beyond the **advisory** role that they should take for the client and **actively speak** on the client's behalf or in support of the client.

By promoting the client's position or opinion too strongly this may mean the accountant's objectivity in the future may be compromised.

example

an advocacy threat to objectivity

Hugh Davies is a qualified accountant who provides a number of services to his clients, including accounting services, management consultancy and taxation advice. Over the past few months Hugh has been providing management consultancy services to Naturally Green, a business that sells organic and environmentally friendly products.

The directors of Naturally Green are in the process of updating their marketing brochures and have asked Hugh to provide a written statement, as management consultant, endorsing the product range that they sell.

Should Hugh agree to provide the requested endorsement?

If Hugh were to provide an endorsement of Naturally Green's products he would be going beyond his advisory role for the client and would be taking a strongly proactive stance on the client's behalf. This would have a seriously negative effect on Hugh's independence.

Consequently, Hugh should refuse to provide the endorsement and should explain to the directors of Naturally Green the reasons for his refusal.

There are two more examples of circumstances that could create an advocacy threat to an accountant's fundamental principles. These are:

- promoting shares in a listed entity when the entity is an audit client
- acting as an advocate on behalf of an assurance client in litigation (legal cases) or disputes with another third party

An accountant must think very carefully before promoting a client or acting as the client's advocate. If there is any question in the accountant's mind as to whether their fundamental ethical principles are being threatened then they should decline to perform these roles for the client.

SAFEGUARDS AGAINST THREATS TO THE FUNDAMENTAL ETHICAL PRINCIPLES OF ACCOUNTANTS IN PRACTICE

How does an accountant in practice ensure that their fundamental ethical principles and objectivity are maintained when accepting or continuing to work for a client? How does an accountant deal with threats to their fundamental ethical principles?

There are a number of possible safeguards and procedures that an accountant could put in place to help reduce the threats to their compliance with the fundamental ethical principles. These are in addition to any requirements provided for by law or by professional rules – for example, the rules that govern the accountancy profession. A list of suggested safeguards is shown below. This list is not exhaustive, but it will help to summarise much of what has been explained in this chapter so far.

- a leadership culture in the accounting practice that stresses how important it is for staff to comply with the fundamental ethical principles
- a leadership culture in the practice that expects all members of staff working on assurance assignments to act in the public interest
- strong quality control procedures which are monitored for all engagements together with a member of senior management being given responsibility for overseeing the adequate functioning of this quality control system
- documented internal policies and procedures requiring compliance with the fundamental principles and a disciplinary mechanism to promote this compliance
- specific, documented policies for identifying threats to compliance with fundamental principles including evaluating the significance of these threats, and devising safeguards to eliminate these threats or reduce them to an acceptable level

- timely communication of a firm's policies and procedures, including any changes to them, to all partner and professional staff, and appropriate training and education on such policies and procedures
- documented independence policies for assurance engagements to ensure that the independence of members of staff is not threatened at any stage
- policies and procedures that will enable the identification of interests or relationships between members of staff and clients
- policies and procedures to monitor and, if necessary, manage the reliance on fees received from a single client
- using different partners on engagement teams with separate reporting lines to provide non-assurance services to an assurance client
- policies and procedures that prohibit individuals who are not members of an engagement team from inappropriately influencing the outcome of an engagement
- advising partners and professional staff of assurance clients that the practice and its members of staff must be independent from the client
- published policies and procedures to encourage and empower staff to communicate to senior levels within the firm any issue relating to compliance with fundamental principles that concern them
- published policies and procedures that ensure both qualified and unqualified staff maintain their technical knowledge by carrying out sufficient, relevant continuing professional development (CPD)

THREATS TO THE FUNDAMENTAL ETHICAL PRINCIPLES OF ACCOUNTANTS IN BUSINESS

Accountants in business will also be faced with threats to their fundamental ethical principles. As with accountants in practice these could be any of the following:

- self-interest threats
- self-review threats
- familiarity threats
- intimidation threats
- advocacy threats

We will now look at some examples of circumstances where these threats may occur.

self-interest threats

These threats may occur where financial interest on the part of the accountant may influence the judgement or behaviour of the accountant. Circumstances that could create self-interest threats for an accountant in business could be:

- an accountant having a financial interest in the business. For example, an accountant may be entitled to compensation and/or incentives such as a bonus linked to their financial reporting and decision-making. As a consequence, their objectivity may be threatened by this conflict of interest
- an accountant may have personal use of an asset of the business which is not part of their employment contract. This could create a self-interest threat to the objectivity of the accountant and also to their integrity and professional behaviour. For example, if an employed accountant was given use of his employer's corporate hospitality at an international cricket match and was able to take his whole family
- where there are concerns over the security of an accountant in business's employment which may threaten his objectivity

self-review threats

An accountant in business could face a self-review threat where they have been involved in preparing data that is then going to be used for making business decisions which the accountant is also involved in. For example, an accountant may be asked to prepare the staff bonus calculations and then be involved in the decisions regarding who should receive these bonuses (this could also result in a self-interest threat if the accountant is eligible for a bonus).

familiarity threats

An accountant in business may face familiarly threats where they have a close personal relation which means the accountant becomes too sympathetic to the interests of that person or persons. There are several possible situations where a familiarity threat may arise:

- where an employed accountant is preparing financial information for their employer which is the ultimate responsibility of an immediate or close family member, this may pose a familiarity threat
- where there has been a long association with a supplier or customer of the employer, this could cause a familiarity threat
- if an employed accountant is offered a gift or some other kind of preferential treatment by an employer, customer or supplier, this could cause a familiarity threat to the accountant's fundamental principle as they may feel an obligation to conform to their wishes as a 'thank you for the gift'

- if an accountant has been working for a manager for a long period, this may cause a familiarity threat

intimidation threats

An employed accountant may feel intimidated and hence their fundamental ethics principles may be threatened in the following circumstances:

- where there is a threat of dismissal to either the accountant in business or one of their close relations because the accountant will not conform to the wishes of their employer
- where a dominant person in the employed accountant's business attempts to influence the decision-making process by forcibly making their point

advocacy threat

As an employee of the organisation, an accountant in business will be expecting to support the legitimate goals and objectives of the business. It would, therefore, be part of the accountant's job to promote the business provided, ensuring of course any statements that they made were not false or misleading. It is therefore unlikely that an employed professional accountant would be faced with an advocacy threat to their fundamental principles.

SAFEGUARDS AGAINST THREATS TO THE FUNDAMENTAL ETHICAL PRINCIPLES OF ACCOUNTANTS IN BUSINESS

In addition to the safeguards that are created by the accounting profession, legislation and regulation, there are a number of safeguards that can be put in place in the work environment to reduce or eliminate the threats to the fundamental principles of a professional accountant in business. Examples of these safeguards are listed below.

- the employer's systems of corporate oversight or other oversight structures
- the employer's ethics and conduct programmes
- recruitment procedures that emphasise the importance of employing high calibre, competent staff
- a system of strong internal controls
- appropriate disciplinary processes
- leadership within the business that stresses the importance of ethical behaviour and the expectation that employees will act in an ethical manner
- policies and procedures to implement and monitor the quality of training and clear training on these policies and procedures

- policies and procedures that encourage employees to communicate any ethical issues that concern them to senior management and also give them the power to do so without fear of retribution
- the opportunity to ask advice from another appropriate professional member of staff

SAFEGUARDS CREATED BY THE ACCOUNTING PROFESSION, LEGISLATION OR REGULATION

Previously we have said that in addition to the specific safeguards for accountants in practice and accountants in business, there are safeguards created by the profession, legislation and regulations. These have been summarised again below.

- educational, training and experience requirements for entry into the accounting profession
- continuing professional development requirements
- corporate governance regulations
- professional accounting standards
- professional or regulatory monitoring and disciplinary procedures
- external review of the reports, returns, communications or information produced by a professional accountant by a legally empowered third party, for example an external auditor

In this chapter we have looked at possible threats to a professional accountant's fundamental ethical principles and safeguards that eliminate these threats or reduce them to an acceptable level. Where safeguards are put in place to reduce threats to an acceptable level then the decision to continue with the assignment must be documented. This documentation should include a description of the threats that have been identified and the safeguards that have been applied to eliminate or reduce them to an acceptable level.

But what if it is not possible to eliminate or reduce the threats to an acceptable level? If the accountant feels that even after the safeguards are put in place the threats are still clearly not insignificant then they must refuse to accept or continue with the work they are being asked to complete.

summary of the threats to fundamental principles

This chapter has looked at the threats to the fundamental principles that can face accountants in practice and also accountants in business. We have also identified the safeguards that can be put in place to eliminate these threats or reduce them to an acceptable level.

While all of the fundamental principles can be affected by any of the five types of threats, the table below summarises the particular threats of each fundamental principle. This table provides a handy revision summary for your synoptic assessment.

Principle \ Threat	Self-interest threat	Familiarity threat	Intimidation threat	Self-review threat	Advocacy threat
Integrity	✔	✔	✔		
Objectivity	✔	✔	✔	✔	✔
Professional behaviour	✔	✔		✔	
Professional competence and due care	✔	✔		✔	
Confidentiality	✔	✔	✔		

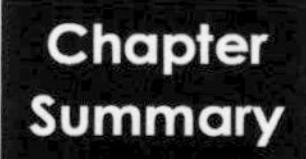

- There are five main threats to the fundamental ethical principles of a professional accountant working in practice or in business which are:
  - self-interest threats
  - self-review threats
  - familiarity threats
  - intimidation threats
  - advocacy threats
- There are a number of safeguards that accountants are able to put in place to eliminate these threats or reduce them to an acceptable level.
- In addition to the safeguards that accountants can put in place to eliminate threats to their fundamental principles, there are also safeguards created by the accounting profession, legislation or regulation.
- Where safeguards will not reduce the threat to an acceptable level the accountant should refuse to accept or continue with the work they are being asked to complete.

Key Terms

conceptual framework	a set of principles to help accountants to act ethically
principles-based approach	this means to use the conceptual framework to identify and evaluate threats to the fundamental ethical principles and put in place safeguards to minimise or eliminate these threats
rules-based approach	the approach to professional ethics that means that you apply any rules exactly as stated regardless of the circumstances
self-interest threat to fundamental principles	the threat caused by a financial relationship between the accountant and a client or an employer
self-review threat to fundamental principles	the threat caused by an accountant having to review or evaluate a previous judgement that they have made
familiarity threat to fundamental principles	the threat caused by a family relationship or friendship. For an accountant in practice, this may be between the accountant and a key member of the client staff. For an accountant in business this may be between the accountant and a supplier, or customer, or where there is a close friendship with a work colleague or manager
intimidation threat to fundamental principles	the real or perceived threat caused by a client exerting undue pressure on an accountant in practice or a dominant employer attempting to influence an accountant in business
advocacy threat to fundamental principles	the threat caused by an accountant going beyond an advisory role and publicly supporting the client in some way

Activities

6.1 'Taking an approach that identifies, evaluates and addresses threats to compliance with the fundamental ethical principles.'

To which of the following does this approach to professional ethics relate?

(a)	A rules-based approach	
(b)	A principles-based approach	

6.2 Samantha is a professional accountant who works as a sole practitioner. One of her larger clients, Red News, has recently taken over one of its large rivals, Blue Media, which Red News intends to continue to operate as a separate entity. It has asked Samantha to take on Blue Media as a client. If she accepts this offer it will mean that the combined fee income from these two businesses will be 25% of her total fee income.

(a) Explain which of Samantha's fundamental principles is most threatened by this situation and the type of threat that she is facing.

(b) Should Samantha accept the additional work?

6.3 Complete the following statement by circling the appropriate word(s) for each option:

'When providing consultancy services to an existing client, professional accountants may face a (**self-interest/self-review/intimidation**) threat to their fundamental ethical principles. They must ensure that they (**do/do not**) make recommendations and (**do/do not**) make management decisions.

6.4 Hayley works for Trott & Cook. She has recently returned from a week's holiday to find a thank you card on her desk from one of her clients, Andrew. The card includes the following note together with a £150 gift voucher.

> Hi Hayley,
>
> Thank you for all your hard work on our financial statements this year. We are delighted that you decided not to raise the significant reduction in our allowance for doubtful receivables with the management at Trott & Cook. This has meant that our profit figure for the year is in line with the forecast we gave our shareholders rather than much lower as it would have been without your help.
>
> Please find enclosed a gift voucher as a small thank you.
>
> Best wishes
>
> Andrew
>
> PS I would appreciate it if we could keep this arrangement between us as it may not look good for you if the partners at Trott & Cook found out about this.

(a) Explain which two of Hayley's fundamental ethical principles are most threatened if she, knowingly, did not raise the reduction in the allowance for doubtful receivables.

(b) What type of threat does Hayley face to her fundamental ethical principles?

(c) If Hayley genuinely believed that the allowance for doubtful receivables was correct are there any reasons that she cannot accept the gift voucher from Andrew?

6.5 Adrian has been employed by Tahil & Emerson, a medium sized accounting practice, since he started training as an accountant. He has now been qualified for four years. Each year since he joined the firm Adrian has been part of the team of accountants working on Tahil & Emerson's largest client, Headstyle Ltd, starting as a junior and currently working as the manager of the assignment. The Managing Director of Headstyle has asked Adrian if he would be interested in becoming the company's new Finance Director. He has asked that Adrian does not mention his offer until after the current year's assignment is complete.

(a) State what types of threats Adrian is facing to his fundamental ethical principles.

(b) Explain which two of Adrian's fundamental ethical principles are most threatened by this situation.

(c) Explain what safeguards he can put in place to eliminate these threats or reduce them to an acceptable level.

6.6 Michael Austin works for Paragon Ltd, a company that manufactures industrial lighting. The managing director, Jules West, has recently leased a hospitality box at the local premiership rugby club for the whole season. Jules has said that Michael, a keen rugby supporter, can use the box for the cup final if he works late for the next week to ensure that the financial statements are completed on time.

(a) Explain what type of threat Michael faces to his fundamental ethical principles.

(b) Explain which two of Michael's fundamental principles are threatened in this situation.

(c) What safeguards he can put in place to eliminate this threat or reduce it to an acceptable level?

6.7 Explain whether professional accountants in business or professional accountants who work in practice are more likely to face advocacy threats to their fundamental ethical principles.

7 Ethical conflict and reporting unethical behaviour

this chapter covers...

This chapter explains how ethical conflicts arise, and the practical approach that a professional accountant takes to professional ethics and the way in which ethical conflicts can be resolved. It also covers what to do if an ethical issue cannot be resolved.

It then covers the key ethical organisational values that should be included in a business's code of practice to ensure that it complies with the spirit of the regulations it must comply with.

The chapter will also look at the consequences of not complying with organisational values, codes of practice and regulations including the internal disciplinary procedures an accountant may face. It will also highlight the opportunity for an accountant to consider whistleblowing if he or she believes that an employer, colleague, or client has acted illegally or unethically.

The final section of the chapter covers professional liability, and how to minimise the risk of professional negligence. It also includes how accountants can take out professional indemnity insurance to mitigate some of the potential costs of a legal case for professional negligence against them.

ETHICAL CONFLICT

ethical conflict between interests of different clients

In Chapter 5 we discussed the issue of **conflict of interest** in relation to the objectivity of an accountant, explaining that accountants should not allow business or personal interests to prevent them from remaining objective and independent. The interests here are clearly those of the **accountant**.

Another situation where a conflict of interest can occur relates instead to the interests of the accountant's **clients**. Accountants who work in public practice normally have several different clients. Consequently, there is a strong chance that at some point there may be a conflict of interest between two or more of these clients. For example, the accountant may have several clients that work in the same market sector, all competing for the same customers, so the success of one client in increasing sales may well have a negative effect on another client in the same sector.

The issues for an accountant who is working for clients where a potential conflict of interest exists are predominantly those of objectivity and confidentiality.

There are two potential problems which the accountant may face:

- the accountant may provide services and give professional advice to one client where they know that this will have an adverse effect on another of their clients (objectivity)
- information gained about one client could potentially be beneficial to another and vice versa (confidentiality)

In many cases, the risk associated with these issues can be reduced to an acceptable level by compartmentalising the responsibilities and knowledge about each of the clients by using different members of staff to work on the client assignments. However, if this safeguard does not reduce the threat to the fundamental principles to an acceptable level, then the accountant should not accept or continue with one or more of the appointments.

When an accountant is considering taking on a new client or where there are any changes in the circumstances of existing clients, the accountant should take all reasonable steps to find out whether a conflict of interest exists or could arise.

If a significant conflict of interest is identified between clients, the accountant should ensure that the clients involved are fully informed of the circumstances. This will then allow each of them to make an informed decision about whether to use the accountant's services.

The issue of conflict between the interests of different clients is illustrated in the example that follows.

example

a conflict of interest

Jim Kirk is an accountant who runs Kirk & Co., a successful firm of accountants in Pineridge. Jim has recently been approached by Robert Redpool, one of the partners in Blackwell & Redpool, a local firm of builders, asking if Kirk & Co. would be interested in carrying out some accounting work for them relating to the potential purchase of a development site in Pineridge. One of Jim's existing clients, Bluebell & Whitelake, is also a building firm located in Pineridge.

What points should Jim consider when deciding whether to accept the assignment for Blackwell & Redpool?

First, Jim must investigate whether there could be a conflict of interest between the potential client and his existing client, Bluebell & Whitelake. If he believes that there is, or could be, a conflict of interest between the two clients, Jim must then decide whether Kirk and Co. have sufficient staff to use separate staff on each of the clients. This would reduce the risk that the interests of either client could be adversely affected if Kirk & Co. took on the new work.

If Jim believes that he can adequately safeguard the interests of both clients he should then contact Blackwell & Redpool and Bluebell & Whitelake and fully explain the situation, including the staffing measures Kirk & Co. intends to put in place. This will then allow the existing client and the potential client to decide for themselves whether they are happy to enter into, or continue in, a relationship with Kirk & Co.

If Jim decides that he could not sufficiently reduce the risks associated with the conflict of interest between the two builders, then he must either decline the appointment with Blackwell & Redpool (the more likely option) or end Kirk & Co.'s relationship with Bluebell & Whitelake.

In this circumstance he must ensure he fully documents the process he goes through.

conflict of loyalties for an accountant

a definition of loyalty

One definition of loyalty is:

> *'being firm and not changing in your support for a person or an organisation, or in your belief in your principles.'*

Society generally views loyalty as a good thing whether it is to friends, family or to employers. Employers are keen for their employees to be loyal to the organisation that they work for as this encourages stability within the workforce and a good team spirit, which in turn contributes to the success of the organisation. It also means that employees will be supportive of decisions taken by the organisation that they work for and will carry out the tasks that are expected of them.

One of the factors that will help to maintain an employee's loyalty to the organisation that they work for is a culture that encourages strong ethical values. We have seen in previous chapters just how important the accounting profession considers ethics to be for its members. But this need for strong ethical values is not limited to the accountancy profession. Every employee, regardless of their seniority in an organisation, should maintain an ethical approach to their work.

conflict of loyalties

Employed accountants are expected to be loyal to their employer; but, as professional accountants, they also owe a duty of loyalty to the accounting profession. There is potential for conflict here. As an employee, it would seem logical that the employed accountant's first priority should be to support their organisation's objectives and the rules and procedures drawn up in support of them, provided that the organisation is acting in a legal and ethical way. However, there may be times when something that the employer expects the professional accountant to do conflicts with their professional and ethical values.

Because of the responsibility to their employer, an accountant may be put under pressure not to comply with the fundamental ethical principles. They may face pressure to:

- break the law
- breach the rules and standards of their profession
- be part of a plan for unethical or illegal earnings
- lie to or mislead (including by keeping silent) auditors or regulators, or
- put their name to, or otherwise be associated with, a statement which materially misrepresents the facts

We can see that all of the above are serious situations. Each one clearly conflicts with the ethical standards expected of a professional accountant.

Breaking the law is obviously not something anyone, never mind a professional accountant, should do. The rules and standards of the accounting professional are clearly there for a purpose and should not be broken by members of the profession. Note that breaching ethical standards includes not only active deception, but also an accountant misleading the auditors by just keeping quiet when they know the auditors have got something wrong.

So, what happens if an employed accountant is put in a position where the employer puts pressure on them to do one (or more) of the above? Possible action that the accountant could take is:

- if the employer has broken the law, the accountant should try hard to persuade the employer not to continue with the unlawful activity and to rectify the situation as soon as possible

- if there is a difference of opinion between the accountant and the employer regarding an accounting or ethical matter, wherever possible this should be resolved with the involvement of more senior staff within the organisation. If necessary, the issue should be dealt with using the employer's formal dispute resolution process
- where the issue between the employer and the accountant cannot be resolved and the accountant considers that they have exhausted all other possible alternatives then they may have no option but to offer to resign. In this case the employed accountant should explain to the employer the reasons for their resignation, and should at the same time maintain the duty of confidentiality to the employer

It is worth noting here that the accounting profession and the code of ethics strongly recommends that the employed accountant should obtain advice from their professional body or legal advice before taking the step of offering to resign. One important reason for this is that the law now protects an employee from dismissal for 'whistleblowing', ie breaking confidentiality. In other words, the employee should not have to be put in the position of having to lose their job when the matter is serious enough to be made public. Only the employed accountant's professional body or a lawyer (or both) can advise in this situation.

The process of dealing with conflicts of loyalty is summarised in the diagram below.

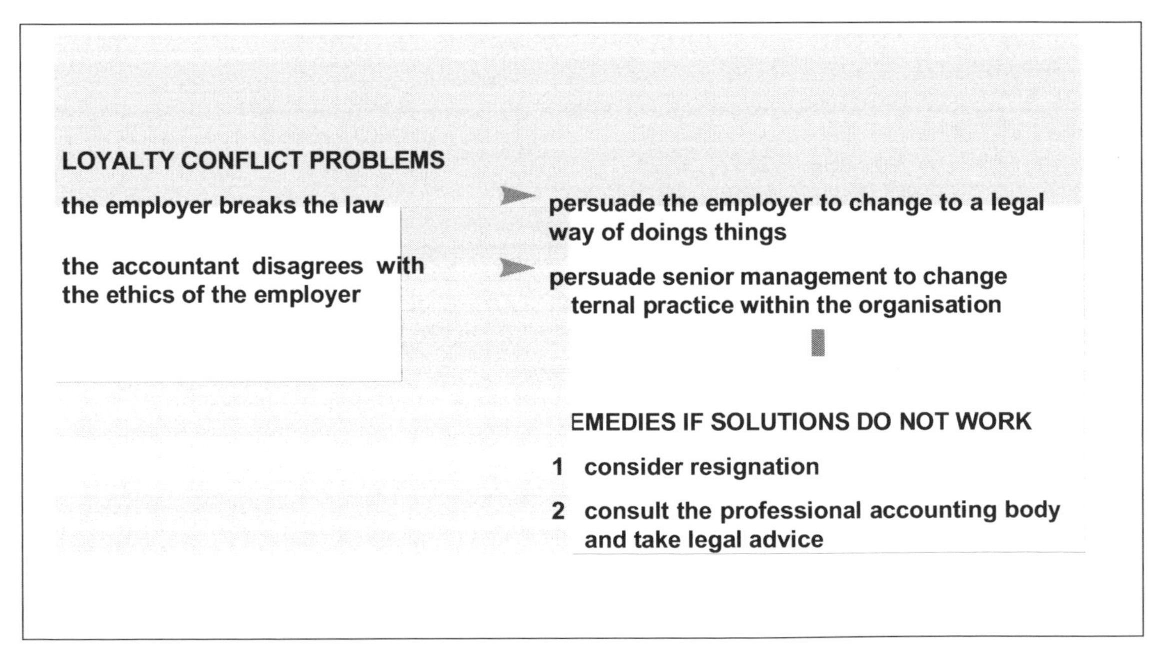

The area of conflict of loyalties and the ethical issues that it raises is illustrated in the example that follows.

example

a conflict of loyalties

Rona Hughes works as an Accounts Assistant in the accounts department of Peters & Son where one of her responsibilities is to prepare the quarterly VAT Return for the company. It is now the end of the financial year, and the Financial Controller has asked Rona to manipulate the figures to be included on the VAT Return so that the company's year-end VAT liability is reduced.

This is clearly wrong, and Rona should take no part in the Financial Controller's request to falsify the data that is to be included in the VAT Return. But what should she do in these circumstances to resolve the problem?

As an employee of Peters & Son, Rona has a duty of loyalty to the company and to the Financial Controller as her line manager, but she also has a duty to follow the rules and regulations of the accountancy profession and adhere to the fundamental principles of professional behaviour, professional competence and due care and integrity. Rona also has a legal duty to prepare an accurate VAT Return.

In this case there is a conflict between her loyalty to her employer and to her profession. In the first instance, Rona should explain to the Financial Controller that she has serious concerns about doing what he has asked and cannot be involved in such activities. If, at this point, the Financial Controller agrees with Rona that she is right, then no further action needs to be taken. However, if, despite raising her concerns with him, there is still a disagreement, Rona would have to raise the issue with a higher level of management.

Finally, if Rona has no success when she raises the matter with the senior management of Peters & Son and the Financial Controller continues to falsify the VAT records, Rona will be faced with no alternative but to consider resigning. Before doing so she should take relevant legal advice.

If, after taking legal advice, she decides that resigning is the only course of action available to her, Rona should explain her reasons for resigning to the management at Peters & Son. She will still be bound by her duty of confidentiality to her employer and so should not tell anyone else these reasons at this stage.

You will see that a number of issues are raised by the example of Rona Hughes above. Firstly, she has been put in a very difficult position as a result of the request made by the Financial Controller. He is more senior than she is and so has the authority to put pressure on her to comply with what he has asked her to do. Raising the issue with more senior management in the organisation is likely to cause a significant amount of tension between the Financial Controller and Rona, which could ultimately make her position within Peters & Son very difficult.

Resigning from the company would also be a huge step for Rona to take. The consequences of this could be that she may not receive a reference from Peters & Son or may find it difficult to find another job.

With all these issues to contend with it is easy to see why some employees choose to remain silent about malpractices that occur within their organisation. They choose instead, to 'keep their heads down' and ignore the ethical issues that this raises.

ETHICAL CONFLICT RESOLUTION

We can see that there will be occasions in an accountant's working life when they may be faced with an ethical conflict in the application of the fundamental principles. In these circumstances the accountant will need to find a method for resolving this conflict. If the organisation that the accountant works for has a formal conflict resolution process (as many large professional accounting firms do) the best approach may be to use this conflict resolution process. Alternatively, the accountant may initially try to resolve the conflict informally.

In either case when attempting to resolve the conflict the accountant should consider each of the following points:

- the relevant facts relating to the conflict
- assess all the ethical issues involved
- the fundamental principles that are involved in the ethical conflict
- whether there are established internal procedures to deal with the conflict and if so, how they can be applied to the situation
- what alternative courses of action are available to the accountant
- seek advice from others

Having considered these factors, the accountant will need to decide the best course of action that is consistent with the fundamental principles identified. They will also need to consider the consequences of each possible course of action.

If the ethical conflict remains unresolved, the accountant may decide to consult with other appropriate colleagues for help finding a resolution. Where an issue is raised with a line manager, the accountant must ensure that this is done discreetly and confidentially.

If, after consulting with a colleague, the accountant is still unable to resolve an ethical dilemma, or ethical conflict, the accountant may decide that they need to seek further advice. If the organisation that the accountant works for is large enough, this may initially be from the employer's ethics helpline. However, for accountants employed in smaller organisations they may need to contact the helpline of their professional accounting body. For example, AAT has a confidential ethics helpline that is available to give advice to its members.

If the ethical conflict is between the accountant and another member of staff or the organisation that they work for, the accountant may need to report this to the persons charged with governance (management) of the business for conflict resolution. This may be the Board of Directors or the Audit Committee.

The accountant must remember that it is important to always document the details of the ethical issue involved together with details of any discussions held or decisions taken, concerning this issue.

The following example illustrates how an ethical issue could be resolved using this approach.

resolving an ethical conflict

a taxing question

Ben works as a manager for Parkinson & Norton, a large accounting practice. One of the partners, Michael Norton, has asked him to personally carry out some taxation work for a client, Ricard Dupre. During the work on Ricard's tax return Ben realises that Ricard is currently setting up a new business venture with another of Ben's clients, Jon Darmery. There are some issues in Ricard's tax affairs that indicate to Ben that Jon may not be fully aware of Ricard's true financial position.

Ben is now faced with an ethical dilemma. Should he break confidentiality rules and tell Jon what he has found out about Ricard or risk compromising his professional competence and due care?

Although Ben may be tempted to go straight to Michael Norton, he should do the following:

- gather all the facts relating to the situation
- assess the ethical principles involved, in this case professional competence and due care and confidentiality
- decide what procedures (formal or informal) are available within Parkinson & Norton for the resolution of ethical conflicts. This could be reporting the issue to a senior member of staff or, if there are legal issues involved, it may require external advice
- decide what alternative courses of action are available and the consequences of each one. This could involve explaining to Ricard that Parkinson & Norton has an issue as it already acts for Jon Darmery and matters arising from its review of Ricard's affairs mean its professional competence has been compromised. It could also be to advise Ricard to fully disclose his financial affairs to Jon or to give Parkinson & Norton authority to disclose the information
- then discuss the issue with Michael Norton and document the results of the discussion and the course of action that has been decided upon. He must be sure that whatever decision is finally made it does not compromise his fundamental ethical principles and those of Parkinson & Norton

The above example identifies an ethical dilemma for an accountant in practice who is dealing with a client. However, there may be occasions when an accountant in business is faced with an ethical dilemma when dealing with a supplier – for example, if a supplier offers to carry out work for the business on a cash basis so that the business avoids paying VAT and the manager of the business accepts the offer. This would create an ethical issue for the accountant. In this case they would have to take the same approach detailed on the previous page to resolve the ethical conflict.

failure to resolve an issue

If an ethical conflict cannot be resolved, a professional accountant may consider obtaining professional advice from their professional accounting body or taking legal advice. This would have to be done on a confidential basis and to ensure that there was no breach of confidentiality.

An example of where this confidentiality issue might arise would be if the accountant suspects that a fraud may have been committed by a colleague, employer or client. In this case they may need to discuss confidential information with advisors from their professional accounting body or a lawyer to confirm whether their suspicions are justified.

Ultimately if the accountant is still unable to resolve the ethical conflict, they may have to dissociate themself from the issue. This could be by withdrawing from the engagement team working on client assignment or actually resigning altogether from the engagement, the firm that they work for or the employer.

ORGANISATIONAL AND PROFESSIONAL VALUES

Professional accountants are expected to comply with the law and with relevant regulations. However, organisations should also comply with 'the spirit' of the regulations, ie how these regulations are expected to work in practice. To do this many organisations will have their own code of conduct. There are a number of key organisational values that should be included in a business's code of conduct, or code of practice. These are:

- **being transparent with colleagues, customers, and suppliers** – eg not hiding things in the small print of contracts, or telling customers that you can provide them with a product or service that is not available
- **reporting financial and regulatory information clearly and on time** – eg producing management accounts promptly and accurately for use by colleagues in the business
- **being open and honest by identifying when it is appropriate to accept and give gifts and hospitality** – eg defining, including specific policies in the organisation's code of practice, that gifts can only be accepted if they are less than £20 in value
- **paying suppliers a fair price and on time** – eg ensuring that all suppliers regardless of size are paid to terms, eg within a 30 day period of receiving an invoice
- **providing fair treatment, decent wages, and good working conditions for employees** – eg ensuring that a regular review is carried out for staff who work on computer terminals to ensure their workstations comply with health and safety regulations
- **appropriate use of social media** – eg a clear guide as to what is acceptable and unacceptable to be included in social media posts made on behalf of the business, or made, personally, by one of its employees

conflict with personal values

In addition to complying with the organisation's ethical values and principles a professional accountant must ensure that they are able to apply their own ethical values and fundamental principles to decide whether behaviour is ethical or unethical.

Although many organisations have well defined codes of conduct and business ethics, there may be occasions where the key personal values of an individual within the organisation may conflict with the values of the organisation itself. In these circumstances it is important that the individual makes their feelings known and discusses the conflict with management in the business using the conflict resolution process detailed earlier in this chapter.

NON-COMPLIANCE WITH ORGANISATIONAL AND PROFESSIONAL VALUES

As we have seen, in addition to complying with regulations, businesses introduce codes of practice and organisational values to try and ensure that their employees work ethically. But what happens if organisations and individuals do not comply with these values, codes, and regulations? We will now look at the consequences of non-compliance.

non-compliance by an organisation

It is one thing to produce a set of ethical organisational values. However, these are only of any use if the organisation actually follows them. It is no use simply 'paying lip service' to a code of practice. The image and reputation of a business will be adversely affected if it does not comply with its values and codes. We will now look at each of the key organisational values highlighted in the previous section to see examples of the consequences of failing to comply with each of these values.

- **being transparent with colleagues, customers, and suppliers** – if an organisation hides unreasonable terms in the small print of a contract that they later try and enforce, this will put customers off trading with that business in the future. Similarly, if a business is not clear in its dealings with suppliers, these suppliers will be reluctant to deal with the business in the future
- **reporting financial and regulatory information clearly and on time** – failure to produce accurate and timely financial information may lead to poor decisions being made by the management of the business. Failure to produce regulatory information such as financial statements on time can lead to the business being fined
- **being open and honest by identifying when it is appropriate to accept and give gifts and hospitality** – a business that gives gifts or hospitality

to customers could be seen as trying to influence the customer's decisions or even to bribe the customer. Similarly, accepting gifts from a supplier could influence the decision-making of the organisation. The consequence of not having clear policies regarding gifts and hospitality could be to adversely affect the image of the business and potentially lead to accusations of unethical business dealings

- **paying suppliers a fair price and on time** – a business that tries to squeeze the lowest price out of a supplier and delays payment can adversely affect the relationship with that supplier. Recently some of the large supermarkets have received some very negative publicity in the press for their control over small farmers and demanding very low prices
- **providing fair treatment, decent wages and good working conditions for employees** – if a business does not treat its employees well, they will leave the organisation which will lead to high staff turnover. Also, poor working conditions will affect staff morale and affect the quality of work and the commitment of the business's staff

Organisational values and codes of practice are implemented within the organisation and are not legally enforceable. However, if a business fails to comply with regulations, it could be subject to fines. For example, if an organisation is found in court to have breached the Health and Safety at Work Act (1974) and its relevant statutory provisions, the court can impose significant penalties on the business.

disciplinary procedures for non-compliance

In Chapter 5 we looked at **the internal disciplinary procedures** that an employer may bring against a professional accountant who fails to adhere to the employer's organisational values or internal codes of practice. These included some or all of the following stages depending on the seriousness of the breach.

- a verbal warning
- a written warning
- a disciplinary hearing
- the opportunity to appeal
- suspension from work
- dismissal

In Chapter 5, we saw that the professional accounting bodies in the UK also expect their members to comply with their codes of ethics and to uphold the high standards that are expected of the accounting profession. Failure by an accountant to comply may result in the accountant being disciplined by their individual accounting bodies or by the Financial Reporting Council (FRC).

Misconduct falls into two main categories:

- bringing the accounting profession into disrepute
- acting in breach of the rules and regulations of the accountant's professional body

Details of the disciplinary procedures that are available to individual accounting bodies in the UK are listed in Chapter 5.

WHISTLEBLOWING

We have looked at the consequences for a business or an individual accountant of breaching ethical codes. But what does an employee do if they suspect an employer, a colleague or a client has committed, or may commit, an act which is illegal or unethical? They must decide the appropriate reporting procedures to follow. The employee may decide to 'blow the whistle' to expose the misconduct that they believe has or may occur.

So, what do we mean by the term '**whistleblowing**'? A whistle blower can be defined as:

> *'a person who tells someone in authority about misconduct, alleged dishonesty or illegal activity that has or may occur in an organisation.'*

The misconduct could be breaking the law – for example, committing a fraud, contravening regulations such as health and safety regulations, or something that is contrary to public interest such as corruption. The allegations of misconduct made by a whistle blower can be made internally within the organisation or externally to regulators or to the police.

internal whistleblowing

Most whistleblowers are **internal whistleblowers**, who report misconduct on the part of a colleague to someone more senior in the organisation.

It is a big decision to internally blow the whistle on an employer or colleague. This action can have a serious impact on the individual's future employment with the business and could ultimately force them to resign. If they decide to blow the whistle, the following points should be considered:

- ensure that they know all the facts surrounding the issue and have evidence to support the facts
- follow the employer's internal procedures for reporting suspected misconduct in order to disclose the malpractice; this may involve reporting unethical behaviour and breaches of confidentiality to a prescribed internal department within the organisation
- ensure that the situation is fully explained to management including the concerns that they have and how the organisation could be affected if they are not addressed

external whistleblowing

An individual is advised to raise concerns internally before going outside of the business. However, if they feel that the issue is not being addressed or that the matter is so serious that it cannot be raised internally, they should report to an appropriate regulator such as the Financial Reporting Council (FRC). Legal protection available to an external whistleblower is limited so it is important to seek third-party advice before blowing the whistle. The AAT ethics advice line will be able to help in these circumstances.

This can be a very serious step especially if the employee decides not to resign after blowing the whistle. In these circumstances the employer is unlikely to be very happy if one of its employees has reported them for something illegal and are unlikely to want the person to work for them any longer. Consequently, is it important that the employee has some protection from dismissal if they choose to blow the whistle on the employer.

The Public Interest Disclosure Act 1998 (PIDA) offers the employee such protection in certain circumstances. PIDA gives an employee protection where they disclose otherwise confidential information which they reasonably believe shows that one of the following has or is likely to occur:

- a criminal offence
- a breach of a legal obligation
- a miscarriage of justice
- endangerment of an individual's health and safety
- environmental damage

In order to be protected from dismissal the employee must also be able to show that:

- the disclosure is made in good faith
- the employee reasonably believes that the information disclosed is true
- the employee would otherwise be victimised, or the evidence concealed or destroyed if the information is not disclosed

The Public Interest Disclosure Act 1998 does make it easier for an employee to report an unethical or disreputable employer, but it still cannot offer complete protection from the employer who is the target of the whistleblowing. Recent cases of whistleblowing have resulted in employees being suspended pending an enquiry, or being dismissed at a later date. The main risk for an individual who has blown the whistle on an employer is the subsequent effect on future career prospects.

The following example highlights the serious consequences of deciding to 'blow the whistle' on an employer.

example

time to blow the whistle?

Stephanie Andrews works as an accountant for Harmsworthy Plc, a large, quoted company. The Finance Director has asked her to help her with a scheme which she and the Managing Director have come up with. The directors have offered to pay Stephanie £5,000 for her help in the scheme which involves illegal dealing in shares of Harmsworthy Plc. The Finance Director has made it clear to Stephanie that if she does not help them, she will lose her job.

What should Stephanie do in this situation?

An employee cannot legitimately be required to break the law by their employer. In the first instance, Stephanie should raise her concerns with the directors of Harmsworthy Plc and make every effort to persuade them not to break the law. However, this option could prove difficult for Stephanie as it is the senior management of Harmsworthy who are involved in the illegal activity.

Assuming Stephanie does not agree to break the law she is faced with two options. First, she could choose to resign from Harmsworthy Plc stating her reasons for doing so. Secondly, she may decide to blow the whistle on the management of Harmsworthy Plc and report them to the appropriate authorities. Under the second option she must be sure that the facts are correct and that she would be victimised and the evidence concealed or destroyed if she did not whistleblow.

seeking advice

If an accountant has exhausted all internal routes to report unethical behaviour by an employer, colleague, client, or customer they may need to seek advice externally.

There are several organisations that can provide confidential advice, including the Citizens Advice Bureau. There is also Protect, a charity that works to support employees in the workplace by giving guidance and support about wrongdoing or malpractice in the workplace. They will help and give advice on how to raise a concern with your employer.

Like all the professional accounting bodies, AAT has a (free) ethics helpline that is available to give advice and guidance based on the ethical code. Before whistleblowing, a member of AAT should seek confidential advice from this helpline about how to report unethical behaviour.

PROFESSIONAL LIABILITY

We have already covered professional competence and due care in Chapter 5. In addition to breaching their fundamental ethical principles, a professional accountant who acts beyond their professional experience, knowledge and experience may be liable to their client.

a definition of liability

Liability means **'having legal responsibility for something with the possibility of having to pay damages'**.

Liability can arise from a number of causes, including criminal acts, breach of contract in the supply of services, breach of trust, professional negligence, and fraud.

In law, **negligence** is a breach of a duty of care that is implied in a particular situation or relationship. For example, a railway company has a duty of care for the safe transit of its passengers and an accountant has a duty of care to carry out assignments in a skilled and professional manner. If the railway company fails to observe safety measures (such as red signals) and the accountant makes mistakes in a tax return, in different ways they are both held to be negligent. We will now look at liability for professional negligence on the part of a member of the accounting profession. **Professional negligence** may occur if a client, to whom the accountant owes a duty to exercise reasonable care and skill, suffers a financial loss that can be proved is the fault of the accountant. Additionally, the accountant will have entered into a contract with the client, so this may be a breach of contract and in certain cases there may even be accusations of fraud, or even money laundering.

We will now look at an example of professional negligence and breach of contract.

Cecil is a professional accountant who works as a sole practitioner. Earlier in the year he prepa the tax return for his client, Amos, which included income that Amos has earned from some comp share transactions. HMRC has now investigated Amos's tax affairs in relation to this return and found that the tax calculations are incorrect, and that Amos has underpaid a substantial amour tax. It has fined Amos for this error and has sent him a demand for the underpaid tax.

In this situation what can Amos do?

If Amos can prove that Cecil has not exercised reasonable care and skill and that he has suffe financial loss, he can sue Cecil for professional negligence. As Amos also has a contract with Cec complete his tax return, he could also sue for breach of contract.

minimising the risk of professional negligence

For all assignments the following points should be covered to ensure that the possibility of a client suing an accountant for professional negligence is minimised:

- accountant should ensure that before taking on an assignment, the exact duties to be included (and equally as important, excluded) in the assignment are written down and agreed by both the accountant and the client. This would normally be done in the letter of engagement
- if further duties are added to an assignment, then the accountant should ensure that these are also written down and agreed by both parties

- where an accountant gives a client advice without having been provided with all the information they need, the accountant must make sure that the client is aware of any limitations to this advice and that this is written down
- if the accountant prepares unaudited accounts or financial statements for a client, they must clearly mark on the documents that they are confidential and solely for the private use of the client
- if an assignment is very complex, an accountant should take specialist advice or suggest that the client does so

professional indemnity insurance

All accountants hope that they will never be put in the position where a client brings a legal case against them for professional negligence. However, it is possible that at some time this may happen. Accountants in practice should ensure that they have adequate **professional indemnity insurance**. This type of insurance is taken out by an accountant (or other professional) as cover against legal liability to compensate a third party (normally a client) who has sustained injury, loss, or damage through a breach in the accountant's duty of care. (**Note**: professional indemnity insurance is strongly recommended for student accountants who undertake self-employed work.)

We will now look at an example where the issue of professional liability could arise.

example

a question of professional liability

Christopher Matthews works as an accountant in practice. He has recently received a request from the Managing Director of one of his clients to provide him with some personal advice on inheritance tax. Christopher has no experience in this area of taxation and has never given advice on inheritance tax before.

Christopher is considering reading up on this area of tax and taking on this assignment. However, he thinks it would be a good idea to make sure his professional indemnity insurance is up-to-date.

Is this appropriate professional and ethical behaviour on Christopher's part?

If Christopher is unsure of his expertise regarding inheritance tax, he should ensure that he gets the necessary advice and guidance from an appropriately qualified person. He should only take on the assignment if he considers that he has the professional and technical competence to carry out the work satisfactorily.

It would be unprofessional for Christopher to rely on his professional indemnity insurance to cover the risk that he may not carry out the work properly. It is also unlikely that a court would allow him to rely on this should the client bring a legal action for damages against him were his advice to result in the client losing money.

All accountants should have professional indemnity insurance. But this should not be used as a 'safety net' in situations where an accountant does not have the necessary skills to carry out an assignment.

Chapter Summary

- Where conflict of interest exists between two or more clients, an accountant should take all possible steps to minimise the risks that could arise.
- Employed accountants have a duty of loyalty to the organisation that employs them and also to the accounting profession. On occasion these different loyalties may conflict.
- Where ethical conflicts arise, accountants should take all necessary steps to resolve these:
  - gather the relevant facts relating to the conflict
  - assess all the ethical issues involved
  - identify the fundamental ethical principles that are involved in the ethical conflict
  - assess whether there are established internal procedures to deal with the conflict and if so, how they can be applied to the situation
  - review the alternative courses of action available
  - seek advice from others
- If an ethical conflict cannot be resolved, an accountant should seek advice from a solicitor, or from their professional accounting body's advice line.
- Professional accountants are expected to comply with the law and with relevant regulations.
- Organisations should comply with 'the spirit' of regulations and should include key ethical organisational values in their code of practice. These are:
  - Being transparent with colleagues, customers and suppliers
  - Reporting financial and regulatory information clearly and on time
  - Being open and honest by identifying when it is appropriate to accept and give gifts and hospitality
  - Paying suppliers a fair price and on time
  - Providing fair treatment, decent wages and good working conditions for employees
- Failure to comply with an employer's organisational values or codes of practice can result in an accountant being disciplined by their employer or professional accounting body.
- Accountants and other employees may decide to report illegal or unethical behaviour on the part of an employer, colleague or client through the process of whistleblowing.
- Providing a member is acting in good faith when they 'blow the whistle' on an employer and so break the duty of confidentiality, they will be protected in many situations by the Public Interest Disclosure Act 1998.
- If an accountant is negligent in their duties, they could be liable ie legally responsible with the possibility of having to pay damages. This could be for a criminal act such as fraud or money laundering, breach of contract, breach of trust or professional negligence.

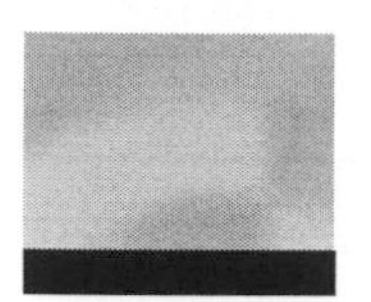

- Members of the accounting profession should have sufficient professional indemnity insurance to cover against legal liability to compensate a client or third party that has sustained loss through a breach of the accountant's duty of care.

Key Terms

conflict of interest — This arises where the business or personal interests of an accountant may influence their objectivity

conflict of loyalty — this arises where an employee's loyalty to their employer clashes with their loyalty to the accounting profession

ethical conflict — this occurs where there is a fundamental disagreement between what has been requested of the accountant and what their ethical principles indicate that they should do

disciplinary action — processes and sanctions that a professional accounting body can carry out if a member is accused of non-compliance with its regulations and the code of ethics; an employer may also carry out sanctions when an employee has not complied with its policies, procedures and ethical values.

internal whistleblowing — telling someone more senior within the organisation about something illegal or unethical within the organisation that the employee works for

Public Interest Disclosure Act 1998 (PIDA) — a statute that protects employees (whistleblowers) who make disclosures of confidential information that they believe to be in the public interest

professional negligence — this may occur where a client, to whom an accountant owes a duty of care, suffers a financial loss that can be proved to be the fault of the accountant

professional indemnity insurance — insurance that an accountant takes out to cover any damages they may have to pay a client due to professional negligence

Activities

7.1 Terry is a qualified professional accountant who has worked for Parks & Co for a number of years. Over the last three years Terry has been working on assignments for two large local building firms, Pentagon Homes and Vale Housing. A large building plot that has space for 100 houses has recently come up for sale and both Pentagon Homes and Vale Housing are putting in a bid for the land. They have each asked Terry to act for them in relation to the bid. Both building firms have now realised that the other is likely to be interested in the land. Pentagon has offered Terry an additional fee of £5,000 to act for Pentagon Homes only; meanwhile Vale Housing has offered £6,000 if Terry will act exclusively for them. Neither of the companies is happy for Terry to act for both building firms in relation to the bid.

(a) Which two of Terry's fundamental principles are threatened by the fact that both Pentagon Homes and Vale Housing are both bidding for the same piece of land?

(b) What process can Terry go through to resolve the ethical conflict he has in deciding how to deal with this situation?

(c) If Terry decides to act for one of the clients, explain two issues that he must consider when carrying out the assignment.

7.2 Esther is a professional accountant who works for Goodrich Ltd. The Accounts Department is currently preparing the year-end financial statements and part of Esther's responsibilities is to prepare the inventory valuation. Esther attended the year-end inventory count and identified £60,000 of inventory that is not in saleable condition and will need to be scrapped. She has highlighted this to her manager, Sam, and suggested that £40,000 should be written off the inventory value.

Sam told Esther that he does not want her to write off the damaged inventory and they will deal with it after the year-end. The total value of the inventory before this £40,000 proposed reduction for damaged stock is £347,000.

(a) Explain the conflict of loyalties that Esther faces in this situation.

(b) What options does Esther have to deal with this conflict of loyalties?

7.3 List the **six** key organisational ethical values that a business should include in its code of practice.

7.4 Babridge Limited employs a number of staff in its warehouse. These warehouse workers have recently been required to do a significant amount of overtime to fulfil an urgent overseas order. Overtime worked is paid to all staff in the business at their standard hourly rate. The Managing Director has decided to give the sales team that secured the order a large bonus, in addition to the overtime they worked to secure the order, but does not plan to give bonuses to the warehouse staff.

Decide whether each of the following statements is true or false

	True	**False**
(a) Because all staff are paid for the overtime that they work, Babridge Limited is automatically considered to be behaving ethically towards its staff		
(b) The Managing Director's decision regarding staff bonuses raises concerns about the ethical nature of the management and leadership of Babridge Ltd		

7.5 Martin is a member of AAT who works for Mejanna Ltd. His manager has recently overheard Martin in the pub, telling a friend, who works for Showman Ltd, all about a confidential matter at work. The manager has told Martin that he will now face disciplinary procedures because he has behaved unethically.

Decide whether or not each of the following organisations can bring disciplinary procedures against Martin for his unethical behaviour.

Select **one** option for each organisation.

	Can	**Cannot**
(a) Showman Ltd		
(b) Mejanna Ltd		
(c) AAT		

7.6 Felicity believes that her colleague, Marcus, has acted illegally and has decided to internally blow the whistle on Marcus's misconduct.

What points should Felicity consider before she decides whether to blow the whistle?

7.7 Michaela, a professional accountant in practice, has provided taxation advice to her client, Nigel. Michaela did not have the necessary technical expertise to provide this advice and Nigel has ended up incurring a fine from HMRC.

If it is proved that Michaela has acted outside her professional competence, on what grounds may Nigel be able to sue Michaela for compensation?

State two grounds.

1
2

7.8 What type of insurance should professional accountants have to cover them against legal liability to compensate a client who has sustained financial loss through a breach of the accountant's duty of care?

8 Money laundering

this chapter covers...

This chapter starts by explaining what money laundering is and the three stages of money laundering: layering, placement, and integration. It also details what activities constitute money laundering.

The next part of the chapter examines the anti-money laundering legislation in the UK and the role that the National Crime Agency takes in enforcing this legislation.

After this, the chapter will cover some of the offences under the money laundering legislation and the importance of reporting suspected money laundering.

MONEY LAUNDERING

a definition of money laundering

Money laundering can be defined as:

> *'to move illegally acquired cash through financial systems so that it appears to be legally acquired'.*

Put simply, this means using money gained illegally – eg through terrorist funding, drug dealing or other criminal activities – so that the money is 'laundered' or 'washed' and then appears to be 'clean' and legally obtained.

stages of the money laundering process

There are three stages of the process of money laundering:

placement: the first stage of money laundering is moving the money into a legitimate financial system. This may be by paying it into a bank account, or in more complex operations, into an offshore account. Placement is the stage where it is most likely that the laundered money will be detected.

layering: the second stage of the money laundering process is to create a complex web of transactions to move the money around the financial system, by layering financial transactions. This then obscures the audit trail and conceals the original source and ownership of the illegal funds.

integration: the final stage of money laundering is to integrate the illegal funds back into the legitimate financial system. Criminals may do this by investing in property and other assets. Integration will be done carefully so that the criminal creates a plausible explanation for where the money has come from.

money laundering activities

Activities related to money laundering include:

- acquiring, using, or possessing criminal property
- handling the proceeds of crime such as theft, fraud and tax evasion
- being knowingly involved in any way with criminal or terrorist property
- entering into arrangements to facilitate laundering criminal or terrorist property
- investing the proceeds of crime into other financial products
- investing the proceeds of crime into the acquisition of property/assets
- transferring criminal property

Criminal property is property which was knowingly obtained as a result of criminal conduct. It may take a number of forms including money, security, tangible, or intangible property. Terrorist property is money or property likely to be used for terrorist purposes, or the process of commissioning or carrying out terrorist acts.

An accountant will be guilty of a money laundering offence if they provide accounting services while 'turning a blind eye' to the client's suspect dealings. This would be viewed as facilitating the client's illegal activities as detailed in the fourth point above. The value of the criminal property will have no bearing on whether or not an accountant should report a money laundering offence as there are no de minimis exceptions or lower limits in relation to money laundering or terrorist financing offences.

Similarly, a professional accountant in business must be vigilant in preventing and detecting money laundering in the organisation they work for.

The next example illustrates a situation where an accountant has to consider money laundering

example

Your client Eric has been given some company shares by his aunt, who bought them with money she did not declare to the tax authorities (ie tax evasion). By accepting these shares, is Eric guil money laundering? Are you as his accountant guilty of a money laundering offence?

The shares will only be criminal property as far as Eric is concerned if he knows or suspects that had originally been acquired as a result of criminal conduct on the part of his aunt. He will then cor a money laundering offence if he deals in them. Conversely, if he has no knowledge or suspi regarding the funds that his aunt used to purchase the shares then he will not be committin offence.

As his accountant you are in a similar position in that you will only be committing a money launde offence if you know or suspect that the shares are criminal property. As Eric's accountant you car be found guilty of money laundering if you knew about the criminal property even if Eric is innocer your client's state of mind has no bearing on your obligations.

anti-money laundering legislation in the UK

The legislation and regulations relating to money laundering, or anti-money laundering regime can be found in the following laws and regulations:

The Proceeds of Crime Act 2002 (POCA): this sets out the principal money laundering offence and the requirements to report suspicious transactions.

The Terrorism Act 2000 (TA): this sets out the principal terrorist financing offences and reporting obligations in similar terms to POCA.

The Money Laundering and Terrorist Financing Regulations 2020 (MLR): these regulations set out further, more detailed, rules including the risk-based approach that accountants must take to customer due diligence (this is covered in more detail later in the chapter). They also seek to prevent new means of terrorist financing, including through e-money and prepaid cards.

National Crime Agency

As the name suggests, the National Crime Agency (NCA) is a crime-fighting law enforcement agency responsible for pro-active operations against serious and organised crime. NCA tackles serious organised crime that affects the UK and its citizens, including class A drugs, people smuggling, human trafficking, major gun crime, fraud, computer crime and money laundering.

money laundering penalties

Under the laws and regulations above, an individual found guilty of money laundering, or the organisation that they work for, can be penalised. Dependent on the severity of the offence this could be an unlimited fine and/or a prison sentence of up to fourteen years.

the accountant's duty to report money laundering

The **Proceeds of Crime Act 2002 (POCA)** and the **Terrorism Act 2000**, require accountants as individuals in the regulated sector to report any suspicion that a client, employer, or colleague is involved with criminal property to the National Crime Agency (NCA) in a suspicious activity report (SAR). If the accountant is working in an organisation which, due to its size, has appointed a Money Laundering Reporting Officer (MLRO), the matter should be reported to the MLRO in an internal report. The MLRO will then review the information they have received and decide if it needs to be reported to the NCA.

Once the nominated officer decides there are reasonable grounds to suspect money laundering, they must tell the NCA at the earliest possible opportunity. The nominated officer should get consent from the NCA to complete the transaction. If it's not possible to delay the transaction to get consent, the nominated officer should inform the NCA of this when they send their report.

terrorist financing

Terrorist financing is the provision or collection of funds from legitimate or illegitimate sources with the intention or in the knowledge that they should be used in order to carry out any act of terrorism, whether or not those funds are in fact used for that purpose. Like money laundering the maximum penalty for this offence is an unlimited fine and/or up to 14 years in prison.

The example on the next page highlights a situation where an accountant may suspect money laundering.

example

terrorist financing

Julia is a qualified accountant who works as a sole practitioner. She has recently started work on the year-end accounts for her client Michael. During her work she discovers a number of payments that have been made to an overseas company that she does not recognise. There is no detailed supporting documentation for these payments. Julia suspects that these payments may relate to terrorist activities.

What should Julia do in these circumstances?

As Julia is a sole practitioner, she will not have a Money Laundering Reporting Office (MLRO) to whom she can report her concerns. She should, therefore, report her concerns to NCA using a Suspicious Activity Report (SAR). Failure to do this could result in Julia being charged with terrorist financing offences. She should not inform Michael of her suspicions.

required disclosure

There are two circumstances where a **required disclosure** in an internal report or a SAR **must** be made by an accountant:

- when the accountant wishes to provide services to a client in relation to property which is known or suspected to relate to money laundering or terrorist financing. In such circumstances, the person making the report must indicate in the report that they are asking for consent to provide such services. They cannot provide the services until consent is received
- when the accountant actually knows or suspects, or there are reasonable objective grounds for knowing or suspecting, that another person is engaged in money laundering or terrorist financing, regardless of whether or not they wish to act for that person. The person in question could be a client, colleague or a third party

As a minimum the standard report or SAR must contain:

- the identity of the suspected person (if known), such as, full name, address, telephone numbers, passport details, date of birth, account details
- the information on which the suspicion of money laundering is based
- the whereabouts of the laundered property if it is known
- details of the person making the report which will normally be the MLRO or sole practitioner

One particular area where this must be considered is where, despite advice from their accountant, the client has failed to disclose an omission or error in their tax affairs. Although it would seem logical to report this to HMRC, an accountant should report this to the firm's MLRO or if they are a sole practitioner, to NCA.

If an accountant believes that a fraud had been committed, then they also have a duty to report this to the police.

Practices and employers must also have training and internal procedures in place to ensure that they comply with the reporting requirements above. If these procedures are not in place, the accountant may be liable for a fine or imprisonment or both.

Clearly this is an important legal issue that the accounting profession takes very seriously. Professional accountants and students must ensure that they are familiar with their employer's internal procedures for reporting suspicions of money laundering. Employers must ensure that all their staff have been provided with adequate training on their legal obligations in respect of money laundering and the firm's anti-money laundering procedures.

protected and authorised disclosure

Where any person, not just an accountant, submits a report providing a required disclosure of a suspicion of money laundering, this is a **protected disclosure**. This means that the person is protected against allegations of breach of confidentiality regardless of how the restriction on the disclosure of the confidential information was originally imposed. For example, as we saw in Chapter 5, an accountant has an ongoing duty of confidentiality to their client. If, however, the accountant has had to include confidential information about the client in a SAR that they submit, the accountant is protected against any allegations of breaches of confidentiality that the client might make.

Any person, not just an accountant, who realises that they may have engaged or are about to engage in money laundering, should make an **authorised disclosure** to the appropriate authority. The disclosure should be made before the act is carried out (and they have obtained consent for the act from NCA, see required disclosure above), or as soon after the act is done with good reason for the delay. This may then provide them with a defence against charges of money laundering.

exceptions to the duty to report

There are certain circumstances where an accountant is **not** obliged to report knowledge or suspicions of money laundering. These are:

- when the information that forms the basis of the knowledge or suspicion was obtained other than in the course of the accountant's business, for example during a social occasion
- when the information came about in privileged circumstances, that resulted from the accountant being asked to provide legal advice, expert opinion, or services in relation to legal proceedings. An example of this would be if an accountant found out information about possible money laundering whilst explaining the client's tax liability. However, a report would have to be made if the advice sought from the accountant was to enable the client to commit a criminal offence or to avoid detection

- when there is a reasonable excuse for not reporting straightaway. In this case the report must be made as soon as reasonable in the circumstances. There is currently no money laundering case law relating to 'reasonable excuse' and it is anticipated that would only be accepted in relatively extreme circumstances, such as duress and threats to safety

money laundering offences

There are three money laundering offences that may be committed by individuals or businesses, which accountants must be aware of when they are dealing with clients. These are:

- **concealing** – concealing or disguising criminal property includes concealing (hiding), or disguising, its nature, source, location, movement, or ownership. A person commits this offence if they conceal, disguise, convert, or transfer criminal property, or remove it from the UK.
- **arrangement** – a person may be guilty of the money laundering offence of arrangement if they enter into, or become concerned with, an arrangement, which they know, or suspect, facilitates the acquisition, retention, use, or control, of criminal property by another person.
- **acquisition** – a person may be guilty of the money laundering offence of acquisition if they acquire, use, or have possession of criminal property.

It is important to note that a person does not commit these offences if they make an authorised disclosure, which we have looked at earlier in the chapter.

failure to disclose

We have already discussed the requirement for an accountant to report their suspicion of money laundering to the firm's MLRO or directly to the NCA. However, it is worth noting that it is an offence of **'failure to disclose'** under the POCA if an accountant does not report their suspicion. This offence carries a maximum penalty of five years imprisonment and/or a fine.

An accountant who fails to disclose a suspicion of money laundering may face disciplinary action by the professional accounting body they are a member of, eg AAT.

prejudicing an investigation

A further money laundering offence may be committed where any person, not just an accountant, knows or suspects that a money laundering investigation is being conducted or is about to be conducted and either:

- makes a disclosure which is likely to prejudice the investigation; or
- falsifies, conceals, or destroys documents relating to the investigation, or causes this to happen.

The person making the disclosure does not have to intend to prejudice an investigation for the offence to apply. However, it is worth noting that there is a defence available if the person making the disclosure did not know or suspect the disclosure would be prejudicial, did not know or suspect that the documents were relevant, or did not intend to conceal facts from the person carrying out the investigation.

If a person is found guilty of prejudicing an investigation, the maximum penalty is five years imprisonment and/or a fine.

tipping off

POCA has created a criminal offence of **'tipping off'**. This is where an accountant who knows, or thinks they know, that a report of money laundering has been made to an MLRO, the NCA, the HMRC Fraud hotline or the police, warns (or 'tips off') the person(s) suspected. Where this happens the person who 'tips off' the suspect is liable to be prosecuted as well as the person who is carrying out the money laundering. The person who tips off does not have to intend to prejudice an investigation for this offence to apply.

An accountant who discovers that an employer or a client is potentially money laundering must report their suspicions to the Money Laundering Reporting Officer or NCA. They must ensure, however, that they do not make the employer or client aware of this as this would be considered tipping off.

Although tipping off is an offence, an accountant is entitled to advise their clients in general terms about the issue of money laundering.

The maximum penalty for tipping off is five years imprisonment and/or a fine.

The following example illustrates the serious implications of money laundering.

example

a case of money laundering

Wilfred Joyce is an accountant in public practice. One of his clients is an antiques dealer called Louis Kans. One Friday Wilfred receives a telephone enquiry from Louis, who says that a customer is in the shop asking to buy a piece of furniture for £11,000. The customer is offering to pay Louis in cash.

What should Wilfred advise in this situation?

Louis has been offered a large amount of cash but does not really know where it has come from. Although the customer may have good reasons for having such a large amount of cash, there is a risk that it may not have been gained through legal means.

As Wilfred's objective in this situation is to ensure that his client does not breach the UK's anti-money laundering regime, he should advise Louis to identify the customer and verify the source of the cash before accepting it, thus satisfying himself that the cash is not the proceeds of some crime.

If, despite Wilfred's advice, Louis then goes on and deals with the customer on a cash basis then Wilfred will have no option but to report him to the NCA.

registration with HMRC

If Money Laundering Regulations apply to a business, it needs to be monitored by a supervisory authority. The regulations apply to a number of different business sectors, including accountants, financial service businesses, estate agents and solicitors. Most accountants will be supervised by their professional accounting body. However, if they are not, they will need to register with HMRC. Failure to do so is a criminal offence.

customer due diligence

Before providing services to a client, accountants must consider whether their services could be used to facilitate money laundering, or to finance terrorist activities. This is done by carrying out **customer due diligence (CDD)**. One definition of due diligence is:

'the process of evaluating a prospective business decision by investigating relevant financial, legal, and other important information about the other party.'

Under the Money Laundering Regulations, there is a requirement on accountancy firms to take a risk-based approach to CDD. Procedures must be followed to analyse the client's potential exposure to money laundering or terrorist financing, and firms must document the process that has been followed to assess the risk of money laundering, and also document that CDD that has been carried out.

The regulations set out a number of situations where an accountant should carry out CDD:

- When the accountant establishes a business relationship with a client
- When an accountant carries out an occasional transaction between an accountant and a customer or client, that does not constitute an actual ongoing business relationship
- When the accountant suspects money laundering or terrorist financing
- When there is doubt about a client's identification information
- When the circumstances of an existing customer or client change or appear to be inconsistent with the accountant's previous knowledge of that customer or client
- When the regulations require an accountant to apply enhanced CDD because circumstances have been identified that create a higher risk of money laundering or terrorist financing

What this means is that an accountant should carry out CDD **before** they enter into a business relationship with a new client; when the accountant suspects that money laundering or terrorist financing might be taking place; where the accountant is dubious about information that the client has previously given them about the client's identity; or when the accountant is entering into a transaction with the client for a significant amount of money.

In order to carry out sufficient CDD the accountant must have a detailed look at the client and the way it operates to decide whether they can enter into a professional relationship with them, confident that there are no ethical issues or any risk that they may be involved in money laundering.

CDD should include:

- verifying the client's identity by looking at documents, data or other information obtained from a reliable source
- where the person who owns the business is not the person who runs it, the accountant should ensure that they fully understand who any beneficial owners are (normally defined as someone who owns 25% or more of the business). In this case the accountant should also carry out the same sort of verification of the identity of the owner
- the accountant should also find out what the client wants from the relationship or the purpose and nature of the transaction

Where the accountant is unable to carry out adequate CDD, they must decline the assignment. If, having carried out due diligence, the accountant has a suspicion that the client may be involved in money laundering or terrorist financing, the accountant must submit a report to the Money Laundering Reporting Officer or submit a Suspicious Activity Report to the National Crime Agency (NCA).

keeping records of customer due diligence

Money Laundering Regulations are clear about the circumstances where customer due diligence (CDD) should be carried out. The regulations also require that records of CDD that has been performed are maintained to assist in any future law enforcement investigating relating to clients. These records will also demonstrate that the accountant has complied with their statutory obligations. Records of CDD carried out should include:

- copies of, or reference to, the CDD evidence that was used to verify the client's identity, for example passport details. These records must be kept for five years starting with the date on which the accountant's relationship with the client ends
- copies or originals of documents relating to transactions that have been subject to CDD or to ongoing monitoring, for example an invoice supporting a client receipt of a large cash payment from a customer. These must be kept for five years starting from the date on which the accountant completed the client's instructions

Chapter Summary

- The process of money laundering has three stages: placement, layering and integration.
- If an accountant has knowledge or a suspicion that a client or an employer is money laundering, they must report this to the National Crime Agency (NCA), or to the firm's Money Laundering Reporting Officer.
- The money laundering rules are set out in the Proceeds of Crime Act 2002, The Terrorism Act 2000, and The Money Laundering and Terrorist Financing Regulations 2020.
- The maximum penalty if convicted of money laundering is 14 years imprisonment.
- A required disclosure of a suspicion of money laundering is a protected disclosure, which means the person is protected against allegations of breach of confidentiality.
- There are certain exceptions to the duty to report knowledge or suspicion of money laundering.
- Failure to disclose a suspicion of money laundering carries a maximum penalty of five years imprisonment and/or a fine.
- The three money laundering offences are concealing criminal property, arranging money laundering, and acquisition of criminal property.
- It is an offence for an individual to make a disclosure which is likely to prejudice an investigation into money laundering or to falsify, conceal or destroy documents relating to the investigation.
- It is a criminal offence to tell someone that they may be investigated for possible money laundering. This is the offence of 'tipping off' and carries a maximum penalty of five years imprisonment and/or a fine.
- Regulated business such as accountants must be monitored for money laundering by a supervisory authority. Most accountants will be supervised by their professional accounting body. However, if they are not, they will need to register with HMRC. Failure to do so is a criminal offence.
- Accountants should carry out customer due diligence before providing services to a client to ensure there are no legal or ethical reasons why they should not enter into a professional relationship with the client. In particular the accountant should ensure that their services are not being used to facilitate money laundering.

Key Terms

money laundering	moving illegally acquired cash through financial systems so that it appears to be legally acquired
placement	the first stage of money laundering where criminally obtained funds are moved into a legitimate financial system
layering	the second stage of the money laundering process that creates a complex web of transactions to move the money around the financial system, by layering financial transactions
integration	the final stage of money laundering which integrates illegal funds back into the legitimate financial system, often by investing in property and other assets
Proceeds of Crime Act 2002	a statute that sets out the law in relation to financial gains made from illegal acts
Terrorism Act (2000)	a statute that sets out the law in relation to terrorism financing
The Money Laundering and Terrorist Financing Regulations 2020	the most recent update to the regulations governing the crime of money laundering, and include the risk-based approach that accountants must take to customer due diligence
National Crime Agency	NCA is a crime-fighting law enforcement agency responsible for proactive operations against serious and organised crime including money laundering
Suspicious Activity Report (SAR)	a report submitted to the National Crime Agency giving details of suspected money laundering
money laundering reporting officer	an official appointed by a practice of two, or more, accountants who is responsible for deciding whether there is sufficient suspicion to send an SAR to the NCA
required disclosure	disclosure of money laundering must be made when an accountant knows or suspects money laundering on the part of a client
protected disclosure	disclosure of a suspicion of money laundering is protected against allegations of breach of confidentiality

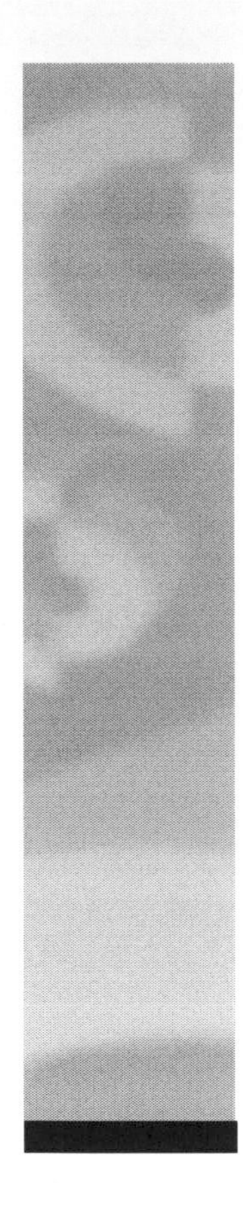

authorised disclosure	disclosure by a person who realises they may have engaged in money laundering or are about to engage in money laundering
concealing	the money laundering offence of concealing or disguising criminal property
arrangement	the money laundering offence of knowingly entering into an arrangement that they know involves criminal property
acquisition	the money laundering offence of acquiring criminal property
failure to disclose	failure to tell the relevant authority about a suspicion or knowledge of money laundering
prejudicing an investigation	making a disclosure that is likely to adversely affect an investigation into suspected money laundering
tipping off	the criminal offence of warning an individual that they are suspected of money laundering
customer due diligence (CDD)	evaluating prospective business decisions by investigating relevant financial, legal and other important information about the other party

Activities

8.1 You have been asked by your manager to produce some notes on what is meant by money laundering for inclusion in the staff training that he is delivering next week. Prepare a paragraph explaining what money laundering is.

8.2 Identify the three stages of money laundering and explain what is meant by each one.

8.3 Which external body should a suspicious activity report (SAR) be sent to?

Select **one** option.

(a) HMRC	
(b) AAT	
(c) National Crime Agency	
(d) The police	

8.4 Jonathon works as an AAT trainee for a medium sized firm of accountants. He has been working with one of the supervisors on the accounts of a local restaurant and is concerned that there seems to be a significant level of cash payments for meals and these payments are a lot higher than he would expect based on the menu prices. He has also noticed that the business pays a number of its supplier in cash.

Jonathon has asked his supervisor about this but has been told that everything is normal and if he doesn't mention it to the manager, he can expect to be able to eat at the restaurant without paying several times in the coming year.

(a) Explain what offence the client may be committing here.

(b) In this situation, who should Jonathon report his concerns to?

(c) What money laundering offence might Jonathon be guilty of, if he speaks to the client about his concerns?

8.5 A money laundering investigation has just started at the business where Melia works. Melia is concerned that she and her manager may be implicated and has shredded some documents that might suggest they are involved. What offence might Melia be guilty of by doing this?

Select **one** option.

(a) Tipping off	
(b) Prejudicing an investigation	
(c) Authorised disclosure	
(d) Placement	

8.6 Georgia is a qualified accountant who works as a sole practitioner. She has just started work on a new client, Opino Ltd. When she took on Opino Ltd as a client she carried out appropriate customer due diligence procedures. Georgia is now completing the VAT Return for Opino Ltd for the current quarter and has found a significant error in the previous quarter's return which has resulted in a large underpayment of VAT by Opino Ltd. This return was completed by their previous accountant, Joe.

Georgia raises this issue with Edgar, the owner of Opino Ltd, who replies 'Well if HMRC hasn't noticed we won't need to adjust it! I'll tell Joe to keep quiet about it'. Despite Georgia strongly advising him to disclose the error to HMRC, he refuses.

(a) Explain what Georgia must do in this situation.

(b) What are the consequences for Georgia if she does not take any action in this situation?

(c) What action should Joe take regarding Edgar's refusal to disclose the error to HMRC?

8.7 Jake works for Delaney & Clarke, a firm of accountants in Sandsville. He has recently been working on the accounts for one of his clients, Thompson Facilities Ltd, that provides security services at large outdoor events. Jake has noticed some unusual large cash transactions going through its accounts for which he cannot find any supporting paperwork. He strongly suspects that the money has come from sales on which Thompson Facilities Ltd has not charged VAT.

What are the consequences for Jake if he raises the issue of the unusual cash transactions with the management of Thompson Facilities Ltd?

9 New technology and data security

this chapter covers...

This chapter explains the impact of emerging and developing technologies on accounting systems, including: automation, AI and machine learning, blockchain, electronic filing and signing of documents and data analytics. It then looks at how new technology has allowed organisations to outsource and offshore elements of their business operations.

The chapter then moves on to the key features of cloud accounting and the benefits and limitations of cloud accounting for an organisation.

The second part of the chapter starts by looking at the key data protection principles and the impact of data breaches on individuals and businesses. It then highlights the importance of maintaining information security through access levels, security controls and integrity controls. The last part of the chapter identifies the risk to data and operations posed by cyberattacks and the importance of cybersecurity to protect against cyber risks.

EMERGING AND DEVELOPING TECHNOLOGY AND ACCOUNTING SYSTEMS

the importance of developments in technology to accounting systems

Technology impacts all aspects of our lives. From onboard computers in the cars we drive, to our mobile phones which are actually mini-computers in our pocket – even some vacuum cleaners and irons have computer chips in them these days. It has also had a significant impact on our working lives, with virtual meetings becoming the norm, and automated telephone systems an everyday occurrence.

But what about the impact on our work as accountants and the accounting systems that we use? Well, the accounting professional has embraced technology which has allowed greater efficiency and improved accuracy in their work.

In the section we will investigate at the impact of developing technology on accounting systems.

automation of accounting processes

Software can be used to automate some of the essential accounting tasks that are carried out by the finance function. This may be sending out customer statements, reconciling accounts, updating financial records, or actually creating financial statements, all without the need from human involvement. Unlike robotic process automation (RPA) this is not simply using machines to carry out repetitive tasks – think production line but for accountants! Instead, it is using the accounting software to streamline the accounting process with as little human intervention as possible.

So what are the benefits of automation? Some of these are detailed below.

- **improved data integrity:** the chance of human error is reduced
- **more efficient approval:** documents requiring approval by management can be automatically sent to the appropriate person, thereby saving time
- **greater internal data visibility:** the business has easy access to data which allows it to quickly see what is working well and what needs to be addressed
- **quicker payment from customers:** potentially quicker customer invoicing resulting in quicker receipt of payment

As accountants it is really important that we don't see automation as a threat. Automation will never completely replace humans, and there will always be a need for accountants. What it does mean is that the role of an accounting professional within a business will change to become more of a business advisor, working more closely with the rest of the business or with clients, rather than simply being viewed as 'number crunchers.'

AI and machine learning

There are a number of definitions of **Artificial intelligence (AI)**, but put simply, it is the concept of a computer, or machine, being able to simulate the way that humans think and behave. This 'intelligence' is developed by the computer processing and analysing large volumes of data so that it can interpret the way it is dealt with by humans and then do the same.

Machine learning is an application of AI that codes computers to learn from data, without being programmed explicitly. Machine learning bases its actions on past events to predict the probability of what will happen next. A social media company will target account holders with specific advertising, based on their viewing history – it has 'learnt' what the person is interested in.

So how does AI and machine learning apply to an accounting system? A simple example would be a purchase invoice is received for inventory that the business has ordered before. When the invoice is scanned into the accounting system, it will recognise the transaction and automatically update the appropriate inventory record and correct supplier account in the payables ledger.

There are many other uses for AI and machine learning in the accounting system. Examples of these include:

- **coding of data** – automatic coding of invoices, receipts and purchases should lead to accurate and prompt reporting
- **audit of information** – large amounts of data can be reviewed quickly, and any 'unusual' items can be highlighted and investigated
- **forecasting future data** – AI could use its predicative capabilities to forecast future events. Examples of this might be price changes, movement in exchange rates, or customer buying trends
- **analysing complex data** – properly developed AI and machine learning can be used to carry out complex analysis, that would require training for finance staff

The impact on the finance function also has to be considered; development costs and running costs for this type of system are expensive, and there will be a constant need to update the systems as technology changes. This may make bespoke machine learning prohibitively expensive for all but the largest businesses. However, more 'off the shelf' cloud accounting systems are now available to smaller businesses with built in machine learning.

There will always be some reluctance on the part of the finance function to embrace the new technology. Trusting the computer system may take time, plus there is the risk that some finance staff may be made redundant, as some of their tasks are carried out by the AI accounting system. However, there is the opportunity to train finance staff to improve their skills, and allow them to analyse and interpret the information generated by the system. Consequently, businesses must think carefully before implementing these kinds of systems.

blockchain

Blockchain is a digital ledger of transactions that is shared across the entire network of computers in the particular blockchain. Because the information is duplicated and shared across a huge number of users within the blockchain, it means that records of transactions cannot be altered, deleted or destroyed.

So how does this work in practice? Well, let's look at the creation of a block chain transaction step-by-step.

1. A user raises a transaction
2. A block is created to digitally represent the transaction
3. The block is distributed to **every** computer in the network
4. **Every** computer validates the transaction to prove it is authentic
5. The now authenticated and complete block is added to the chain

The next question is why are blockchains created? In traditional systems changes to data can be carried out by one user. This means that it is much easier for the system to be hacked. Blockchain can protect against hacking because of the following features:

- each transaction is shared across the internet by a number of users in the blockchain (each one in the blockchain)
- all the details of the transaction are recorded by all the users in the blockchain. For example, if money is paid into a bank account all users would know the amount, date, time, location, bank name, account number, etc.
- the ledgers of all the users in the blockchain will be updated for the transactions, but only when they have **all** agreed it is consistent. This decentralised network of computer transactions prevents a single system from adding new blocks to the chain
- when a new block is added to the blockchain it is linked (hence the chain) to the previous block using a cryptographic hash that is generated from the previous block in the chain. This encrypts the data so that only authorised users can access it

This process protects the data in the chain so that any attempt to manipulate the data by an unauthorised user will be rejected.

Blockchain can be very useful in accounting systems by:

- providing certainty about the ownership of assets
- maintaining ledgers of accurate information
- reducing costs and improving efficiency by taking on the record keeping so that staff can carry out other work

electronic filing of documents

Traditionally, organisations have kept paper documentation. However, increasingly, businesses are opting for electronic file management systems which can be specifically designed to meet their needs.

The benefits of electronic filing are:

- instant access is available to any authorised users, at any time. The user can access the data remotely rather than having to be in the same location as physical documents
- frees up physical space which can be used for other things, and may save money
- reduces the need to make copies of documents as multiple users can access the files
- files will be better organised
- better version control as the business will have a full document history
- files are automatically backed up and less susceptible to natural disasters such as fire or flood
- productivity will improve as files are more easily accessed

However, there are some disadvantages of this method of filing:

- software used to maintain the filing system will need to be kept up-to-date
- there is likely to be a significant initial cost to set up the system
- there will be a risk of data breaches which will need to be addressed

signing documents electronically

As the business world increasingly moves online, organisations are swapping physical signatures on documents for electronic signatures. This way of signing documents has the advantages of being quick and efficient. However, businesses must be confident that documents that have been signed electronically are valid and remain secure and confidential.

There are several ways in which documents can be signed electronically:

- **simple electronic signatures** – such as scanning a physical signature or using tick boxes with a declaration from the signatory that they agreed to the terms, or similar. An example might be an attachment to an email has been prepopulated with a box where the signatory can automatically generate a signature. Simple electronic signatures can only be used by individuals rather than organisations.

- **advanced electronic signatures** – these will be uniquely linked to the signatory by an electronic identifier. This might be an application on their mobile phone that they need to use in order to validate their signature on an electronic document.
- **qualified electronic signatures** – this is effectively an electronic version of getting the signature witnessed. Similar to an advanced electronic signature, it has the additional security of electronic validation by a third-party trust service provider (TSP) which checks the associated matching criteria and validates the signature.

A good quality electronic signing will be a useful tool for the finance function, speeding up the processing of documents such as customer contracts, and authenticating the link between the signatory and the document. However, it is worth remembering that the more important, or sensitive the transaction, or the higher its value, the more important it to use a legally enforceable method of signing.

data analytics

Data analytics is the process of collecting, organising and analysing large amounts of data. A business will gather internal and external information, and then organise and store it for future use. It will then analyse the data to identify patterns in the data. The four types of data analytics are:

- **descriptive** – what has happened in the business? This type of data analytics looks and reports on past performance, with no further explanation. For example, a report detailing the monthly sales of each division of the business.
- **diagnostic** – why did it happen? This digs a bit deeper by doing detailed analysis on the causes of things that have happened. A simple example might be analysis of why the sales of each product have changed month on month.
- **predictive** – what is likely to happen next? Predicative data analytics is very important for business to produce accurate forecasts. It uses large volumes of data to make its predications but it important to remember that, like human forecasting, it can never be 100% accurate
- **prescriptive** – what action do we need to take now? Prescriptive data analytics may use a combination of machine learning, algorithms (complex mathematical tools) and rules set by the business to make recommendations or for problem solving.

Does data analytics have an impact on the accounting function? Well, its ability to handle large volumes of data quickly can speed up the reporting processes in accounting function so decision-making will be quicker.

Data analytics may also reduce the risk of fraud as it can identify anomalies in information and then diagnose why these may have happened. For example, certain customers may be getting higher levels of discounts than the business normally offers. Data analytics would be able to identify if these customers were all dealing with the same salesperson.

Data analytics can also help a business to decide which activities to focus on and prioritise them. This may be due to their profitability, or it may be because the analytics have identified trends in the market that indicate certain products will be popular going forward.

It is worth noting that using predictive and prescriptive data analytics can be expensive, particularly if algorithms need to be written to undertake the analysis, so a business needs to carefully consider the benefit before introducing them to the business.

OUTSOURCING AND OFFSHORING

outsourcing

When businesses use a third party to carry out tasks, provide services or handle operations that the business has previously done in-house, this is known as outsourcing. Example of things that a business may outsource include:

- certain manufacturing processes
- human resources tasks
- finance functions such as bookkeeping and payroll
- legal services
- facilities management
- catering
- cleaning

Outsourcing has become more common in recent years, particularly for support functions that are not part of the core operations of the business, such as cleaning and catering. By outsourcing this work it allows the business to focus on 'what it is good at'. However, it is important for a business to think carefully before outsourcing any of its core operations as this could have a negative effect on the business. For example, a business that manufactures bicycles may decide to outsource the manufacture of the gear system. If the outsourcing business gains knowledge from producing the gears it may then be able to produce the same quality for competitors of the business.

Advantages of outsourcing include:

- potential cost savings, such as lower payroll costs due to reduced staff numbers, reduced training costs, and reduced capital expenditure. However, this change in cost structure will mean that, whilst capital costs reduce, expenses will increase
- staff time freed up to carry our core operations
- benefitting from the expertise of the business to which the work has been outsourced
- the business may no longer need to comply with certain regulations and legislation if it no longer carries out certain operations itself

Disadvantages of outsourcing include:

- if core operations are outsourced then the business may lose expertise
- quality issues may arise if the outsourcing business does not have the same level of skills as the business
- difficulties in moving the work back in-house, should the business want to, at a later date
- data security – for example if the outsourcing business needs to see product designs, or have access to confidential business data such as payroll records
- outsourcing may adversely affect staff morale if outsourcing results in redundancies
- cost increases from the outsourcing company once the business has started to rely on it
- depending on the location of the outsourcing business, there may be a delay in the delivery of the outsourced items, which could disrupt supply

offshoring

Offshoring is the relocation of some of the organisation's operations to another country. This is normally done by businesses in developed countries to less developed counties with the intention of reducing cost.

As technology has improved and communication across the world has become high quality, instant and reliable, offshoring has become much easier for businesses. Typically, services that are offshored by UK companies include call centres, data processing and some manufacturing processes.

One advantage of offshoring can be higher visibility for the business in the overseas country; this could ultimately result in increased business in that country. However, there may be disadvantages of offshoring, including cultural and language barriers, which the business will need to overcome.

CLOUD ACCOUNTING

Cloud computing delivers computer resources 'on demand' via the internet. Users of cloud computing will log in to their account to access and update their files via remote servers. An example of cloud computing is iCloud, a service from Apple that securely stores users' photos, files, notes, passwords, and other data in 'the cloud'. Data is kept up-to-date and can be accessed from any compatible device using the person's login details and can be shared with other users.

A more traditional, business-based computer accounting system stores data on a server that is based in the building. This system is accessed by desktop computer and laptops via a local, private network. **Cloud accounting** systems have become more popular in recent years and are increasingly replacing traditional systems.

Cloud accounting is an accounting system that is accessed via the internet, with information stored on remote, secure servers, owned by the system provider. Users will subscribe to the system and all their accounting records will be held in the cloud.

features of cloud accounting

- **remote access** - users can access the software from anywhere, as long as there is a stable internet connection. If employees are unable to travel, this means they can work at home, saving travelling time and money. Organisations that operate in several locations nationally or internationally, will also benefit as all parts of the business can access data and information, as if they were in the same place.
- **remote data storage** – data is not held in the business and the accounting system is automatically updated as each piece of data is added, and therefore, automatically backed up to the cloud.
- **shared access -** finance often needs to share reports with different parts of the business. In a business-based system, large reports might be emailed, slowing down the system, or put onto a USB stick, which may be lost or stolen. Cloud accounting allows all parts of the organisation to see the same information at the same time.
- **multi-user access** – several employees can access data and files from different locations and see the same data.
- **automation capabilities** – some cloud accounting systems will incorporate an element of AI and machine learning. For example, if it is linked to the business bank account it will recognise transactions and automatically post them to the appropriate expense, or revenue account.

- **availability of apps/plug-ins/add-ins** – cloud accounting apps allow users to access the system from tablets or phones, adding to the flexibility of access to the system. Many cloud accounting providers will offer plug-ins and add-ins that allow the user to customise the reports that the cloud accounting software produces to fit with the needs of the business.
- **interaction with stakeholders** – most cloud accounting software packages include a dashboard that allows accounting data to be presented in a clear, easy to understand format, using charts, graphs and tables. This 'data visualisation' allows non-financial staff, including managers, within the business to interact with the financial information provided by the accounting system. For example, the sales manager can easily download graphs showing the split of sales across the departments, or month on month. We will look at data visualisation in more detail in Chapter 10. However, there may be issues for some stakeholders of the business if they do not have access to the software it uses.
- **real-time data** – the data held in the cloud accounting system is always up-to-date. This means the current position can be checked at any time. This may be the bank balance, the amount owed by a customer or the sales of a specific division or the business as a whole.

further benefits of cloud accounting

In addition to the benefits that have been outlined as part of the features of cloud accounting, further benefits include:

- **lower IT costs** – the business does not have the cost of buying and maintaining its own server. There is also a reduced need for IT expertise in the business and no back-up processes are required, all of which will reduce the overall IT costs.
- **improved sustainability** – cloud accounting reduces an organisation's use of paper, as many systems can send invoices and statements of account to customers electronically.
- **better security** – any cloud accounting software companies will use a data centre, with sophisticated levels of security to protect both the software and the data. There is no need to back up the data periodically, as this is automatic, which is particularly beneficial to smaller businesses.

disadvantages of cloud accounting

Having detailed a number of features and benefits of cloud accounting, there are also some disadvantages:

- **reliance on internet access** – users will only be able to access the computer accounting system if they have a strong and stable internet connection. If the wi-fi connection is poor, then the business operations may be disrupted.

- **data security** – the business is putting sensitive and confidential data in the hands of a third party, via the internet, which increases the risk of unauthorised access.
- **software requirements** – all stakeholders will need to have the same cloud accounting software installed on their computers or devices to allow them to access the information produced.
- **switching may be difficult** – once a business has moved its accounting system to a particular cloud accounting software, it may be difficult to then switch to an alternative system in the future.

DATA PROTECTION, INFORMATION SECURITY AND CYBER SECURITY

the principles of data protection

In May 2018, the Data Protection Act 2018 came into force, which incorporates the requirements of the EU General Data Protection Regulation (GDPR). This legislation details the following principles about data:

- **lawfulness, fairness, and transparency** – whenever a business is processing personal data it should have good reasons to do so and should be open and honest about these reasons.
- **purpose limitation** – personal data should be used only for the explicit purpose for which it was given.
- **data minimisation** – personal data that is collected by an organisation should be only what is necessary for the specific purpose. For example, if a request is made to subscribe to a business's marketing emails, the business should only ask for necessary information such as name and email address, rather than unnecessary information such as phone numbers, home or work address, or date of birth.
- **accuracy** – a business that collects personal data is responsible for ensuring that the data is accurate and that it is kept up-to-date.
- **storage limitation** – any personal data stored by a business must not be kept any longer than is necessary. Business should be able to justify how long it holds on to this data.
- **integrity and confidentiality** – a business must keep personal data that it holds secure from internal and external threats and protect it from unauthorised access, unlawful processing, accidental loss, destruction, or damage.

- **accountability** – a business must have appropriate measures and records in place to prove that it is complying with data processing principles. Supervisory authorities can ask for this evidence at any time, so it is important for the business to have a documented audit trail that proves it is complying with regulations if required.

breaches in data protection

The sheer volume of information that organisations now hold about individuals means that there is greater risk of data security breaches. Breaches may occur due to errors made by those handling the data, or by deliberate, criminal attacks. This may result in the personal data held by the business being shared with unauthorised persons who misuse the information.

The UK has nominated the Information Commissioner's Office (ICO) to regulate and enforce GDPR and has given it greater powers to regulate organisations that fail to comply. The maximum fine that can be imposed for breaches of the data protection principles in the EU is the greater of €20 million, or 4% of the organisation's annual global turnover – this applies to UK businesses if they process personal data of EU residents. In the UK the maximum fine for breaches of data protection principles in the processing of UK residents' personal data is the greater of £17.5 million, or 4% of annual global turnover.

If an organisation discovers a personal data breach it must report this breach to the relevant supervisory body within 72 hours of becoming aware of it. If the breach is likely to result in a high risk of adversely affecting individuals' rights and freedoms, the organisation must also inform those individuals without undue delay.

Organisations must also ensure that they have robust data breach detection, investigation, and internal reporting procedures in place. This will make it easier for the organisation to decide whether it needs to notify the relevant supervisory authority or the affected individuals, or both.

The organisation must keep a record of any personal data breaches, regardless of whether it has been required to notify the relevant supervisory authority or the affected individuals, or both.

maintaining information security

A business must ensure that it protects data that it holds from **physical risks**, such as fire or flood, and the risks associated with **unauthorised access**, such as hacking, fraud or viruses.

In order to maintain information security and keep the risks of data breaches to a minimum, business must implement certain controls which are detailed below.

- **accounting systems access levels** – businesses will have passwords that only allow authorised employees to access parts of the system. For example, access to sensitive and confidential personal information that is held on the payroll will be restricted so that only those members of staff who need to view it are able to do so. Businesses may also have electronic access logs which will provide a record of who has accessed different parts of the system.
- **security controls** – to protect data held by a business, it will implement security controls including firewalls to protect access from outside the organisation. A **firewall** is a network security device, or 'barrier' that sits between a business's internal network and the public internet. Its main purpose is to monitor incoming and outgoing traffic, allowing non-threatening traffic in, but keeping dangerous traffic out ie hackers and viruses.
- **integrity controls** – data integrity refers to the accuracy and completeness of data that is held and processed by an organisation. Integrity controls are an integral part of computer applications, designed to manage and maintain the integrity of data.
  - **input controls** will provide reasonable assurance that transactions are complete, and have been properly authorised before they are processed by the system. This may include sequence checking for documents such as invoices or good received notes, reconciling batch totals.
  - **processing controls** ensure that data that is entered into the system is processed properly. This may be data matching of two, or more, items before the system will carry out a process, eg matching an invoice to a goods received note. It could also be controls that prevent more than one user updating the same data record at the same time.
  - **output controls** are designed to ensure the integrity of the data that is output from the system. This may be by reconciling data in the system, eg the Receivables Control account to the Receivables ledger, or review and sign off by a user of the system, eg review of the BACS payroll payment by the payroll manager before submission to the bank for payment.

cyber security, cyber risks, and the risk of cyberattacks

In Chapter 2 we looked at **cyber risk** and the fact that the increased use of technology in all aspects of business operations has meant that cyber risk for most businesses has increased. A **cyberattack** is a malicious and deliberate attempt by someone outside the organisation to access its information system. Although often for financial benefit, the attack may be designed simply to disrupt the operations of the business.

We saw in Chapter 2 that the key examples of cyberattacks are:

Phishing – where an attacker sends a message to a person within the business which attempts to trick them into opening the email or an attachment. Once opened, this will release malware or ransomware into the system, or will identify information that will allow the attacker to access the organisation's network and data.

Malware – software that is often inserted into computers when attachments, on phishing emails are opened, or when links are clicked. It finds weaknesses in the business's network and attempts to introduce viruses, worms, or ransomware. Once in the system malware can multiply and spread, ultimately causing the system to stop operating.

Ransomware – this is malware that locks a user out of their own information systems and then asks for a 'ransom' to be paid to the attacker. Failure to make the payment may lead the attacker to retaliate by posting the business's confidential data online.

Denial-of-service attack (DDoS) – this overwhelms the organisation's central server with huge numbers of data requests, simultaneously. This then causes the system to freeze up, and effectively holds the business hostage until the attacker's demands are met.

Spyware – if this gets into an organisation's system it allows the attacker to spy on its operations and gather information without been seen.

Keylogging – once this gets into the system it records every keystroke made by users. Hackers can then recreate these keystrokes to identify passwords and other sensitive information.

A cyberattack poses significant risks to the operations of a business. These include:

- loss of data – this could relate to customers, supplier, or employees
- disruption to business operations – due to IT failure caused by malware or DDoS

To protect its systems from the risk of cyberattacks, businesses must implement **cyber security** measures including:

- **firewalls** – which we covered earlier in the chapter
- **antivirus software** – this is software that, once installed, runs in the background, and is designed to provide real-time protection against virus attacks by scanning, detecting and deleting viruses from a system
- **data encryption** – this software translates data into another form, or code, so that only authorised users with a 'decryption key', or password, can read it. Its main purpose is to protect data confidentiality when it is stored on a system or transmitted using the internet, to another network

Chapter Summary

- Technological change will have an impact on the accounting system.
- Automation of the accounting system improves data integrity, leads to a more efficient approval process, ensures greater internal data visibility, and sometimes results in prompter payment by customers.
- Intelligent accounting software can use artificial intelligence (AI) and machine learning programmes to increase efficiency of recording day-to-day transactions. It can also audit large volumes of data and be used to create models to forecast data.
- Blockchain duplicates and shares data across a huge number of users within the blockchain, so that records of transactions cannot be altered, deleted or destroyed.
- Filing documents electronically can be beneficial, as this will save physical space, allow instant access, reduce the need for multiple copies and automatically back up files. However, it is important to keep the software that stores the documents up-to-date and ensure that all information is protected from data breaches.
- Businesses and individuals may choose to sign documents electronically. If they do, it is important to ensure that documents that have been signed electronically are valid and remain secure and confidential.
- Data analytics are software that can be used to analyse data to find out:
  - What has happened in the business? (descriptive)
  - Why did it happen? (diagnostic)
  - What is likely to happen next? (predictive)
  - What action do we need to take now? (prescriptive)
- Data analytics are costly and are used for large volumes of data.
- Organisations use outsourcing and offshoring to reduce costs and to allow them to focus on their key business activities.
- Cloud accounting, accessing the accounting system via the internet, has several benefits including supporting home working, file sharing, multiple user access and improved sustainability. IT costs may be lower and there may be better security of data and backups.
- The risks associated with cloud accounting are loss of control of data, security breaches over the internet and reliance on internet access.
- The Data Protection Act 2018 incorporates the requirements of the EU General Data Protection Regulation (GDPR). The seven principles about data protection included are:
  - lawfulness, fairness, and transparency
  - purpose limitation

- data minimisation
- accuracy
- storage limitation
- integrity and confidentiality
- accountability

- Breaches in data protection can result in substantial fines. An organisation must report any breach as soon as it becomes aware of it.
- Maintaining information security is very important, so data must be protected from physical risk such as fire or flood, and risks from unauthorised access. This can be done through accounting system access controls such as passwords, security controls, including firewalls, and integrity controls over inputting, processing, and outputting data.
- When an organisation holds data there are cyber risks of criminals attacking the system using cyberattacks such as phishing, malware, ransomware, denial-of-service attacks, spyware, and keylogging. Firewalls, antivirus software and data encryption will all help to protect against the risk of cyberattacks.

Key Terms

artificial intelligence — the concept of a computer that can simulate the way humans think and behave

machine learning — the application of artificial intelligence that allows computers to learn from data, without explicit programming

blockchain — transactions that are shared across an entire network of computers in a particular blockchain. Because the information is duplicated and shared across a huge number of users within the blockchain, it means that records of transactions cannot be altered, deleted or destroyed

simple, advanced, and qualified electronic signatures — the three levels of electronic signature that can be used to sign documents, with a qualified signature being the most secure

data analytics — the process of collecting, organising and analysing large amounts of data

outsourcing — when a business uses a third party to carry out tasks, provide services or handle operations that the business has previously done in-house

offshoring — the relocation of some of an organisation's operations to another country

cloud computing — delivers computer resources 'on demand' via the internet

cloud accounting — an accounting system accessed via the internet, with information stored on a server owned by the system provider

Data Protection Act (2018) — legislation that incorporates the requirements of GDPR and protects personal data that an organisation holds about individuals.

firewall — a network security device that sits between a business's internal network and the public internet, to monitor incoming and outgoing traffic, allowing non-threatening traffic in, but keeping hackers and viruses out

integrity controls — controls in a computer system that are designed to manage and maintain the integrity of data. They include input, processing, and output controls

cyber risk — risk associated with financial loss, disruption, or damage to the reputation of an organisation from failure, unauthorised or erroneous use of its information systems

phishing	an email pretending to be from a valid source, that is designed to trick the user into either opening it, or an attachment that comes with it. Once opened, it will release malware into the computer system
malware	viruses attached to emails that can damage, destroy, or gain entry to the computer system
ransomware	a programme designed to lock the users out of the system and open it only once a ransom is paid
denial of service attack (DDoS)	a malware attack that overwhelms the organisation's central server with a large number of simultaneous data requests until the system freezes up
spyware	malware that allows the attacker to spy on its operations and gather information without been seen
keylogging	malware that records every keystroke made by users. Hackers can then recreate these keystrokes to identify password and other sensitive information
cyber security	the measures in place to protect information stored on computers from unauthorised access
antivirus software	software that runs in the background of a computer system, and provides real-time protection against virus attacks by scanning, detecting and deleting viruses from a system
data encryption	software that protects data confidentiality by translating the data into another form, or code, so that only authorised users with a 'decryption key', or password, can read it

Activities

9.1 Which of the following are benefits of using artificial intelligence and machine learning as part of the accounting systems of a business?

Select **all** options that apply.

(a) Large amounts of data can be processed quickly and accurately	
(b) Correct programming will lead to more accurate forecasting of likely future events	
(c) High initial set up costs	
(d) Manual data entry and coding will reduce	
(e) Requires significant amount of manual supervision	

9.2 What is being described here?

Information is duplicated and shared across a huge number of users which means that the records of transactions cannot be altered, deleted or destroyed without all the computers validating the change.

Select **one** option.

(a) Artificial intelligence	
(b) Data analytics	
(c) Blockchain	
(d) Machine learning	

9.3 Which category of data analytics can be used to record high volumes of data and produce monthly reports, comparing actual and budgeted information?

Select **one** option.

(a) Descriptive	
(b) Diagnostic	
(c) Predictive	
(d) Prescriptive	

9.4 Which category of data analytics can be used to produce forecasts of likely future trends?

Select **one** option.

(a) Descriptive	
(b) Diagnostic	
(c) Predictive	
(d) Prescriptive	

9.5 For the last 20 years, Freedman & Sons, a large manufacturing business, has operated a staff canteen that caters for its 350 production workers and administrative staff. It has decided to make all of the staff in the canteen redundant and has signed a contract with Marvellous Menus to provide all the catering services for the business.

Decide whether each of the following statements is true or false.

	True/False
(a) This is an example of Freedman & Sons offshoring its catering function	
(b) This is an example of Freedman & Sons outsourcing its catering function	
(c) In the first year after this change Freedman & Sons can expect to save money	
(d) It may be difficult for Freedman & Sons to take back operating its canteen and employ its own catering staff in the future	
(e) Most of the responsibility for complying with health and safety and food hygiene regulations will be passed on to Marvellous Menus	

9.6 Which of the following are features of cloud accounting?

Select **all** options that apply.

(a) Only accessible on desktop or laptop computers	
(b) Data and information can be accessed from anywhere	
(c) Data is updated in real-time	
(d) Data is stored on the organisation's own server	
(e) Apps, plug-ins and add-ins are sometimes available	

9.7 Identify which of the following are valid data protection principles.

Select **all** options that apply.

(a) Data should be used only for the explicit purpose for which it was given	
(b) Any data stored by a business must not be kept any longer than is necessary	
(c) As well as the personal data it requires, a business may request additional information that it feels might be useful in the future	
(d) A business must keep personal data that it holds secure from internal and external threats	
(e) Businesses must ensure that all personal data is deleted after three months and requested again if necessary	

9.8 What is the maximum fine that can be imposed for breaches of data protection principles in the processing of UK residents' personal data?

£ [ ] or [% of annual global turnover]

9.9 Complete each of the following sentences about cyberattacks.

(a) A cyberattack that locks a user out of their organisation's information system until a payment is made is known as ____________________ attack.

(b) __________________ is a virus that allows the attacker to watch a business's operations without being seen.

9.10 What are the three measures a business can put into place to minimise the risks associated with a cyber attack?

10 Communicating information to stakeholders

this chapter covers...

This chapter starts by looking at the attributes of good quality information, using the acronym ACCURATE. It then considers the different information that is needed at the strategic, managerial, and operational levels of a business.

The next section of the chapter is about big data. It looks at the characteristics of big data, and then identifies the benefits and limitations to businesses of collecting, processing, and managing big data. The importance of applying professional scepticism to big data is also highlighted.

Data visualisation is a good way of making financial, and non-financial, information understandable for non-financial managers and staff. The chapter will explain different formats that can be used to present information visually, including tables, matrices, diagram, images, graphs and charts. It will then look at how to decide which method of presentation is most appropriate to use in different situations.

Dashboards are an integral part of computerised accounting software and are particularly helpful for managers and owners of small organisations to identify areas in the business to focus on, even if they do not have a financial background.

The final section of the chapter covers communicating information. It considers the attributes of good information and then goes on to look at some of the different methods of communication that are used by the organisation, both internally and externally.

GOOD QUALITY INFORMATION

the attributes of good quality information

In the previous chapter we looked at data and how it must be held securely, and protected. But what turns the raw facts and figures that are **data** into information, and what makes that information good quality? Processing data so that it is organised, structured, and well presented converts it into useful and meaningful **information** for the user.

The attributes of good quality information are often remembered using the acronym **ACCURATE**.

A ccurate	Decision-making relies on accurate information. Therefore, information should be free from errors, free from bias, and sufficiently accurate to be relied upon.
C omplete	Information that is provided to managers and decision-makers must be complete. This means that they should be provided with sufficient information for their purposes, with nothing missing. However, the amount of information provided should not be excessive.
C ost effective	The usefulness and value of information must be greater than the cost of producing it.
U nderstandable	The style, format, detail, and complexity of information should fits the user's needs, ie user-targeted.
R elevant	Information should be fit for purpose, and communicated to the right person, ie the person who has responsibility for the decision-making based on the information.
A uthoritative	Information should come from a reliable source. This may relate to the qualifications and experience of the person providing it, or the reliability of the computer program that has analysed the data to produce the information.
T imely	Information should be communicated in sufficient time for the user to make the necessary decisions based on that information.
E asy to use	Information should be provided in such a way that is easy to use.

information at different levels of an organisation

There are typically three levels of management within an organisation: corporate/strategic, managerial, and operational. We will now look at the of information that is required at each of these levels, including its characteristics and purpose.

information at strategic/corporate level

This is the highest level of the organisation where strategic decisions are made. The management at this level will be concerned, primarily, with planning the future direction of the business, and setting goals. Information for strategic planning and decision-making will need to include analysis of what has happened in the past so that management can make **longer-term** decisions for the future. A strategic goal may be financial, such as aiming to grow revenue by 30% in the next 12 months, or it may relate to business behaviour, such as setting a sustainability target.

Strategic management will require internally generated information about the performance of the business, the resources available, and internal factors that may affect the way the business performs in the future. However, it is likely to focus more heavily on **external information** that affects the business, such as competitor activities, government policies, or the economic environment, including interest rates, exchange rates and inflation.

The information provided at the strategic level of an organisation will be **summarised** rather than detailed. Senior management will want to know the headline figures and will rely on lower levels of management to carry out the analysis before it is presented to them. The information is also likely to be required on an **ad-hoc** basis rather than a regular basis.

information at managerial level

The managerial, or tactical, level of an organisation will be responsible for making decisions about how the organisation will achieve its strategic goals. It is the middle level of management that translates the strategic vision into a practical, tactical plan. Managerial decision-making relies on being provided with **regular**, operational information to monitor the progress towards the organisation's goals. Information required at this level will be mostly generated **internally**, for example, a twelve-month rolling budget, or analysis of sales by division, or by product. Some external information may be required at this level of the business, for example competitors' pricing and product range.

The information at this level will need to be **sufficiently detailed** for planning and allocation of resources. For example, at managerial level, decision-makers may need a budget showing the required number of labour hours for the next 12 months in each production department to allow the available labour resources to be allocated effectively.

information at operational level

At the operational level the management are involved in the day-to-day running of the business. Operational management will be given explicit, detailed information, and will be expected to implement strategic and tactical decisions that have been made at the higher levels of the organisation. At this level management relies on **regular**, **detailed** information from **internal sources** which will be used to make immediate decisions. Information at the operational level of the business tends to relate to **past events**. For example, operational management may receive details of production levels in each production department to assess labour efficiency.

BIG DATA

The term **big data** has become increasingly common when referring to large volumes of data collected by organisations. Big data can be defined as:

'A collection of data which is so large and complex, and which accumulates so quickly, that it is difficult to store, and process using traditional data processing software.'

sources of internal and external big data

Big data can come from a variety of sources, and can be financial or non-financial data. Three primary sources of big data are social data, machine data and transactional data.

Social data comes from tweets (and retweets), likes, comments, videos, and other media that is uploaded onto social media platforms such as Facebook, Twitter, and Instagram. Social data provides organisations with invaluable insight into the ways customers think and behave. If this data can be analysed and processed it will help business to focus their marketing, and develop products and services, to appeal to their target markets.

Machine data, as the name suggests, is data that is generated by machines. This may be from any kind of machine, for example, sensors in medical equipment, handheld scanners used by delivery couriers, checkout scanners in supermarkets that record what customers have purchased, domestic electricity smart meters, satellites, and online computer games played via the internet. Because this type of data is machine generated, it will, generally, be well structured and easier to analyse.

Transactional data is generated from the daily transactions that take place in a business. This will be all the data that is included in the sales and purchases, payments and receipts, and other transactions of the business. It will include huge amounts of data about every individual transaction, including information about customers, suppliers, products, prices, locations, and importantly, the links between each of these.

characteristics of big data

The characteristics of big data are often referred to as 'the five Vs'. These are explained below.

Volume The most obvious characteristic of big data is its volume. The sheer amount of data that organisations now process has skyrocketed in the last ten years, with some businesses now handling so much data, from so many different sources, that it has almost become unmanageable.

Velocity As well the volume of data that a business is able to process, the speed (velocity) at which that data can be processed is equally, if not more, important. Organisations will need information to flow quickly, and as close to real-time as possible. In certain situations it will be better for businesses to have limited data in real-time, rather than large volumes of data at a slow speed.

Variety Organisations are able to obtain data from lots of different sources ranging from internal information collected from customer transactions to external information about consumers' preferences collected from social media networks. The variety of data needed by an organisation will depend on what business sector it operates in. A business that sells to a mass-market will need to monitor data from social media networks to ensure that it is aware of changes in consumer tastes. By contrast, this information will not be as important to a manufacturing business.

There will also be variety in the way in which the data is generated. For example, data may be text, images, audio, or video. It will be difficult to identify any interrelationship between these various types of data without the algorithms used by big data to sort and process them into a meaningful form.

Veracity By this we mean how accurate, or truthful, the data is. The variety and volume of the data, together with the speed at which it is being generated, means that there is an increased risk of inaccuracies, or bias. Therefore, it is important for data to be obtained from a trusted source and that the way the data is processed removes things like bias, duplication, anomalies, or inconsistencies, to ensure the veracity of the data.

Value There is no point in a business collecting huge amounts of data unless it can be processed and transformed into useful and valuable information that can then be used to add value to the business.

benefits of using big data

There are a number of benefits for businesses of collecting, processing, and managing big data. These include:

- **Attracting and retaining customers**: using big data allows a business to pinpoint exactly what its customers are looking for. It can identify patterns in consumer behaviour and use these patterns to promote brand loyalty and maintain customer satisfaction. Businesses will be able to suggest items that they think a customer will like, based on their previous purchases, and also be able to offer items that other customers with a similar profile have purchased.
- **Focused marketing**: rather than spending money on advertising and marketing that may not work, businesses can use big data to analyse trends in the market and focus their marketing.
- **Gain competitive advantage**: as a result of the first two points above, managing big data effectively will allow businesses to gain an advantage over businesses in the same market due to improved decision-making.
- **Identification of areas of potential risk**: effective analysis of big data will allow businesses to identify riskier areas in the business and act promptly before the risk becomes too great.
- **Faster innovation**: the speed with which big data can be collected and analysed means that businesses can react more quickly to changes in tastes and market trends.
- **Improved business processes**: by analysing big data, businesses will be able to streamline their operations to improve processes such as inventory management, supply chain, and distribution, all of which will help businesses to control their costs.
- **Fraud detection**: by implementing machine learning technologies, banks and other financial institutions are better able to detect fraudulent transactions, including fraudulent purchases with stolen credit card details.

limitations and risks of using big data

Having identified the characteristics of big data and the positive impact that big data can have on a business's performance, it is worth looking at its limitations.

- **Lack of knowledge and skills**: to manage big data businesses need to employ skilled data professionals. These data analysts, data scientists and data engineers need to be up-to-date with the constantly evolving data handling tools that businesses are using. Unfortunately, there are two issues here: insufficient skilled professionals to take on these roles, and a lack of ongoing training to ensure that the data professionals employed by businesses keep their skills and knowledge up-to-date.

- **Difficulties integrating data from different sources**: whilst it is good to be able to gather data from a number of different sources, and in a variety of formats, this can overwhelm data analysis tools and result in information that is incomplete and/or inaccurate.
- **Data protection**: as the amount of data that organisations collect about individuals continues to grow at a rapid rate, businesses must ensure that they adhere to the data protection principles that we looked at in Chapter 9.
- **Data security**: collecting such large amounts of data increases the need for data security. Businesses must ensure that they have sufficient resource to protect the big data they collect against the risks of data leaks, hacking or data losses.

professional scepticism in relation to big data

Just because a huge amount of big data has been collected, this does not necessarily mean that the data is trustworthy, accurate and/or fit for purpose, ie for decision-making. We have already looked at **professional scepticism** in Chapter 5 and identified how important it is that we do not to take things at face value but instead ask questions until we are satisfied that information is correct. Professional scepticism must be applied before big data is used as the basis of key business decisions. If professional experience indicates that the results of data analysis are not right, then the results need to be questioned. Further analysis may need to be done, rather than just assuming that because it's been analysed 'it must be right'.

data analytics from external sources

We have already identified that gathering, analysing, and interpreting big data requires significant resources and high levels of skill and expertise. Large businesses will have the resources to generate their own big data and employ staff with the necessary expertise to analyse it, but for smaller organisations this may not be economically viable. Consequently, some businesses will use professional data analytics companies with the specialist skills to provide analysis.

Whilst using external sources for data analytics will reduce the costs for the business, there are some drawbacks to this option. First, the professional analytics company may be excellent at the mechanics of data analysis, but may not have the specialist knowledge of the sector in which the business operates. This means that it may not be able to provide an in-depth understanding of the market without clear instructions from the business. Second, the business must rely on the professional analysts to maintain the security of the data it has collected, some of which is likely to be personal data protected by the Data Protection Act, which will require permission from the data subject to be shared with a third party.

VISUALISING INFORMATION

Data visualisation is the term given to images, diagrams, graphs, tables, matrices and charts that are used to present information in an accessible and usable way. It is often used to summarise and simplify large amounts of complex information, and can be particularly useful for making financial information understandable for non-financial managers and staff.

different formats for visualising information

There are a number of ways that information can be presented visually using images and diagrams, rather than simply using lists of figures. This section will detail some of the formats that are commonly used by businesses.

tables

Presenting data in a table is one of the simplest ways of making information clear and easy to understand. Tables will normally arrange data in rows and columns, and are often generated using spreadsheet software. The simple table below has been prepared using spreadsheet software, and shows the sales of a business by division for the four quarters of the year, together with a total for the year.

Quarterly sales by division (£000)

	Quarter 1	Quarter 2	Quarter 3	Quarter 4	Total
	£000	£000	£000	£000	£000
Scotland	421	479	512	410	**1,822**
North	745	711	645	722	**2,823**
Midlands	1,121	1,041	1,245	924	**4,331**
South	1,274	1,144	1,578	1,431	**5,427**
Total	3,561	3,375	3,980	3,487	**14,403**

Advantages of using tables to present information include:

- **clear presentation** – large amounts of information can be summarised and presented clearly
- **easy to compare figures** – in the table above it is easy to compare the sales of each division with the other three divisions, or with its own sales in different quarters
- **patterns can be identified** – a table will make it simple to identify patterns in data, for example total sales peak in Quarter 3, or sales are highest each quarter in the South division

- **anomalies can be identified** – like patterns, it will be easy to identify anomalies, for example, sales are highest in Quarter 3 for all divisions except the North, where sales fall in this quarter
- **easy to prepare and understand** – spreadsheet software is widely available, making tables easy for businesses to use to present information, and for the user to navigate

Although there are advantages to using tables to display data, there are also disadvantages. These include:

- **too much data** – some tables may include so much information that the user is overwhelmed, and unable to process what the table is showing. Imagine if the table in example was on a monthly basis and the business had twenty divisions – this would make the information much more difficult for the user to process
- **data may get lost** – if a table is large, this may mean that key points cannot be easily identified
- **two dimensional** – although a table shows the figures in a well organised way, if further analysis is required, for example, the percentage of total sales that each division represents, further tables will need to be prepared

matrices

A matrix takes information that is shown in a table and simplifies it by using colour, icons, or pictures rather than the actual figures, making it easier to understand. The matrix below uses the same information from the table above but uses symbols to identify the quarters in which each division made its highest (filled spot) and lowest sales (hollow spot).

Quarterly sales by division

	Quarter 1	Quarter 2	Quarter 3	Quarter 4
Scotland			●	○
North	●		○	
Midlands			●	○
South		○	●	

The user can quickly identify the anomaly in the sales in Quarter 3 where the North division makes its lowest sales compared to the other three divisions where sales are highest in Quarter 3.

The advantages of using a matrix to present data are:

- **key data stands out** – the user is not distracted by the actual figures shown in a table and can focus on the key message from the data

- **visually appealing** – presenting data in a matrix appeals to less numerate or financial users

The main disadvantage of a matrix is the **lack of detail**. For example, in the matrix above we have no way of knowing which division had the highest or lowest sales or the value of these sales.

Consequently, a matrix presentation should really only be used where a focussed message is required – for example, if the sales director specifically wanted to present the peaks and troughs in the sales of each division.

graphs and charts

One of the most popular ways of showing data visually is using graphs and charts. This can be in a business context to present financial, and other commercial, information in a simple, understandable way. Graphs and charts can also be used in advertising and marketing, magazines or on websites to make a visual impact.

There are a number of different types of charts and graphs that can be used to present information visually. You will cover these in the Management Accounting Techniques unit of this qualification.

We will look at the way in which each of these can be used to present information below.

column and bar charts

Columns and bar charts are very similar in the way that information is presented. The height of the columns, or the length of the bars, represent the value of each item. We can see this in the images below which show the sales by division as a bar and a column chart.

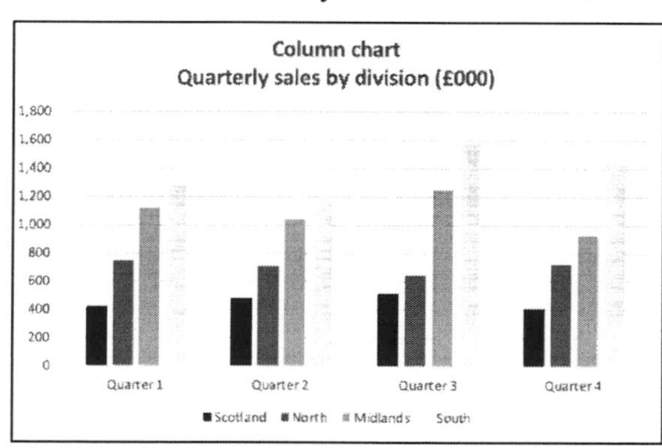

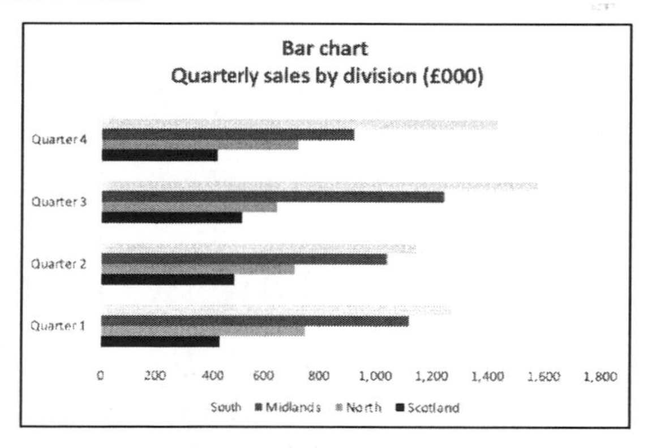

Column and bar charts are useful where several sets of data are being compared, as they provide an instant, visual presentation of the relative success of each variable, in this case each division. However, if there are too many bars or columns, or if the information is not sufficiently different between columns or bars, it may be difficult for the user to interpret what the chart is telling them.

Column and bar charts can be made visually clearer by making them three dimensional (3D). This is shown in the example on the next page.

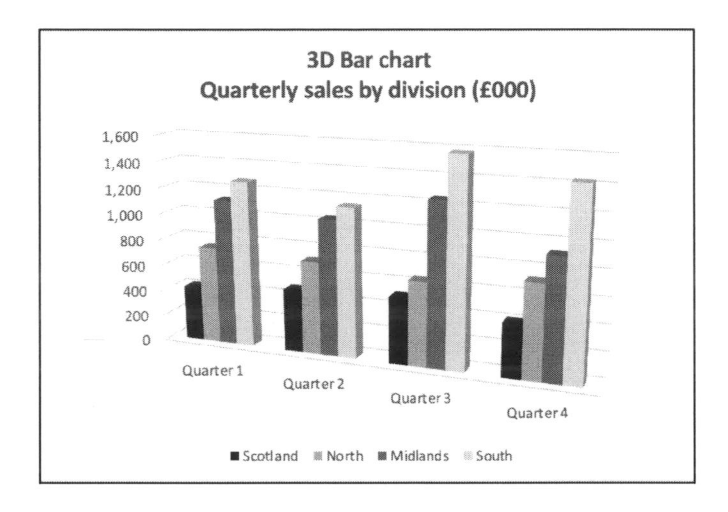

pie charts

A pie chart is a circle divided into sectors to represent the proportion each part makes up of the whole – like a pie divided into slices. A pie chart can be used to visually present one set of data values, for example the split of total expenses into various categories.

In the pie charts below the total annual sales are split by division. Users can easily identify the division that has the highest sales. However, to make things even clearer the pie chart can be exploded and the percentage that each division represents can be added, as shown in the right-hand chart.

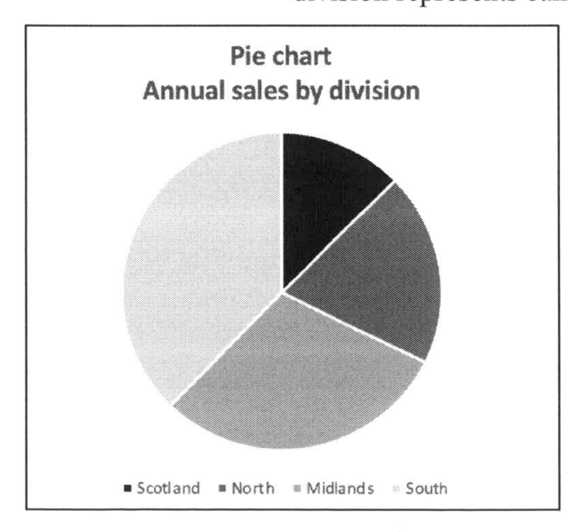

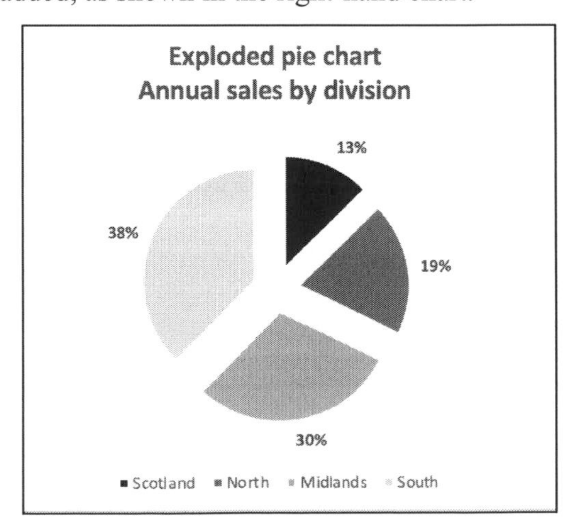

Pie charts can also be shown as a doughnut as shown on the next page. Whilst this does not make a huge difference to the information presented, it may provide some variety if several pie charts have already been used.

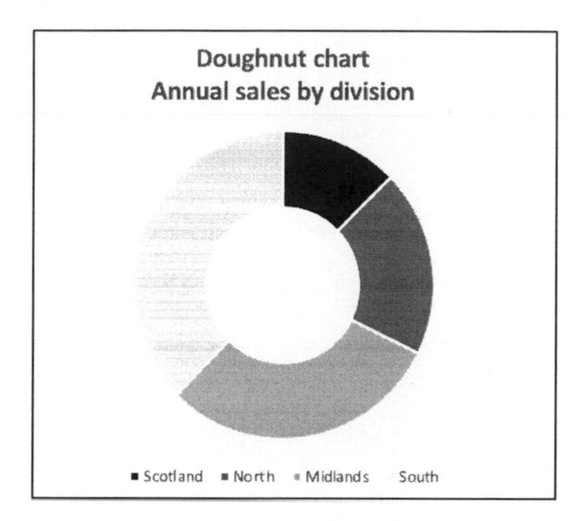

line graphs

Line graphs are particularly useful to plot continuous data and will give the user a good insight into general trends. The line graph below, shows the value of sales and total costs as the number of units sold increases. Users can see that the gap between the two lines, which represents profit, increases as the number of units sold increases. This may be because the fixed costs of the business are being shared across more units as sales volume increases.

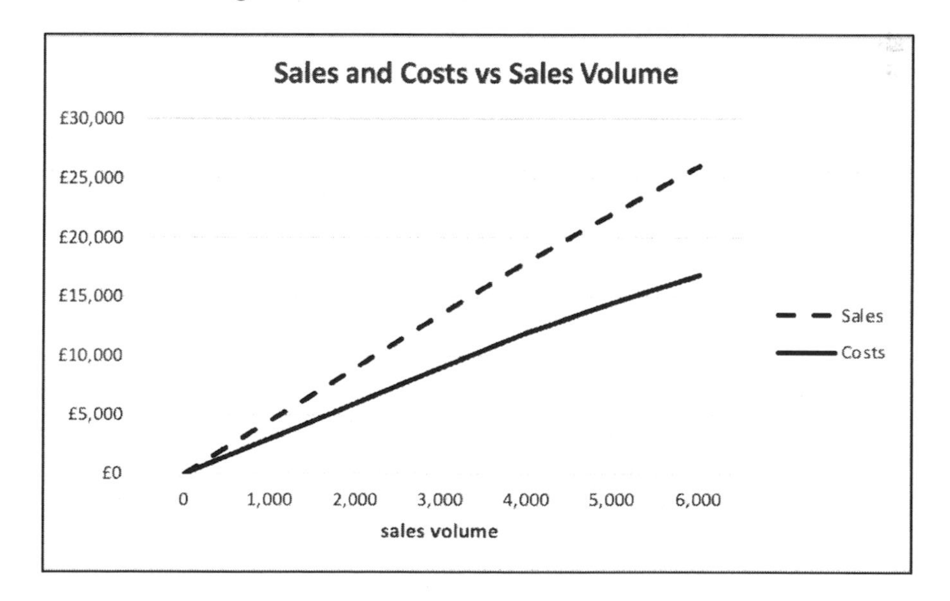

diagrams

Sometimes a diagram is a useful way of presenting information visually. This will help the user to see the relationship between information, and is particularly helpful where there is a movement of information through a process. The diagram below shows the working capital cycle. The use of the arrows to show how cash moves through the cycle, as it is received from receivables, paid to payables, and used to purchase inventory, gives the user a clear indication that working capital changes constantly. In this example, the working capital figures on 31 December are calculated at £90,145 – £254,500 +£214,120 + £274,150 = £323,915. However, using the diagram makes a more visual impact of what this figure represents than simply showing the calculation.

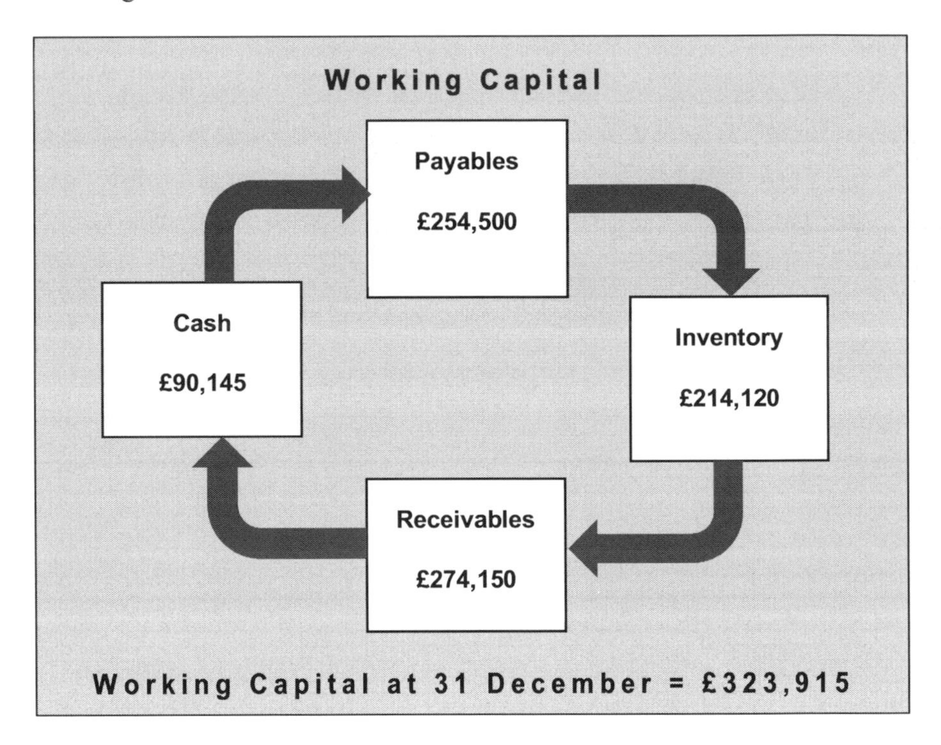

images

An image is a picture or photograph. Whilst these are not widely used in data visualisation, there are certain circumstances where a business may choose to use a photograph to reinforce the message it is trying to put across. For example, a house building company may include 'before and after' images of a particular site in an area of regeneration. Images will sometimes be used to support figures and increase the impact of the message they are trying to put across, and are particularly useful to where the users do not have a specialist knowledge of the data.

choosing the most appropriate form of visualised data

We have looked at tables, matrices, graphs, charts, diagrams and images as a means of presenting information visually. But the important thing is to ensure that the correct method is used. This will depend on three questions:

Who? The way in which data is presented will depend on who it is for. If it is for a strategic level presentation, for example to the board of directors, then graphs and charts that clearly show trends may be appropriate. However, if it is detailed financial information that is needed by the finance manager, this might be better presented in a table.

What? The type of data will have a significant effect on the way it is presented. Where trends, such as the monthly sales over a 12 month period, are being presented, a line graph will make a clear, visual impact showing whether the trend is constant, going up, or going down. If the data needs to show proportions of a total, for example the split of total sales by product, then it might be better to use a pie chart. If detailed analysis needs to be shown, for example profit margins for a number of products, then the best presentation may be a table.

How? The way in which the data is going to be presented will also influence how it is displayed. If it forms part of a presentation, then graphs and charts might be appropriate, as the presenter will explain what these diagrams show. However, if the information is to be included in a report, it may be better to produce a table with some written analysis and explanation, if necessary. This will allow the reader time to look at as much detail as they need.

DASHBOARDS

One of the roles of the finance function is to present information clearly and simply so that it can be understood by non-financial managers. Most businesses now use computerised accounting software which will often have built-in functionality that presents data visually using graphs, charts, diagrams, and tables. The image at the top of the next page is an example of what a dashboard might look like. In one page the user can see the amounts owed by receivables, split by age, a comparison of actual and budgeted revenue for the first three months of the year, a breakdown of expenses, profit for the month, and the current bank balances at the end of the month.

There are a number of benefits of having dashboard functionality in a computerised accounting system:

- data is easy to understand, and for many smaller businesses this will provide sufficient detail for owners or managers to control the business even if they do not have a financial background
- most dashboards can be customised so that the information presented is relevant to the business and users
- the dashboard can be produced in real-time whenever it is required, so the information will always be up-to-date
- if the business uses cloud-based accounting software, the dashboard can be accessed from any device and any location with internet access

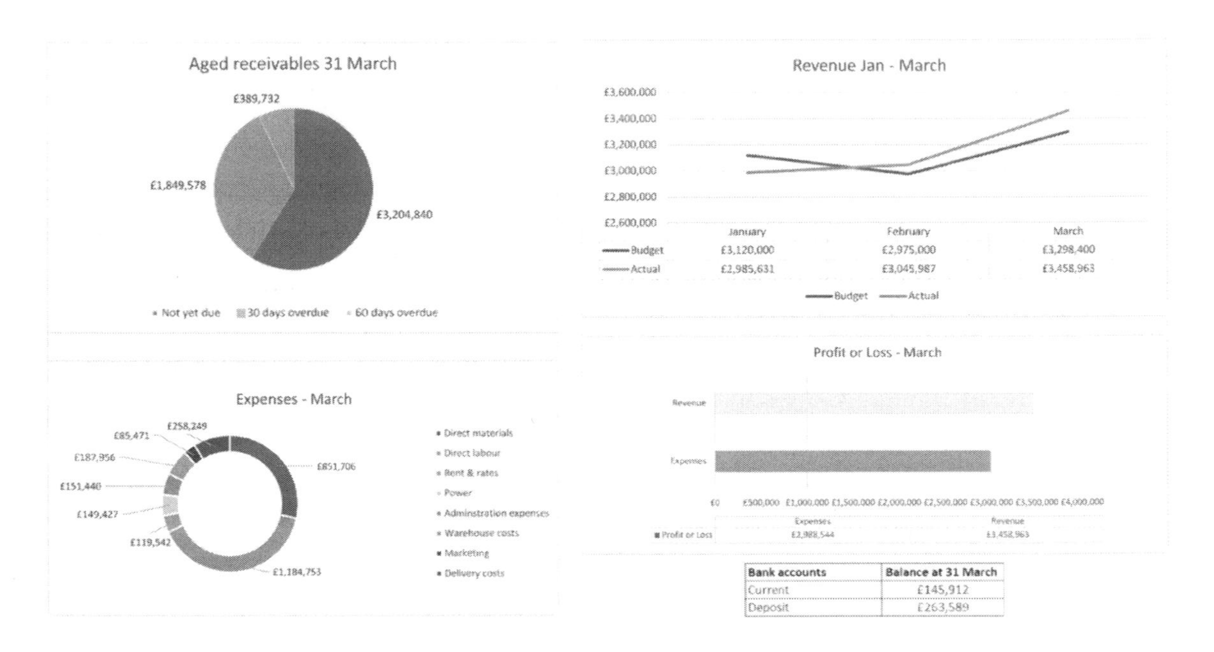

Bank accounts	Balance at 31 March
Current	£145,912
Deposit	£263,589

interpreting relationships and trends in visual information

We have already looked at the benefits for users of information being presented visually. But visual information will only be useful if the user can understand what it is telling them. This does not simply mean that they are able to read the information; they must also be able to interpret what the information is telling them. Visual information should allow the user to see relationships between different sets of information. Earlier, we saw a line graph showing how total costs did not rise as quickly as total sales when the volume of sales increases. If the user sees a trend like this, it will prompt them to ask questions to establish why costs are not increasing as quickly as the sales volumes increase.

Depending on the way information is presented, it may also allow the user to identify trends, for example a column chart of monthly sales for a business that sells fireworks might be showing higher sales in October, November, and December each year, to reflect celebrations such as Diwali, Bonfire night and New Year's Eve.

In the case study that follows we will see how an owner of a business that produces environmentally friendly cleaning products uses a dashboard created by its computerised accounting software to monitor the performance of the business.

Case Study

MOREECO LTD: INTERPRETING VISUAL INFORMATION

situation

Today's date is 15th August.

MoreEco Ltd is a business that produces environmentally friendly cleaning products for domestic customers and commercial cleaning. The business was set up eight years ago by its owner, Zach Morenci, when he started selling environmentally friendly polishes and sprays that he produced at home.

The business has grown significantly and now has a manufacturing site with a team of around 20 members of staff across production, despatch, sales, and administration. The part-time bookkeeper who has always maintained its manual bookkeeping system has recently retired, and Zach has recruited you to run the accounting function using the new cloud accounting package that has recently been installed.

The increasing importance of environmental protection, sustainability and being 'green' has meant that sales have increased significantly in the last couple of years. However, four months ago a large cleaning product supplier announced that all its products were now environmentally friendly and that it was offering the option to buy refills to reduce packaging waste.

Commercial cleaning customers, who buy directly from MoreEco Ltd, have, generally, remained loyal to the brand. However, they are increasingly paying invoices beyond MoreEco Ltd's 30 days agreed credit terms. The business has seen a drop in website orders from domestic customers who order and pay for their goods directly from its website.

MoreEco Ltd's budget has not been adjusted since the beginning of the financial year.

The cloud accounting package has provided the dashboard at the top of the next page that shows current key financial information:

required

Zach has asked you to use the data in the dashboard to explain any conclusions or concerns you have about the performance of MoreEco Ltd over the last six months.

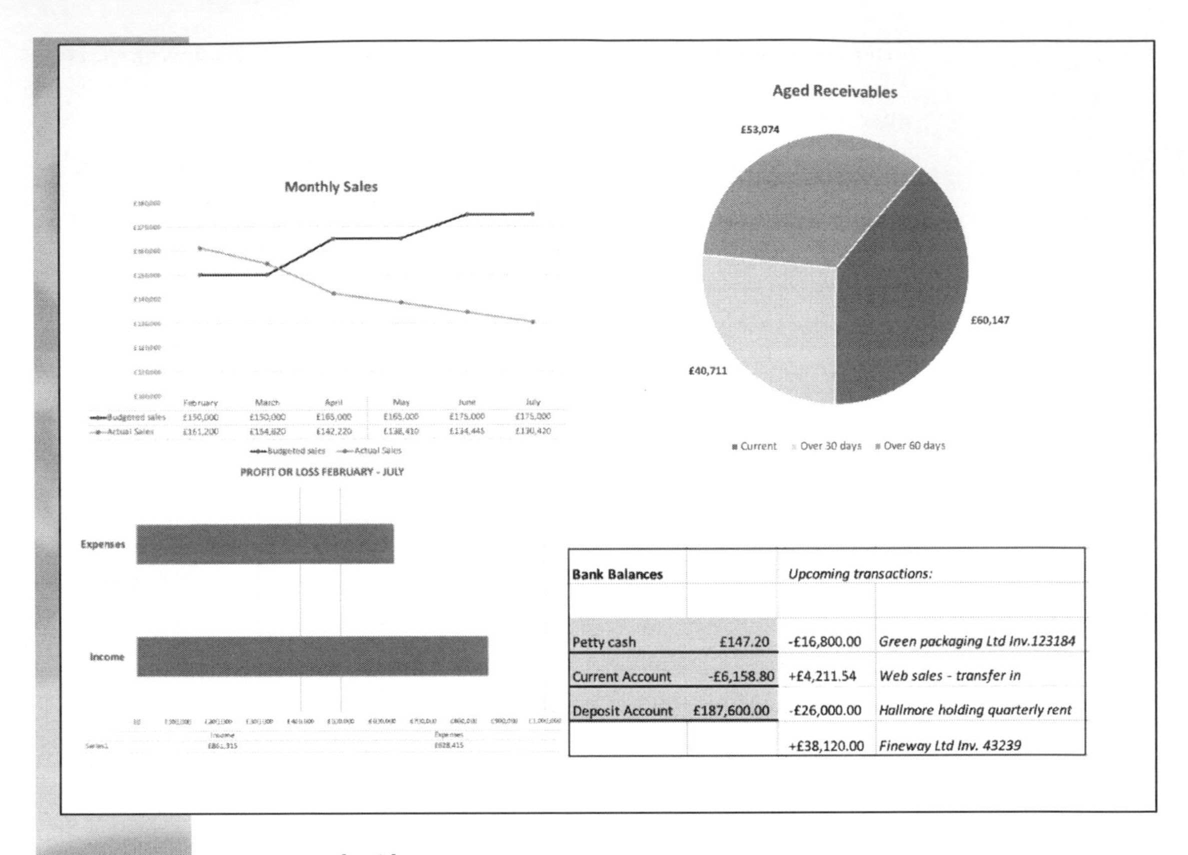

Bank Balances		Upcoming transactions:	
Petty cash	£147.20	-£16,800.00	*Green packaging Ltd Inv.123184*
Current Account	-£6,158.80	+£4,211.54	*Web sales - transfer in*
Deposit Account	£187,600.00	-£26,000.00	*Hallmore holding quarterly rent*
		+£38,120.00	*Fineway Ltd Inv. 43239*

solution

Sales and marketing

Sales were above budget for February and March. However, from April onwards sales have decreased month-on-month, and by July were 25% lower than budget. It appears this may be as a result of lost sales to the large competitor who is adopting more environmentally friendly processes.

It would be useful for the dashboard to show the split between website sales and commercial sales to enable the business to assess the impact of the announcement by its large competitor.

Zach may wish to revisit the budget as it has not been revised since the beginning of the year.

If sales continue to reduce compared with budget the business may have an issue with cashflow.

The business may have to consider carrying out some online marketing to try and regain some of the website sales that it has lost.

Bank

The business does not appear to be managing its cash well and should consider transferring some of the funds from its deposit account to the current account, which is currently overdrawn. Upcoming transactions detailed in the dashboard indicate that its overdraft is likely to further increase.

The business should ensure that it has an agreed overdraft facility with the bank to avoid necessary bank charges.

Aged receivables

Because website sales are all paid for when the order is placed, all aged receivables will relate to business customers. A significant proportion of the total aged receivables are more than 60 days overdue. The business is aware that these customers are increasingly going beyond the agreed credit terms. Credit control procedures should be tightened up to ensure that customers pay more promptly, but care must be taken to ensure that this does not result in loss of business.

MoreEco Ltd could consider carrying out some cash flow forecasting to see whether offering a prompt payment discount may be beneficial.

Profit

The profit for the six months is currently £232,900. Zach needs to be aware that whilst the business is currently making a profit on paper, the deterioration in actual sales compare with budgeted sales, together with the large amount of overdue receivables, may mean that there is an issue with both reducing profit and cash flow in the future.

COMMUNICATING INFORMATION

In order to ensure the smooth flow of ideas, facts, decision-making, and advice, it is important for a business and its staff to communicate effectively and professionally. This may be internally with other members of staff or managers, or externally with suppliers, customers, HMRC, banks, or other external stakeholders of the business.

Effective, professional communication should have the following attributes:

- clear and easily understood
- concise – avoid overloading the recipient(s) by including any unnecessary information
- unambiguous – avoid technical language, or anything that could be misinterpreted or misunderstood
- complete – include everything that needs to be communicated
- accurate
- timely – provided at the right time
- appropriate – ensure it meets the needs of the person, or people, who the communication is with
- in the most suitable format

methods of communication

You will have learned about the different methods of communication that are used by businesses in the Business Environment unit at level 2, and the fact that they can be classified as verbal or written:

- **verbal communication** includes telephone calls and meetings
- **written communication** can be paper-based or electronic:
  - **paper-based**: letters and reports
  - **electronic**: emails, messaging, intranet, and social media

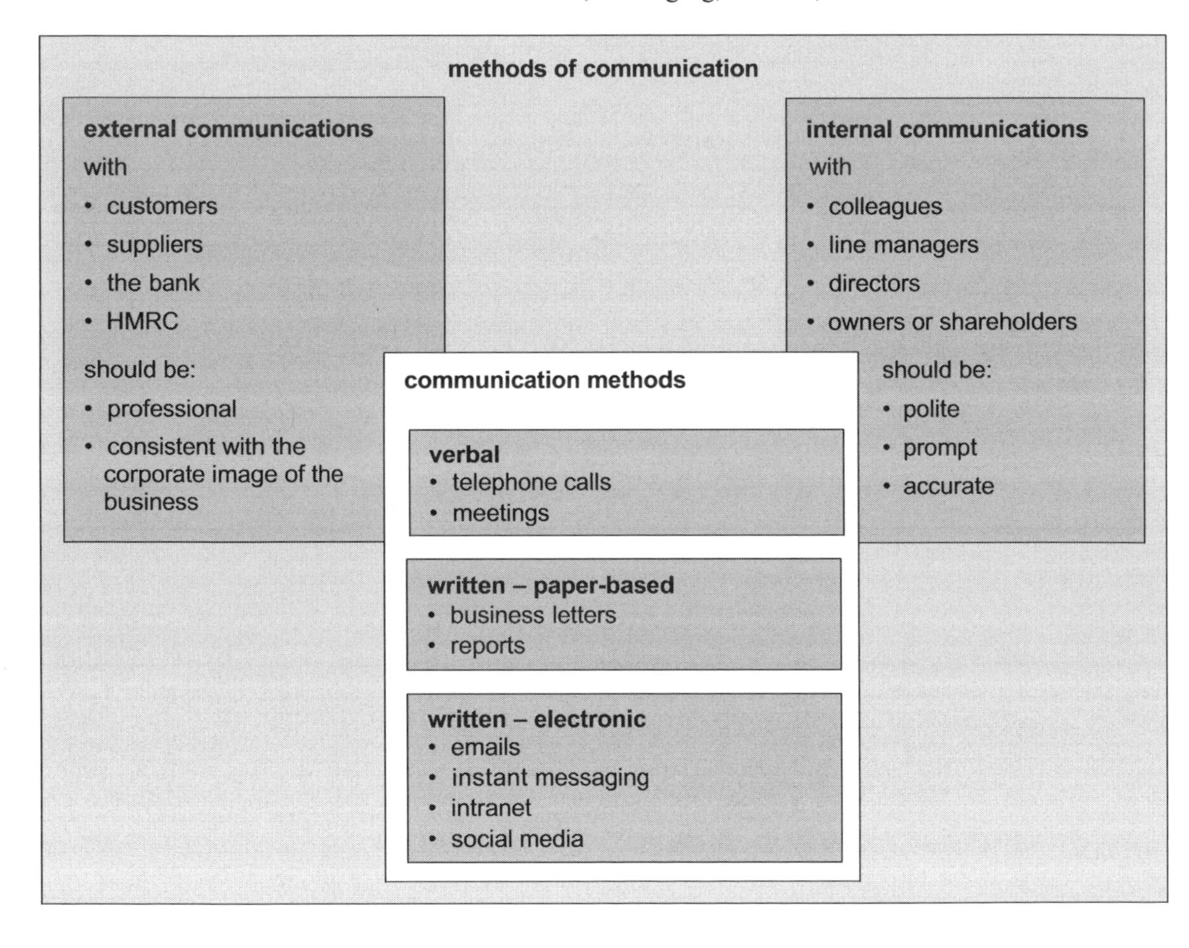

We will now look at the different methods of communication that are used by businesses, and how to determine the appropriate method for communicating internally and externally.

report

Reports are used to communicate information to individuals, or groups of people, on a specific subject. Routine reports may be produced regularly, for example a regular sales report produced for the monthly sales meeting that analyses sales by division and product. One-off reports may also be produced at the request of a particular user, for example a detailed report on the performance of a division to assist management to decide whether the division should be closed or remain open.

Business reports should follow a clear structure with sections covering:

- **title page**: what the report is about, who wrote it, who it is for, and the date it has been prepared
- **summary:** a brief summary of what the report covers, and the conclusions and recommendations it makes
- **introduction**: who requested the report, why and when it was completed
- **findings**: the main body of the report, including all the information gathered as part of the process, presented in a clear and logical way
- **conclusions**: this will be based on the findings in report and should be justified by logical reasoning
- **recommendations**: these are the actions that the writer(s) of the report recommends should be taken based on the conclusions
- **appendices**: figures, including spreadsheets and tables, will be attached as an appendix to the report so that the detailed information included does not distract the reader

Reports are, primarily, used to communicate with internal stakeholders of the business, including managers and directors. However, a business will sometimes need to produce a one-off report for an external stakeholder. For example, a report for the bank to support a loan application, or a corporate social responsibility report that will be used by the general public.

email

Emails are probably the most common way of communicating in a business environment. Emails can be set up so that they automatically include an electronic 'signature', which will normally include the sender's name, job title, business name, and the sender's contact details. Whilst there is no prescribed format for an email, a business email should be professional and, therefore, avoid using slang words, emojis, or lots of exclamation marks.

Emails can be used to communicate internally and externally and are a quick and efficient way of communicating. In an increasingly paperless work environment, attachments can also be added to emails which can be useful to transfer documents without the need to print them out. However, businesses must be careful to ensure that the email is sent to the correct recipient and that confidentiality is maintained.

Emails will be routinely used for internal communication between individuals or groups of colleagues. They will also be used to communicate with suppliers and customers, to send documents such as terms of trade, invoices, statements, or credit control letters.

Some email systems will have an encryption function. This will help to ensure confidential information is protected by translating the email into another form, or code, that can only be accessed by the authorised recipient(s) using a 'decryption key', or password.

letter

Although emails are normally used to communicate with external stakeholders, such as customers, suppliers, or the bank, a more formal business letter may be required in certain circumstances. Any letter sent by the business should be presented using the organisation's 'house style'. This means that the appearance and format of each letter is in a uniform style, and on standard printed stationery that shows the name, address, and details of the business. The elements of the letter, including headings, paragraphs and signatures, will all be presented in a uniform way.

Although letters are normally used for external communication, they may sometimes be used internally if something formal needs to be communicated to an employee or manager. An example of this would be a letter to an employee where the business needs to terminate their employment.

meeting

Communication is sometimes better done verbally. One of the ways of doing this is to hold a meeting. Meetings can be held in person, or over the internet using technology such as Zoom, Microsoft Teams, Skype, or Google Hangouts. They can be formal or informal, and can be between two individuals, or a group of people.

Team meetings, project meetings, management meetings and board meetings are all examples of internal meetings. External meetings may be held between a business and a customer or supplier, to discuss things like terms of trade, new products, or to negotiate discounts.

Meetings should be well structured, with an agenda, so that it is clear what is being discussed, and whether anything will be presented to the meeting. Everyone who is attending should be given the opportunity to contribute during the meeting, and the person chairing the meeting, or presenting, must be aware of non-verbal signs, or body language, during a meeting. Positive non-verbal signals may be nodding and smiling, whereas negative signals may include frowning, lack of eye contact or tone of voice.

telephone call

Telephone calls are used internally by staff as a quick way of confirming arrangements, raising or resolving queries, or discussing issues with another member of staff who does not work in the same location. Increasingly, these calls will made be across the internet with cameras on, so they become more like a meeting.

Telephone calls can also be used externally to contact customers, suppliers, or other external stakeholders. This may be because a discussion is considered better, or because the other party has requested a telephone call.

social media

Social media is now one of the most widely used methods of communication. Most businesses have a social media presence, including Twitter, Instagram, and Facebook, which can be used to attract new customers, engage with existing customers, promote corporate social responsibility, or to maintain a business's reputation.

Once a customer, supplier, or other business, engages with an organisation on social media, they will be able to see all the content that it posts. Consequently, businesses must be careful that the content they post is appropriate and does not cause offensive. An ill-judged social media post may negatively affect the reputation of the business, which will be difficult to reverse. Businesses that use social media for external communication should, therefore, have rules and guidance on the use of social media, and all content should be reviewed and approved before it is posted.

intranet and instant messaging

An intranet is a secure, private network that is used for sharing information and accessing and sharing files. It allows secure communication, back up of data, and data security within an organisation. Usually it does not allow external access which helps to ensure that confidential information remains confidential.

An organisation's intranet can also have a chat function which allows easy and quick communication between employees via instant messaging, rather than using emails.

confidentiality

Although we have touched on confidentiality when we have looked at different methods of communication, it is worth reiterating the importance of keeping information confidential. It is important that information is only communicated to the correct recipient, or group of recipients. An email or report that is sent to a senior manager, or director, may well be opened by their assistant, so sensitive, or confidential, information should be marked 'private and confidential', or delivered in person, to ensure that it remains confidential.

Chapter Summary

- Processing data so that it is organised, structured, and well presented, makes it useful and meaningful for the user.
- Good quality information should be ACCURATE:

  Accurate

  Complete

  Cost effective

  Understandable

  Relevant

  Authoritative

  Timely

  Easy to use
- Information at the strategic level of the organisation needs to analyse what has happened in the past, both to the business itself, and also in the market and business environment in which it operates. This will allow the management to make longer-term decisions about the future direction of the business.
- The managerial level of the organisation requires regular information, to monitor the progress towards the organisation's goals.
- At the operational level of the business, information will need to be regular and detailed to allow immediate decisions to be made about the day-to-day operation of the business.
- Big data systematically analyses information that is so large and complex, and accumulates so quickly, that it is difficult to store and process using traditional data processing methods.
- Big data can be social data that comes from social media, machine data that is generated by machines, or transactional data which is generated from the business's transactions.
- The characteristics of big data can be described as the 'five Vs': volume, velocity, variety, veracity, and value.
- Big data has a number of benefits, including:
  - attracting and retaining customers by analysing customer behaviour to establish exactly what they are looking for
  - focused marketing by analysing trends
  - improved competitive advantage from the previous two points
  - identification of potential risk areas
  - faster innovation by reacting more quickly to changes in customer tastes
  - improved business processes
  - fraud detection

- Limitations of big data include:
  - lack of knowledge and skills: managing big data requires skilled data professionals who are up-to-date with data handling tools. These types of individuals are in short supply, and once employed the business will need to ensure their skills remain current
  - difficulties integrating data from different sources: data from a number of different sources, in a variety of formats, can overwhelm data analysis tools and result in incomplete and/or inaccurate information
  - data protection and security: as the amount of data that organisations collect increases, businesses must ensure that they adhere to data protection principles. They must also protect the big data collected from the risks of data leaks, hacking or data losses

- Professional scepticism must be applied before big data is used for making key business decisions. If professional experience indicates that the results of data analysis is not right, then the results need to be questioned and further analysis carried out.

- Data visualisation presents information in a visual way using charts, images, diagrams, matrices, graphs, and tables to summarise and simplify complex information.

- Most computerised accounting systems will now have built-in functionality that presents data visually using graphs, charts, diagrams, and tables. A dashboard will often provide sufficient detail for owners or managers to control the business, even if they do not have a financial background.

- Effective, professional communication should be:
  - clear and easily understood
  - concise
  - unambiguous
  - complete
  - accurate
  - timely
  - appropriate
  - presented in the most suitable format
- Communication can be verbal or written. Common methods used for business communications include:
  - reports
  - emails
  - letters
  - meetings
  - telephone calls
  - social media
  - intranet and instant messaging

- A business must ensure that it chooses the appropriate method of communication for its stakeholders and that confidential information remains confidential.

Key Terms

ACCURATE — an acronym for good quality information: accurate, complete, cost effective, understandable, relevant, authoritative, timely and easy to use

strategic/corporate level — the highest level of the organisation, where strategic decisions are made

managerial level — the level of an organisation that is responsible for making decisions about how the organisation will achieve its strategic goals

operational level — the level where the management are involved in the day-to-day running of the business

big data — systematic analysis of information that is so large and complex, and accumulates so quickly, that it is difficult to store, and process using traditional data processing methods

social data — big data that is generated from social media platforms, including tweets (and retweets), comments, videos

machine data — big data generated by machines, such as handheld scanners used in supermarkets to check inventory levels, or record data on customer spending

transactional data — big data generated from the daily transactions that take place in a business, including sales and purchases, and payments and receipts

five Vs — the characteristics of big data are sometimes referred to as the five Vs:

- **volume** — the sheer volume of big data makes it difficult to analyse
- **velocity** — because of the volume of big data, the speed (velocity) at which it is processed is important in order for it to be useful to the business
- **variety** — useful big data will be generated from a variety of sources, both internally and externally

veracity big data needs to be accurate, or truthful. Therefore, it should be obtained from a trusted source, and processed so that any bias, duplication, anomalies, or inconsistencies are removed

value big data will only be useful if it can be processed and transformed into useful and valuable information that can then be used to add value to the business

professional scepticism an attitude that includes a questioning mind, being alert to conditions which may indicate possible misstatement due to error or fraud, and a critical assessment of evidence. Professional scepticism should be applied to the results of any analysis of big data

data visualisation images, tables, matrices, diagrams, graphs, and charts that are used to present information in an accessible and usable way

tables tables normally arrange data in rows and columns, and are often generated using spreadsheet software

matrices a matrix takes a table of information and simplifies it by using colours, icons, or pictures rather than the actual figures

column and bar chart a chart where the height of the columns, or the length of the bars, represent the value of each item

pie chart a circle divided into sectors to represent the proportion each part makes up of the whole – like a pie divided into slices

line graph points on a graph connected by lines, which show how something changes over time, or as volumes increase or decrease. Line graphs can have one line or a number of lines, for example a graph showing a line for budgeted sales figures and a line for actual sales figures

diagram a useful way of showing the movement of data through a process

image a picture or photograph used to visually reinforce the message the data is trying to put across

dashboard functionality that is built in to computerised accounting software which will present data visually using graphs, charts, diagrams, and tables

Activities

10.1 Complete the table below to identify the attributes of good quality information which form the acronym ACCURATE.

A	
C	
C	
U	
R	
A	
T	
E	

10.2 Simone, the sales manager, receives a monthly report showing the value of total sales made by each of her sales team. The business sells over 30 products across three quality levels: value, standard, and premium. She has asked for the report to show a breakdown of sales for each salesperson by product and also by quality level.

The additional analysis of the sales will help to ensure that the information is.......

Select **one** option.

(a) Cost effective	
(b) Timely	
(c) Authoritative	
(d) Relevant	

10.3 Briefly explain what is meant by social data as a source of big data.

10.4 Which of the following is not a characteristic of big data?

Select **one** option.

(a)	Variety	
(b)	Velocity	
(c)	Visualisation	
(d)	Volume	

10.5 Decide whether the following statement is true or false.

'Professional scepticism should be applied to the analysis of big data if professional experience indicates the analysis is not correct.'

True	False

10.6 List **three** advantages of presenting data visually.

10.7 Charlie has been asked to prepare a report for the senior management team, some of whom do not have a financial background. Charlie's manager has advised her to present some of the information visually to make it easier to understand.

Match each of the following pieces of information to the most appropriate presentation method, using each option once.

Information	Presentation method
The trend in monthly sales compared with budget over the last 12 months.	Pie chart
Detailed monthly profit or loss for the last 12 months.	Line graph
The proportion of total expenses made up by rent and rates, materials, labour, distribution costs, and administrative expenses.	Table
A comparison of sales by each of the four sales staff for each of the last four quarters.	Column chart

10.8 Briefly explain three benefits of having dashboard functionality in cloud-based computerised accounting software.

10.9 Today's date is 5th October. You work for Gorgeous Gardens, a business that sells outside furniture sets for pubs and restaurants.

- Gorgeous Gardens is a sole trader business owned by Milla Harding.
- The customer base of the business is expanding, as its products are stylish and unique, and are increasingly being purchased by boutique hotels, gastro pubs and restaurants.
- There are four product ranges sold by Gorgeous Gardens: basic, standard, premium and luxury.
- Sales are at their peak during the summer months, as this is when businesses expect their customers will want to eat outside.
- The business had a sales promotion at the end of the summer on the premium and luxury ranges.
- Gorgeous Gardens employs six salespeople who are managed by Rehana, the sales manager. Each salesperson is responsible for a geographical area of the country.
- Gorgeous Gardens' customers regularly make purchases, and the business offers them a standard 30-day credit term, once appropriate credit checks have been carried out.
- As a lot of the products that the business sells are shipped from abroad, many of its suppliers allow Gorgeous Gardens' 60-days' credit.

Sales data for the business has been provided in the dashboard, shown on the next page, for the last six months.

Milla has asked you to provide some analysis, based on the visual sales data on the dashboard. She is specifically interested in:

- the performance of the business over the past six months
- any further information that might be useful in assessing the performance of the sales team and products

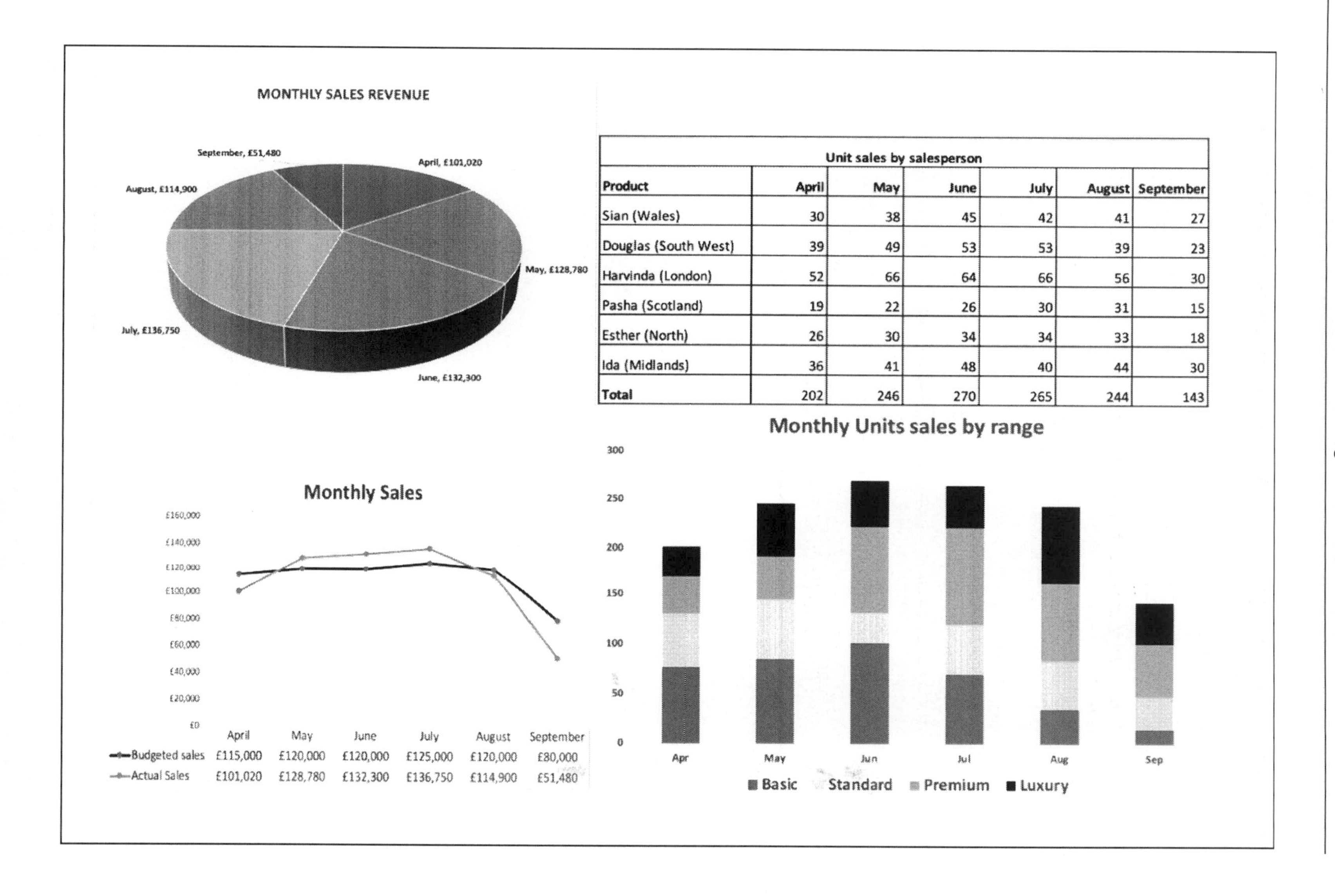

Unit sales by salesperson						
Product	April	May	June	July	August	September
Sian (Wales)	30	38	45	42	41	27
Douglas (South West)	39	49	53	53	39	23
Harvinda (London)	52	66	64	66	56	30
Pasha (Scotland)	19	22	26	30	31	15
Esther (North)	26	30	34	34	33	18
Ida (Midlands)	36	41	48	40	44	30
Total	202	246	270	265	244	143

10.10 For each of the following stakeholders, identify which is the most appropriate method of communication.

	Email	**Meeting**	**Social media**	**Telephone call**
A promotion by a restaurant offering its customers a free meal if they follow its Twitter page.				
A presentation of the company's annual results. All members of staff can be involved if they wish.				
Confirmation of terms of trade, including credit terms, for a new customer.				
Contact with a customer who continues not to pay its overdue account despite having been contacted several times by email.				

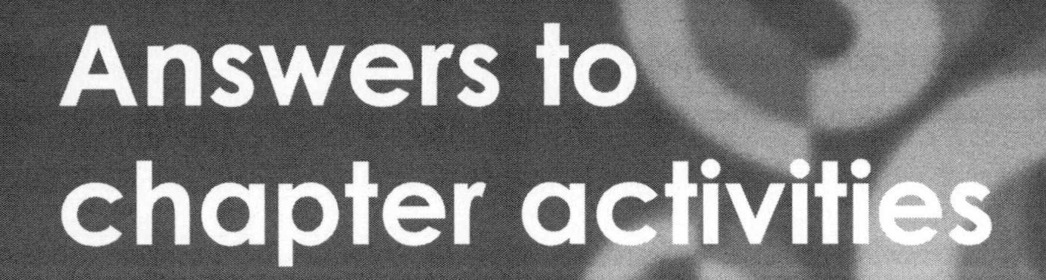

Answers to chapter activities

CHAPTER 1: UNDERSTANDING BUSINESSES

1.1

(a) The owner is independent and can run the business as they wish without consulting others	✔
(b) The owner has limited liability	
(c) The financial statements are made up of a statement of profit or loss and a statement of financial position	✔
(d) The sole trader must make an annual return to Companies House	
(e) The investment in the business by the owner is known as capital	✔

1.2

(a) The way in which profit will be shared	✔
(b) Details of partners' salaries	✔
(c) The location of the partnership's offices	
(d) The rate of interest allowed on partners' capital	✔
(e) The rate of interest charged on partners' drawings	✔

1.3 Goodwill

1.4 **(a)** Incorporation means a company or other organisation being formed into a legal entity separate from its owners. Examples are limited liability partnerships (LLPs) and limited companies.

(b) Advantages of incorporation (two from):

- a limit on the liability of members (LLPs) and shareholders (limited companies) for the debts of the business
- the continuing existence of the business as a separate legal entity
- an enhancement of the credibility of the business
- access to finance may be easier than a sole trader
- transfer of ownership may be easier than a sole trader

Disadvantages of incorporation (two from):

- more complex requirements to set up the business
- higher costs of keeping up with record keeping and annual returns
- information filed with Companies House is in the public domain
- business finances must be kept entirely separate from those of the owners

1.5 **(a)** A charity is an organisation which uses its resources to fund charitable activities under its control.

(b) The main rules governing charities are:

- they must follow charity law, the Charities Act 2011, and the Charity Commission regulations
- for financial reporting they must follow either the Statement of Recommended Practice, or Financial Reporting Standard 102
- their purpose must be for the public benefit
- they are governed by a trust deed
- they are run by trustees
- they are independent of other organisations

1.6

	Loan	**Working capital**	**Retained earnings**
Expansion of the business by opening a distribution centre in Scotland.			✔
Purchase of a new machine for production line C which is expected to cost £220,000 and last for eight years.	✔		
Payment of the business' corporation tax liability.		✔	

1.7

	Internal stakeholder	**External stakeholder**
Directors	✔	
Customers		✔
Suppliers		✔
Finance Providers eg banks		✔
Owners	✔	
General public		✔
Employees	✔	
The Government		✔

1.8 Risk **tolerance** is how much risk a stakeholder is able to withstand, whereas risk **appetite** is the level of risk a stakeholder is prepared to accept to achieve their objectives. Risk **threshold** is the level up to which risk is acceptable – often measured as amount of money that could be lost.

CHAPTER 2: ORGANISATIONAL STRUCTURE AND GOVERNANCE

2.1

	Functional	Divisional	Matrix
Dessus Ltd, an accountancy practice with individual teams that are responsible for audit, taxation, accounts preparation and consultancy services.		✔	
Fabulous Phones and Tablets Ltd, a mobile phone business that sells exclusively on the internet, with teams for sales and marketing, finance, production, administration, and human resources, that all report to the board of directors.	✔		
Pharmacular plc, a pharmaceutical company that has autonomous businesses in different countries all over the world that report to the managing company.		✔	
Jenious Ltd an engineering business that has a number of project teams that are developing new products.			✔

2.2 A manager who works in a business with a **flat** organisational structure is usually responsible for a larger number of employees and is said to have a **wide** span of control.

A manager who is responsible for a smaller number of individuals is said to have a **narrow** span of control and will usually work in a **tall** organisational structure.

2.3

	Centralised control	Decentralised control
Decisions are made at higher levels of the organisation's management.	✔	
Senior management will be distanced from the day-to day running of the business.	✔	
Authority for decision-making is given to lower levels of management.		✔
This 'bottom-up' structure often leads to a more collaborative working atmosphere.		✔
This 'top-down structure' has less flexibility.	✔	

2.4

(a) Centralised control	
(b) Corporate governance	✔
(c) Companies Act	
(d) Corporate goals	

2.5

Type of cyber risk	Option
An attack that locks the user out of their information system and asks for money to be paid to the attacker to prevent further disruption.	Ransomware
This allows the attacker to watch the operations of the business without being seen by the user.	Spyware
An email stating that the user's bank details have been compromised, with a link asking them to input their existing password so the bank can supply them with a new one.	Phishing
The attacker uses automatic software to generate huge numbers of word and number combinations in the hope that they will 'guess' the user's password.	Password attack
If this type of malware gets into a computer, it can record every keystroke made by users. This then allows the hacker to identify passwords and access sensitive information.	Keylogging
The user's default homepage or search engine changes so that the attacker can feed the user with unwanted pop-ups and advertising.	Browser hijacking
The general term for malicious software, often inserted into computer via phishing emails, that can introduce viruses, keyloggers, spyware, worms, or ransomware.	Malware
This type of cyber-attack overwhelms the organisation's computer systems with a huge number of data requests simultaneously. This then causes the system to freeze up.	DDoS

2.6

(a)	Legal and regulatory risk	
(b)	Reputational risk	✔
(c)	Operational risk	
(d)	Financial risk	

2.7

(a)	Failure to comply with health and safety regulations	
(b)	An increase in the interest rate on a business loan	
(c)	Management deciding to introduce a new product to the market without carrying out any market research	✔
(d)	Employing staff without the necessary qualifications or experience	

2.8

(a)	Legality	
(b)	Impact	✔
(c)	Scope	
(d)	Likelihood	✔

2.9

A music festival that takes place in the summer regardless of whether it rains or not.	Accept
A freight business insures all the cargo on its ships against damage or loss at sea.	Transfer
A business ceasing clothing production overseas due to the risk to its reputation of using child labour.	Avoid
Regular staff training in a business where there is a risk of wastage of raw materials if the staff do not operate the machines effectively.	Reduce

CHAPTER 3: THE EXTERNAL AND INTERNAL ENVIRONMENT

3.1

(a) Economic	
(b) Environmental	
(c) Efficiency	✔
(d) Social	

3.2

(a) Public spending	
(b) Government policy	
(c) Taxation	
(d) Currency exchange rates	✔

3.3

(a) Currency exchange rates	
(b) Inflation	
(c) Unemployment	
(d) National minimum wage regulations	✔

3.4

	Political	Economic	Social	Techno-logical	Legal	Environ-mental
The minimum wage rate is due to rise in April of next year by more than the rate of inflation.					✔	
More people working from home has led to an increase in the number of deliveries.			✔			
The business is considering updating its website which has not changed for several years				✔		
The Government has a new subsidised scheme to help pay for people to get their heavy goods vehicle driving license.	✔					
Most of the business's vehicles have been bought using loans and bank interest rates have increased over the last 18 months.		✔				
The business is considering replacing all its small delivery vans with electric vans.						✔

3.5

Issue	Action
Political	
Import costs have increased significantly which will increase the cost of the products that Rose & Bumble imports.	The business should consider sourcing its products from within the UK.
There have been delays in delivery due to border control issues. This may mean that inventory is not available when retailers order it.	Rose & Bumble should build additional time into its ordering and delivery schedules to ensure that the goods arrive on time.
An increase in taxation has reduced disposable income. Given that these are handmade, luxury goods this may result in reduced sales.	The business should investigate the possibility of selling other products that are not luxury items to maintain sales levels.
The increased corporation tax will have a negative impact on the business's profit.	The business may have to consider increasing prices to ensure that it maintains margins, although this may not be effective given the reduction in disposable income due to tax rises.
Economic	
Unpredictable exchange rates have meant that it is difficult to predict the price that will actually be paid for the goods. This means that some products may not be profitable.	Rose & Bumble could negotiate prices in £s with its overseas suppliers.
Social	
Customer needs have changed so that they want to buy directly from Rose & Bumble online. However, this is not currently an option so the business may be losing sales.	The business should investigate updating its website and adapting its systems so that customers can buy online.
There is an increasing number of people who want to buy vegan products rather than leather. This means the business's products may become less fashionable.	Rose & Bumble should consider extending its range so that it includes luxury vegan leather products.
Technological	
Rose & Bumble does not currently have a website where customers can buy directly.	As was said in the social section above, the business should investigate updating its website so that it can sell direct to customers.
Competitors are using machines to produce goods of similar quality at a lower price.	Rose & Bumble should consider extending its product range so that it has a cheaper, machine-produced range to appeal to customers with less disposable income, whilst continuing with its prestige range of handmade products.

Legal	
Employment law means that the business has to offer flexible working to the employee returning from maternity leave, which it will find difficult.	The busines may have to employ and train an additional member of staff to cover some of the role of the member of staff who is returning from maternity leave.
Environmental	
Rose & Bumble disposes of all the packing that the products arrive in, before repackaging with its own branded recyclable packaging. Although the business is being 'green' with its own packaging, the fact that it disposes of non-recyclable packaging and then repackages is not environmentally friendly.	Rose & Bumble should consider asking its overseas suppliers to use environmentally friendly packaging. Alternatively it could provide the supplier with Rose & Bumble branded, recyclable, packaging which would cut down on the need to unpack and repackage products.
The delivery company that Rose and Bumble uses runs a fleet of diesel vehicles which causes damage to the environment.	The business should look into alternative delivery options that use electric vehicles or other, more environmentally friendly options.

3.6

Boom
Downturn
Recession
Recovery

3.7

Definition	Option
Goods that consumers will buy regardless of whether their income changes.	Necessity goods
Cheaper goods for which demand generally decreases as income rises.	Inferior goods
Two, or more, goods or services that can carry out the same purpose for the consumer.	Substitute products
Goods for which demand increases when income increases and goes down if income decreases.	Normal goods

3.8

(a) A decrease in the price of a substitute good	
(b) An increase in the price of a substitute product	✔
(c) An increase in the cost of raw materials	
(d) A decrease in the cost of raw materials	

3.9

(a) An increase in demand for Aye	
(b) A decrease in demand for Aye	✔
(c) An increase in demand for Bee	
(d) No change in demand for Aye	

3.10

(a) An increase in demand for Aye	✔
(b) A decrease in demand for Aye	
(c) No change in demand for Aye	

3.11 The forces of supply and demand determine **a price mechanism** to reach **an equilibrium price**. This is the point on a graph where the supply curve and the demand curve bisect.

CHAPTER 4: SUSTAINABILITY

4.1 **(a)**

1	Objective: **economic growth** Examples: • try to use locally sourced materials • generate profit whilst still supporting social equality and without compromising the sustainability of the environment
2	Objective: **environmental protection** Examples: • recycling paper and printer cartridges used in an organisation's offices • promoting car-sharing schemes and 'cycle to work' incentives
3	Objective: **social equality** Example: • ensure that businesses with which it trades provide reasonable pay and decent working conditions, particularly if they are based overseas • sponsor local sporting events

(b) 'development that meets the needs of the present without compromising the ability of future generations to meet their own needs.'

4.2 **(a)** Corporate social responsibility (CSR) reports.

(b) The public and investors are keen to see a business's attitude to sustainability and will look more favourably on organisations which have made progress towards achieving their CSR goals.

4.3

COST CUTTING METHODS
1 Move manufacturing to a factory in Bangladesh. Issues: • ensure that the employees in the Bangladesh factory have decent working conditions and fair rates of pay • assess the impact on staff in the UK of moving manufacturing to Bangladesh, such as redundancy • consider the effect on the environment, such as increased CO_2 emissions, of transporting the goods from Bangladesh to the UK
2 Close three of their four sales offices and have one central office which will result in a significant increase in business mileage for three quarters of its sales force. Issues: • consider the effect on the environment of the increased travelling for its sales staff • consider the effect on the working conditions of the sales staff if they have to travel further and longer during the course of their working day • quantify the reduction in the costs of power and other running costs of centralising the sales office to one location
3 Change supplier of packaging material from its current supplier that is based locally and uses recycled plastic, to a new overseas supplier who is offering Alecon Ltd a 25% discount. Issues: • investigate the sustainability credentials of the new supplier to see whether they use recycled materials and offer decent working conditions to their staff • consider the effect on local employment of sourcing the material from overseas • assess the effect on the environment of the potential new supplier transporting the packaging materials greater distances

4.4 Reputational risk is the risk of loss resulting from damage to an organisation's reputation.

An organisation will include its sustainability targets in its corporate social responsibility (CSR). When it produces a CSR report this will show its progress towards these targets. There is a risk to an organisation's reputation if it reports negative results. However, the fact that a business is prepared to report its progress towards its sustainability targets and CSR will have a positive effect on its reputation.

4.5 The answer should cover four of the six points detailed below.

ENCOURAGING SUSTAINABILITY

1 **Products and services** – explain to clients that they should try to ensure that their products or services are produced from sustainably resourced materials

2 **Customers** – help clients to supply to their customers in a sustainable manner

3 **Employees** – encourage clients to provide good working conditions for their staff

4 **The workplace** – suggest green policies that clients can introduce including recycling and conservation of energy

5 **The supply chain** – encourage clients to research the sustainability credentials of their suppliers

6 **Business functions and processes** – explain to client management that they should constantly review the way in which they operate to ensure it continues to support and encourage sustainability and sustainable development

CHAPTER 5: PRINCIPLES OF PROFESSIONAL ETHICS

5.1 The International Ethics Standards Board for Accountants (IESBA), which is part of the International Federation of Accountants (IFAC).

5.2 All options apply

5.3
- Integrity
- Objectivity
- Professional competence and due care
- Confidentiality
- Professional behaviour

5.4 **(a)** Integrity

(b) Objectivity

5.5 'A professional accountant who complies with the law and does not bring the accounting profession into disrepute is upholding the fundamental principle of **professional behaviour**'.

5.6 False. The accountant's duty of confidentiality to a client extends to the period after the relationship has ended.

5.7 Robert has a duty of confidentiality to his client, James. Therefore, he cannot disclose the financial information that Zeena has requested. In order for him to do so he would have to obtain authority from his client, James, which is very unlikely to be given.

5.8 Findlay should request authority from his client to disclose the information. Verbal authority is acceptable, but it would be better if this authority were given in writing. He can then give information to the office supplies company. He should include a disclaimer making it clear that this is for the use of the office supplies company only and is given purely to help them to make a decision about whether or not to supply goods on credit to his client. He should also explain that the information is given without any financial responsibility on the part of his firm of accountants.

5.9 An accountant has a professional duty to disclose confidential information to protect their **professional** interests in **legal proceedings**.

5.10

(a)	A questioning mind	✔
(b)	Taking things at face value	
(c)	Being alert to conditions which may indicate possible misstatement due to error or fraud	✔
(d)	Making critical assessment of evidence that is provided	✔
(e)	Assuming that everything is false or deliberately fraudulent	

CHAPTER 6: THEATS AND SAFEGUARDS TO FUNDAMENTAL ETHICAL PRINCIPLES

6.1

(a)	A rules-based approach	
(b)	A principles-based approach	✔

6.2 **(a)** If Samantha accepts the new company as a client, the fee income from this assignment will represent a substantial proportion of Samantha's total fee income. This could represent a self-interest threat to Samantha's objectivity as she could be reliant on the fees from Red News and its subsidiary.

(b) Samantha should not accept the additional work for Blue Media as she cannot reduce the self-interest threat she would face to an acceptable level.

6.3 'When providing consultancy services to an existing client, professional accountants may face a **self-review** threat to their fundamental ethical principles. They must ensure that they **do** make recommendations and **do not** make management decisions.

6.4 **(a)** The two fundamental ethical principles that are most threatened by this situation are:

Integrity: if Hayley knows that the allowance for doubtful receivables was too low, she has deliberately produced incorrect financial information which is both misleading to the users and dishonest.

Professional behaviour: knowingly allowing inaccurate and misleading information to be included in Andrew's financial statements breaches accounting regulations and consequently brings the accounting profession into disrepute.

(b) Hayley faces an intimidation threat from Andrew's statement that 'it may not look good for you if the partners at Trott & Cook found out about this'.

(c) Professional accountants should use their professional judgement to decide whether it is appropriate to accept gifts or hospitality from clients. Even if Hayley believes that she has not done anything wrong, the comments that Andrew has made in the thank you card, together with its significant value, mean that Hayley cannot accept the gift voucher from Andrew.

6.5 **(a)** **Self-interest threat** – from the job offer at Headstyle Ltd.

Familiarity threat – from the length of time that Adrian has worked on the Headstyle Ltd assignment. Also, the fact that the Managing Director has asked him not to mention the job offer until the assignment has been completed.

(b) **Objectivity** – having a long and close working relationship with the management of Headstyle Ltd together with the offer of a senior position in the company will threaten Adrian's independence and hence his objectivity.

Professional behaviour – if Adrian does not declare his interest in Headstyle Ltd to his employers, Tahil & Emerson, then he could be accused of bringing the accounting profession into disrepute.

(c) If Adrian does not intend to accept the job offer from Headstyle Ltd he should politely decline the offer from the Managing Director. If he is interested in the job offer, he should explain the situation to a partner at Tahil & Emerson who can then decide whether to remove Adrian from the assignment or to put an additional level of review in for all the work that Adrian is responsible for.

6.6 **(a)** **Self-interest threat** – Michael faces a self-interest threat to his fundamental ethical principles from the offer of the corporate box at the rugby. He must be careful to ensure that his judgement and behaviour are not influenced by this.

Intimidation threat – Jules is putting time pressure on Michael to complete the work within the next week.

(b) **Objectivity** – as Michael has an interest in completing the work within the time available his objectivity may be threatened.

Professional competence and due care – if Michael is put under time pressure to complete the work allocated to him, this may threaten his ability to carry it out competently and with appropriate due care.

(c) Michael should ensure that the offer is available to all members of staff, ie he is not getting preferential treatment.

He should also make it clear to Jules that if he accepts the offer of the corporate box, it will not influence any decisions he is asked to make.

Michael must ensure that he has adequate time to complete the work he has been allocated and if he does not then he should request additional help to complete the work or inform Jules that the work will be delayed.

6.7 Professional accountants who work in practice are more likely to face advocacy threats to their fundamental ethical principles if they are seen to support a client's point of view or to promote the client's position too strongly.

A professional accountant in business will be expected to support the legitimate goals and objectives of their employer and so would be expected to promote their employer's position. It is, therefore, unlikely that an accountant in business will face advocacy threats to his/her fundamental ethical principles.

CHAPTER 7: ETHICAL CONFLICT AND REPORTING UNETHICAL BEHAVIOUR

7.1 (a) **Objectivity –** acting for both clients with the same aim of securing the building land would be difficult for Terry. Even if he manages to remain independent there may be a perception by each of the two clients that he is favouring the other.

Confidentiality – it will be difficult for Terry to keep information about each client confidential. Again, each client may perceive that he will use confidential information about it to benefit the other.

(b) The process Terry should go through is:

- consider the relevant facts and ethical issues that this situation raises
- consider whether Parks & Co has established procedures for dealing with conflicts of interests between clients
- decide what alternative courses of action are available to him
- select the course of action that is most consistent with his fundamental principles
- discuss the issue with senior management at Parks & Co and document the issue and the discussion

(c) If Terry decides to act for one of the clients, he must consider what safeguards he can put in place so that his relationship with the other clients does not affect his professional judgement and his objectivity. These safeguards must also ensure that he does not breach the other client's confidentiality.

It should be noted that it is very unlikely that the threats to his fundamental ethical principles can be eliminated or reduced to an acceptable level. If this is the case then Terry will not be able to act for either of the clients.

7.2 (a) Esther is employed by Goodrich Ltd and therefore is expected to be loyal to her employer; however, she also has a duty of loyalty to her profession. She is being put under pressure by Sam to act contrary to accounting standards and overvalue the year-end inventory.

(b) Esther should try and resolve the difference of opinion between her and Sam.

If this is not possible Esther should raise this issue with a more senior member of staff in the Accounts Department of Goodrich Ltd.

If Goodrich Ltd has a formal dispute resolution process, Esther should follow this.

Esther can consult with her professional accounting body and take legal advice.

Ultimately if there are no other options open to her, Esther may have to offer to resign from Goodrich Ltd.

7.3

- being transparent with colleagues, customers, and suppliers
- reporting financial and regulatory information clearly and on time
- being open and honest by identifying when it is appropriate to accept and give gifts and hospitality
- paying suppliers a fair price and on time
- providing fair treatment, decent wages and good working conditions for employees
- appropriate use of social media

7.4

		True	False
(a)	Because all staff are paid for the overtime that they work, Babridge Limited is automatically considered to be behaving ethically towards its staff		✔
(b)	The Managing Director's decision regarding staff bonuses raises concerns about the ethical nature of the management and leadership of Babridge Ltd.	✔	

7.5

		Can	Cannot
(a)	Showman Ltd		✔
(b)	Mejanna Ltd	✔	
(c)	AAT	✔	

7.6 Felicity should consider the following:

- does she know all the facts surrounding the issue?
- does she have evidence to support these facts?
- she must follow her employer's internal procedures for reporting misconduct
- she must fully explain her concerns to management

7.7
1 Breach of contract
2 Professional negligence

7.8 Professional liability insurance

CHAPTER 8: MONEY LAUNDERING

8.1 Money laundering is the process that criminals use to convert the proceeds of their crimes into assets that appear to be legitimate. This is usually done through a series of complex transactions to make the funds appear 'clean'.

8.2 **Placement**: this is the first stage of money laundering where criminally obtained funds are moved into a legitimate financial system.

Layering: the second stage of the money laundering process that creates a complex web of transactions to move the money around the financial system, by layering financial transactions.

Integration: the final stage of money laundering which integrates illegal funds back into the legitimate financial system, often by investing in property and other assets.

8.3

(a) HMRC	
(b) AAT	
(c) National Crime Agency	✔
(d) The police	

8.4 **(a)** The client may be committing money laundering by processing criminally obtained funds through the accounts of the business.

(b) Jonathon should report his concerns to the Money Laundering Reporting Officer (MLRO) at the firm where he works. They will assess the issue and decide whether to report the matter to the National Crime Agency.

(c) Tipping off

8.5

(a) Tipping off	
(b) Prejudicing an investigation	✔
(c) Authorised disclosure	
(d) Placement	

8.6 **(a)** Georgia must tell Edgar that she can no longer act for Opino Ltd. This is because the money that it has not paid to HMRC relating to the VAT error constitutes criminal property. By retaining it Opino Ltd could be charged with money laundering.

Georgia must not tell Edgar why she can no longer act for Opino Ltd as this could constitute tipping off. As Georgia is a sole practitioner, she must submit a Suspicious Activity Report (SAR) to the National Crime Agency (NCA).

(b) If Georgia continues to act for Opino Ltd, she is facilitating its retention of the money it should have paid to HMRC relating to the VAT error. In this situation she will be engaged in money laundering. She may also be guilty of the crime of failure to disclose.

(c) Once Joe becomes aware of the error, he should report to the NCA that he suspects Opino Ltd of money laundering. In these circumstances he will be protected from a claim of breach of confidentiality as he has made a protected disclosure. As Joe is aware that he may also have been involved in money laundering, he needs to make an authorised disclosure regarding Edgar's refusal to disclose the error to HMRC.

8.7 If Jake raises the issue with the management of Thompson Facilities Ltd, he could be guilty of the offence of tipping off. Even if he does not intend to prejudice an investigation into possible money laundering by Thompson Facilities Ltd, this offence could still apply.

CHAPTER 9: NEW TECHNOLOGY AND DATA SECURITY

9.1

(a)	Large amounts of data can be processed quickly and accurately	✔
(b)	Correct programming will lead to more accurate forecasting of likely future events	✔
(c)	High initial set up costs	
(d)	Manual data entry and coding will reduce	✔
(e)	Requires significant amount of manual supervision	

9.2

(a)	Artificial intelligence	
(b)	Data analytics	
(c)	Blockchain	✔
(d)	Machine learning	

9.3

(a)	Descriptive	✔
(b)	Diagnostic	
(c)	Predictive	
(d)	Prescriptive	

9.4

(a)	Descriptive	
(b)	Diagnostic	
(c)	Predictive	✔
(d)	Prescriptive	

9.5

		True/False
(a)	This is an example of Freedman & Sons offshoring its catering function	False
(b)	This is an example of Freedman & Sons outsourcing its catering function	True
(c)	In the first year after this change Freedman & Sons can expect to save money	False
(d)	It may be difficult for Freedman & Sons to take back operating its canteen and employ its own catering staff in the future	True
(e)	Most of the responsibility for complying with health and safety and food hygiene regulations will be passed on to Marvellous Menus	True

9.6

(a)	Only accessible on desktop or laptop computers	
(b)	Data and information can be accessed from anywhere	✔
(c)	Data is updated in real-time	✔
(d)	Data is stored on the organisation's own server	
(e)	Apps, plug-ins and add-ins are sometimes available	✔

9.7

(a)	Data should be used only for the explicit purpose for which it was given	✔
(b)	Any data stored by a business must not be kept any longer than is necessary	✔
(c)	As well as the personal data it requires, a business may request additional information that it feels might be useful in the future	
(d)	A business must keep personal data that it holds secure from internal and external threats	✔
(e)	Businesses must ensure that all personal data is deleted after three months and requested again if necessary	

9.8 £17.5 million or 4% of annual global turnover

9.9 **(a)** A cyberattack that locks a user out of their organisation's information system until a payment is made is known as a **ransomware** attack.

(b) **Spyware** is a virus that allows the attacker to watch a business's operations without being seen.

9.10 Firewalls, Antivirus software, Data encryption

CHAPTER 10: COMMUNICATING INFORMATION TO STAKEHOLDERS

10.1

Accurate
Complete
Cost effective
Understandable
Relevant
Authoritative
Timely
Easy to use

10.2

(a)	Cost effective	
(b)	Timely	
(c)	Authoritative	
(d)	Relevant	✔

10.3

Big data from social data come from activity on social media. This can be tweets, likes, comments, videos, and other media uploaded to social media platforms.

This data can be analysed and processed to help businesses to focus their marketing and to develop products and services that will appeal to their target markets.

10.4

(a)	Variety	
(b)	Velocity	
(c)	Visualisation	✔
(d)	Volume	

10.5 True

10.6

Makes the data easier to understand
Allows users to identify trends and anomalies
Makes comparison of data easier

10.7

The trend in monthly sales compared with budget over the last 12 months.	Line graph
Detailed monthly profit and loss for the last 12 months.	Table
The proportion of total expenses made up by rent and rates, materials, labour, distribution costs, and administrative expenses.	Pie chart
A comparison of sales by each of the four sales staff for each of the last four quarters.	Column chart

10.8 Three of the following points, or any other sensible suggestion.

1. Data is presented visually which makes it easy for owners and managers without a financial background to understand.

2. Up-to-date data can be produced in real-time.

3. Dashboards can normally be customised so that the information presented is relevant to the business and users.

4. If the business uses a cloud-based accounting software, the dashboard can be accessed from any device and any location.

10.9 **Performance**

Sales were below budget in April but then were above budget in the next three months. By August sales were slightly below budget (5%), and this difference has increased by September, when sales were significantly below budget (35%).

Harvinda has made the highest unit sales in each of the six months, whilst Pasha has made the lowest unit sales.

Total budgeted sales for the six-month period were £680,000, and total actual sales were 2.2% lower at £665,230.

The discount on the premium and luxury ranges in August and September have led to increased unit sales of these products in these months. However, this appears to have had an adverse effect on total sales revenue for these months, which is lower than budgeted.

Further information

A breakdown of the unit sales of each product range by salesperson.

Sales price per item sold and the contribution that each product makes per unit sold.

Sales value per salesperson for each month, and for the six months. Despite units sales being good for certain people, this may be the lower value ranges, or ranges with the lowest contribution.

The number of customers that each salesperson manages and the geographical spread of these customers. Harvinda may be performing best because he has a larger customer base located in a smaller geographical area. Pasha may be covering a large geographical area with fewer customers.

Details of any discounts given to specific customers.

10.10

	Email	Meeting	Social media	Telephone call
A promotion by a restaurant offering its customers a free meal if they follow its Twitter page.			✔	
A presentation of the company's annual results. All members of staff can be involved if they wish.		✔		
Confirmation of terms of trade, including credit terms, for a new customer.	✔			
Contact with a customer who continues not to pay its overdue account despite having been contacted several times by email.				✔

Index

for your notes

for your notes

for your notes

for your notes

for your notes

for your notes

for your notes

for your notes

for your notes

for your notes

for your notes

for your notes

for your notes

for your notes